The Rotten State of Britain

Eamonn Butler

GIBSON SQUARE

London

This edition first published in by

Gibson Square

UK Tel: +44 (0)20 7096 1100
       Fax: +44 (0)20 7993 2214

US Tel: +1 646 216 9813
       Fax: +1 646 216 9488

Eire Tel: +353 (0)1 657 1057

info@gibsonsquare.com
www.gibsonsquare.com

ISBN 9781906142377

CONTENTS

ACKNOWLEDGEMENTS

Thanks are due to Caroline Porter, Cate Shafer and Sophie Shawdon for their help on the research. I am also grateful for the insights of Matthew Elliott and Mark Wallace of the Taxpayers' Alliance, Helen Evans of Nurses for Reform, Tim Evans of the Libertarian Alliance, Claire Fox of the Institute of Ideas, David Green and Anastasia de Waal of Civitas, Andrew Haldenby of Reform, Philip Johnston, Nicholas Jones, Dominic Raab, Gabriel Stein, and my colleagues at the Adam Smith Institute.

FOREWORD

TO THE PAPERBACK EDITION

When I started working on *The Rotten State of Britain*, most people thought we were in pretty good shape. Certainly, Northern Rock had failed and a few American banks were looking a bit shaky. Central banks were saying that growth would be down a bit this year. But Gordon Brown continued to assure us that, thanks to ten years of his 'prudent' economic management, Britain was in an enviable position – perhaps the country best placed to weather any passing economic storm.

Complacency also abounded on the political front. There was a consensus that the country was being managed broadly along the right lines. Gordon Brown was a safe pair of hands. The government was, broadly speaking, in tune with the people. David Cameron's Conservatives of course insisted that they could run things better. But they gave every impression that they could find no higher aspiration in life than to mimic Gordon Brown's spending plans and carry on pretty much as we were.

Perhaps for this reason, I struggled to find a publisher for *The Rotten State of Britain*. I was told that it would be hard to find an audience for my views that the economic and political fabric of Britain had rotted away, that the state had been captured by a political clan who ran it in their own interests and not in ours, that our rights and liberties had been so weakened that they could no longer save us, and that our fortunes rested only on debt and deception.

It was an uncomfortable and unwelcome message, and I was fortunate to find the one publisher, among many, who did not flinch from publishing it. Even then, it came in for agitated criticism. For many people, it fulfilled my purpose of putting daily events into their context, so that people could see the wood without being blinded by the trees. But others caricatured it as just grumpy criticism of a Britain that, apart from a few hiccups, was working perfectly well.

But reality has a habit of reasserting herself, though she sometimes takes a little time over it. I take no pleasure in the fact, but my original charge has been proven. Britain's economics and politics were indeed both rotten. The difference is that this has now become obvious to anyone who cares to look.

An economy steered onto the rocks
People in finance say that when the tide goes out, you can see who has been swimming naked. I would say, rather, that when the tide goes out, you can see which ships have been floating and which have simply been stranded on the rocks. The financial crisis showed that our economy was indeed on the rocks. The scandal over MPs' expenses showed that our political system was deeply holed below the water line too.

Far from being the country in best shape to weather a downturn, we are the one in worst shape. Our apparent prosperity has proved entirely illusory. It has been built on the shifting sands of cheap credit. Instead of saving and investing during the good times, we have spent and then borrowed and then spent some more – deluded by our politicians into believing that all that debt-financed spending was actually 'investment'. But it wasn't.

Now we have run out of money. Real investment – investment by businesses, the sort that might actually add to our future prosperity – is the lowest it has been since 1965. Firms are going bust, and those that survive are pulling in 40% less business than a year ago. Unemployment is edging up towards 3 million. Britain's economy has shrunk, month on month, for five quarters. We are producing 6 per cent less than we did in Spring 2008. It is a recession twice as deep as that in the early 1990s. If we really had been prudent, and really had invested – or, better, saved – then we would not be in this fix.

With businesses failing, tax receipts are down and benefit expenditures are up. Inflation remains stubbornly high. Vast sums have been spent on bailing out the financial sector – creating zombie banks, kept alive only by the injections of taxpayers' money.

To close the hole that has opened up in the public finances, the government are simply borrowing even more – trying, in fact, to borrow their way out of a crisis that was caused by excessive borrowing in the fist place. Four months deep into the current financial year, we had already borrowed as much as in the whole of the year before. And that was a record, even then. This year, Britain will have to borrow around £200 billion – twice as much as our near neighbours France or Germany. So much for being 'best placed' to weather a downturn. Our income is falling, and a huge proportion of what we do earn is having to be spent on servicing all this extra debt – as it will for years to come.

A bloated public sector

It is no surprise, therefore, that every part of the British economy is suffering a recession. Apart from the public sector, that is. As the real, productive economy sheds jobs, public-sector numbers just grow and grow. And that is not just because of the extra 230,000 Lloyds and Royal Bank of Scotland workers who suddenly discovered themselves to be public employees when the government nationalized their banks. Even if you exclude all those, you find that there are still 615,000 more people on the public payroll than there were in 1997.

The pay of public employees has grown in leaps and bounds too. Police, health workers, teachers, local authority staff and even our discredited MPs can look forward to pay rises between 2.3 per cent and 2.5 percent this year, even while workers in the private sector are suffering pay cuts as a result of the faltering business environment.

Local authorities do their best to conceal how much council officers are paid, but the Taxpayers Alliance discovered that 1,089 people in town halls earn more than £100,000 – in fact averaging £122,539 (or £2,356 a week, roughly four times the average wage). Some earn twice that. And the number of council high rollers is increasing: back in 2006-07 there were just 873 people on £100,000+ packages. Indeed, nearly 200 people in local authorities now earn more than Cabinet ministers do.

And absence seems to make civil servants' hearts grow fonder of their jobs. Staff turnover in the public sector is much lower than in the private sector, where businesses face the chill wind of change and competition. And public-sector absenteeism is chronic. Each public-sector worker takes an average 9.7 days off sick each year (for healthcare workers it is 11 days), compared to only 6.6 days in the private sector. Even when they do show up, public employees are less productive than private-sector ones. In August 2009, the Centre for Economic and Business Research calculated that this productivity shortfall costs taxpayers £58.4 billion a year.

The public pensions scandal

One argument for giving civil servants more generous pensions was that they earned less during their working lives. That excuse has now gone, of course – public employees earn, on average, slightly more than private-sector workers, and the gap is widening. But the generous public-sector pensions still remain.

Facing higher taxes and more onerous regulations – not to mention a downturn in business as the recession bites – companies have rushed to close their unaffordable final-salary pension schemes (where the worker's pension is set as a fixed proportion, say two-thirds, of their final salary level at the company). About 20 million private-sector workers retire without a final-salary pension plan, but these generous arrangements are still the norm in the public sector.

So one of those 1,089 town hall officials on £100,000 can look forward to a pension of two-thirds of that – £66,000. Fully indexed against inflation, naturally. Oh, and public employees normally retire earlier too, at 60 rather than 65. But then the early-retirement arrangements are also more generous, so quite a few of those 1,089 council officers will probably never even make it to 60 before collecting their pension. By contrast, most people in private business – if they have a pension plan at all – have only what is called a defined-contribution pension. They save into a pension pot, which is then converted into an annual pension when they retire. Under this system, a £100,000-a-year private sector worker could realistically hope to retire today, at age 65, on a pension, not fully indexed against the ravages of inflation, of just £7,000.

The generosity of public pensions means that the total amount of money that taxpayers will have to stump up to pay all these benefits is estimated at £1,000 billion. Nobody knows for sure: it depends on how long our retired council officers, teachers, and civil servants live for. And on average, they live longer than the rest of us.

Every four years, the government's actuaries look at the public-sector pension arrangements to check how much cash will be needed to keep paying them. It is usually a dull exercise, and nobody notices. In 2009, however, ministers have made a huge song and dance about it. They at last recognize the amount of resentment that is building up between private-sector workers who see their businesses failing, their hours lengthening or their wages or jobs being cut and their pension investments falling in value, while the public sector seems to carry on regardless. So they are talking about ending the generous plans for new employees, and making civil servants retire at 65 like the rest of us. Good luck to them: the last time they tried that, they had strikes for six months, and eventually gave up.

Even the civil-service unions seem unusually willing to show they are prepared to make sacrifices, such as paying a bit more towards their own pensions. That willingness to make a few concessions, of course, is precisely because public-sector employees are so desperate to keep the index-linked, final-salary arrangements that will deliver them a retirement income worth ten times what a comparable private worker could ever hope for.

A record of failure

Of course, when the economy is booming, and workers are bringing in good money, they pay less attention to how much of their pay goes out in taxes, or how big and expensive the government happens to be. Right now, however, with the chickens of a wild tax-and-spend binge coming home to roost, people are looking more critically at what they get for their tax money.

And they are disappointed in what they find. Despite all the optimistic talk of the late 1990s, and all the extra taxes – a total of £1,200 billion or more – that we have paid, the results can hardly be said to represent good value for money. In healthcare, the budget has roughly doubled, but we still have 250,000 people waiting over 18 months for operations, and some of the worst cancer and stroke survival rates in the developed world, worse even than Eastern Europe. The extra money seems to have gone more into staff pay, and hiring more extra supervisors than extra nurses. But after all that extra spending, the NHS remains largely unreformed. The service seems more focused on targets and protocols than on patients – one reason why the Patients' Association, in August 2009, described the treatment of elderly people in particular as 'cruel'.

Similar criticisms can be made of education. Again, the budget has almost doubled. And indeed, examination grades continue to improve. But parents wonder whether much of this is simply grade inflation; educators believe that much of it is simply drilling kids to pass exams, rather than giving them a real education; and universities and employers are rejecting the government's tests as worthless, and introducing their own.

On welfare, the largest spending item, we were told, correctly, that a paying job was the best anti-poverty policy known to humanity, and that the priority must be on getting people off benefits and into work. Child poverty, in particular, would be targeted and virtually eliminated. But today, one in six children still live in workless households, and the numbers are increasing. Welfare-to-work schemes, along with innumerable benefit changes, have been tried, have failed, and have been scrapped or re-branded and re-introduced. Our welfare system now makes it economically advantageous for couples to split up – which of course they do. The number of men under 50s who claim to be too ill or disabled to work is three times that of Germany. It is clear that our welfare system has become too big and too complicated to manage.

Centralization and its discontents

But these are just symptoms of the problem. The source of the
rot is that government itself has become too big and too
complicated – or at least, too big and to centralized to run the
over-complicated institutions that it has itself created.

In August 2009, four former Cabinet secretaries – former
heads of the civil service – each complained to a House of
Commons committee that the machinery of government had
become too centred on Downing Street. Of course, this isn't
just a criticism of the present government. People rightly
complained that Mrs Thatcher over-centralized decision-
making, and it can be traced long before that.

But New Labour made it systematic. The Party had spent so
long in the political wilderness that they were determined to get
back into office – even if it meant biting their Old Labour
tongues and backing the toothy young reformer Tony Blair.
Blair, Gordon Brown, and the backroom strategists Peter
Mandelson and Alastair Campbell, knew full well what past
disunity had cost them, and what it was now doing to John
Major's Conservatives. They knew that they had to present the
image of a united front – particularly in this age of hungry 24-
hour TV news channels.

It worked better than they could have dreamt of. And they
applied exactly the same mentality to running themselves as a
government as they had in opposition. They had gone to the
country and been given a mandate to enact their ideas. They
were the People's Government, and nothing would stop them
delivering what they believe the People wanted. Not the civil
service. Nor wayward MPs. Not the different views within
Cabinet. Not even the courts. Decisions would be made at the
centre, by the Prime Minister and the Chancellor. Others would

be expected to fall in. No deviation would be allowed. They were decent people, who had meant to make government more open. But in the attempt to make it more effective, they made it more closed.

With the tide of government rising, there were few objections. Countless Party apparatchiks, MPs, and ministers owed their jobs, and in some cases their grace-and-favour homes, to the patronage of the Prime Minister and Downing Street officials. The media too depended on this seamless Party machine for their supply of scoops and stories – as indeed they still do. It all worked to the mutual benefit of the political clan – each supporting the other, and each prospering all the more as this centralized, controlled system of government expanded.

But with politicians identifying themselves so precisely with the will of the People, it was not long before the boundary of Party and State became lost. The institutions of government – Parliament, the civil service, the courts, the rights of trial by jury, free speech and the like – were developed over the centuries specifically to protect the public from the potentially unrestrained power of their leaders, and to protect minorities from the baying mob of populism. But now, in a matter of just years, such restraints have been eroded or pushed aside in the name of that populism. They have been ousted by the need for politicians to look good in the media by reacting instantly and 'doing something', even if what they do is not merely counter-productive, but indeed unjust.

The confusion of State interests with Party or even purely personal interests explains so much of what has corrupted our political system in recent years, or indeed decades. It explains the sclerotic centralism in our public services, the leaking of public information to buy favourable media stories, the sleazy cash-for-favours culture, the willingness of MPs to enrich themselves by abusing their expenses – and then, most remarkably of all to feel themselves genuinely indignant when we complain about it. That is how distant the political clan has grown from the rest of us.

Stopping the rot

With all the resignations that the expenses scandal has precipitated, there will be even more fresh faces in the new Parliament than there was after the New Labour landslide in 1997. Are they likely to stop the rot?

It's possible, if unlikely. Opposition parties always call for governments to be restrained, but once in government themselves, they start to see, understand, and enjoy the powers and influence of office. Yet the only solution to an over-concentration of power is to give power up. A stronger Cabinet, Parliament, and civil service, stronger courts and local decision-making – all these would help, but all of them require the occupants of Downing Street to accept that their word is no longer law – and that it would indeed be far better for the country if it isn't. It needs politicians brave enough to tell the public that it is just none of their business to comment on certain things, whatever personal views they might have. Leaders brave enough to admit that they have no instant solutions to every problem, and need time to think through the right solution, and even to explain why it is often better for them to do nothing at all, however loud were the calls for action.

Human nature being what it is, that seems a lot to expect. And yet, if any politician were indeed brave enough to take this stance, it would define a new age of how we preserve the rights and freedoms of individuals in a 24-hour-news democracy. Far more than any amount of the tinkering we have seen during the last two decades, it would be something a politician would be remembered for.

1

STILL IN A ROTTEN STATE

Things could only get better

Things, they said, could only get better. History and progress would push aside the Tory sleaze-bags. A People's Government, in tune with how ordinary people lived, would oust the elitist clique that cared only for its fatcat supporters in business and the media. Decision would replace dithering. Cool would supplant conservatism. A society broken down by the pursuit of profit would be rebuilt. The social infrastructure would be repaired. Community and opportunity would be restored through personal responsibility and accountability – a new 'Third Way' between Thatcherism and Socialism. Vision and enterprise would regenerate Britain's debt-ridden economy. Britain would again be able to hold its head up high before the world.

Bliss was it in that dawn to be alive. But to be New Labour was very heaven. The Party's all-night election rave in the Royal Festival Hall underlined the coolness and inevitability of it all. The young crowd danced and sang to New Labour's campaign song: no dreary anthem like 'The Red Flag', but the upbeat, ecstasy-inspired D:Ream club hit 'Things Can Only Get Better'.

The revellers had much to celebrate. New Labour had ended eighteen years of Conservative rule with their largest-ever election win. At 5.11am the People's Prime Minister, Tony Blair, swept in to tell them 'We've Done It! The British people have put their trust in us. A new dawn has broken… [it just had – hence the timing] …we shall make this country as proud of us as we are of them.'

The warning signs

Next day I, and hundreds of others, stood in Whitehall to await the new prime minister's arrival. Party workers lined Downing Street, three deep. The plan was that they should all wave New Labour flags. But some spin doctor realized that would look too triumphant. They were hastily issued with Union Jacks, to give the impression of a spontaneous throng of ordinary British people who were enthusiastically welcoming the new order.

Throughout the election, the Blair family's campaign vehicle was a Ford Galaxy. It was not just a car, but a new kind of car, a people carrier. It summed up what New Labour was about – new, democratic, for the People. So it was a disappointment when the Blairs arrived in a mundane, bullet-proof official Jaguar, flanked by motorcycle outriders. They swept through the gates of Downing Street, which would not look out of place outside the imperial palace of St. Petersburg, and were lost from view.

Perhaps we should have suspected then that, safely wrapped up in the trappings of office, the new order would not actually make things better. But what few of us ever imagined, on that dawn, was that it would actually make them worse.

What they wanted to change

Indeed, that possibility certainly did not occur to Will Hutton, the leftist editor, writer, think-tanker, broadcaster and critic. In 1995, he caught the mood of the times with his book *The State We're In*. It shredded the record of Margaret Thatcher and John Major, and called for a new government and a stronger constitution to keep the excesses of such out-of-touch rulers in check.

The book became the gospel of the chattering classes. And yet Hutton's critique of the Conservative years makes hilarious reading today. Every evil he complains of so passionately is still with us today, despite more than a decade of his dreamt-of government and the expenditure of an extra trillion pounds worth of taxpayers' money.

Britain in 1995, he says, is a proud nation living in a tarnished country. Its industry is stagnating, unemployment is rising, its prestige is rock bottom, and it has become isolated in Europe and the world, in thrall to America.

Its political system is sick. A weak and divided opposition allowed the government to grow arrogant and over-bearing. Decision-making has become centralized. Parliament is sidelined: it does not even discuss important issues. The judges' independence has been undermined. The civil service is politicized, and public money is used to promote private or party purposes (as when the Cabinet Secretary, Robin Butler, released public funds to help the Chancellor, Norman Lamont, evict the embarrassing tenant Miss Whiplash from his rented-out flat).

Patronage, continued Hutton, has replaced accountability, with ministers controlling thousands of lucrative quango jobs and public appointments. Public services are hidebound by targets: even the police care more about meeting their targets than helping the community.

Meanwhile, our industrial research and development is lagging behind the rest of the world; investment has fallen; a weakened UK economy is now at the mercy of the forces of globalization and international competition. Pensions have been slashed in value. People and the government are deep in debt; families are suffering negative equity, stress and despair.

The promise of reform
That was 1995. If it sounds familiar, it should – because every

point is even more true of our economy and society today.

I derive no pleasure from this. Colleagues and I at the Adam Smith Institute were willing to give New Labour the benefit of the doubt. 'We were elected as New Labour and we will govern as New Labour,' said Blair. Perhaps they really had accepted the merits of markets, enterprise, localism, and public service reform.

And indeed there were some promising signs. The new government declared that it would not raise income tax rates. Interest-rate decisions were made less political by handing them over to the Bank of England. There was to be 'prudence' in the public finances. And there was much talk of change in the public services. It really did seem like a radical, reforming administration.

But the illusion did not last long. The new ministers looked and sounded exactly like the old ones as they announced policies and reacted to events on television. The neat suits, the tidy hair, the reassuring language... It felt like George Orwell's Animal Farm, where the porcine revolutionaries become indistinguishable from the humans they replaced.

Worse, perhaps. When Conservative ministers spoke at public meetings, like the ones that we and other think tanks regularly arrange, they usually had at most one political adviser in tow. They were confident enough to take questions and debate. The new ministers all came with a complete retinue of civil servants and spin-doctors. They would announce some new initiative, and leave. It looked very much as if the pigs were now warmly wrapped up in the comforts of the farmhouse, no longer part of the common herd.

The turning point came just a year later, on 27 July 1998, when Frank Field, the Minister of State for welfare reform, was reshuffled into oblivion. Blair had asked the veteran anti-poverty campaigner to 'think the unthinkable' on welfare reform. He did: he wanted an attack on benefit fraud, tighter controls on incapacity benefit, and the end of the perverse incentives that he thought created a dependent, work-shy underclass. But his proposals were by then far too radical for an administration that had already settled comfortably into power and did not want to frighten its own left wing.

Since then, things have unravelled spectacularly. Despite raising more than an extra £1,200,000,000,000 from taxpayers since 1997, the government has cured very few of those ills that Will Hutton promised they would. Things have not got better. Most things have got very much worse.

Lions led by poodles

I'm not sure that anyone would describe Britain today as a 'proud nation', as Will Hutton did back in 1995. It's hard to take pride in a country that has been steadily slipping down the league tables of economic performance and up the league tables of crime. It's hard to take pride in public services that focus more on administrative targets than on serving the public. It's hard to share any respect for politicians who simply lie to us and sell public honours for party donations.

In fact, it's hard to be proud of Britain at all when its leaders are so weak and venal. The political process no longer attracts independent people who want to improve society. Politicians are now a self-sustaining professional class. Few of them have any experience of the real world outside politics, trade unions, journalism or public relations. The political process breeds identikit state administrators, rather than anyone with any real flair or contact with the public. Who these days can even name more than two members of the Cabinet?

Britain's standing in the world

It's no wonder that Britain's standing in the world is so feeble, and so much more so than in 1995. Even our European Union 'partners' seem to wish we would just go away. The government promised we would be 'at the heart of Europe' and signed us up to the Social Chapter and other costly regulation to prove the point. In return, we didn't even get a chance to air our views on the hugely wasteful Common Agricultural Policy. A cosy deal between France and Germany in 2003 secured its future for another decade, before we even got to the table.

The Arab and Islamic worlds, meanwhile, hate us with a vengeance. Britain may have been quite right to unseat Saddam, who had gassed 40,000 Kurdish people and pledged to destroy Israel as well as the rest of us. But it was all rushed through to fit George Bush's timetable: the decision was expedited on the basis of 'dodgy' out-of-date intelligence dossiers, 'sexed up' by government spin doctors; and Parliament was given only seven hours to discuss the matter. (They spent a hundred times longer discussing foxhunting.) It made Britain look like America's poodle, rather than a principled world leader.

Even the Commonwealth regards us as an embarrassing elderly relative. The government says nothing about the awful situation in Zimbabwe, for instance, because they know it would be counter-productive among the other African nations, who regard us as racist colonialists. Britain's leadership role has collapsed.

A sick political system

The rot, as Hutton put it, starts from the top. From Magna Carta in 1215, our rights and liberties have been built up over the centuries. Trial by jury, habeas corpus, the presumption of innocence – all these and more grew up to restrain our leaders and prevent them from harassing us. Yet within a decade, almost all these protections have been diluted or discarded. Our leaders are no longer restrained by the rule of law at all.

They argued that our liberties must be curbed if we are to

combat terrorism. That our rights get in the way of efficient government. That the law got in the way of doing what the public really wanted. But now that political populism has replaced Britain's liberal principles, there is nothing to protect us from the self-serving actions of our leaders. And this power elite has shown every willingness to harass, bully, spy on, arrest, and imprison us without trial whenever they deem it appropriate.

Decisions are now made by the Prime Minister and a large coterie of unelected, political advisers within Downing Street. The Cabinet no longer makes executive decisions, but has degenerated into a weekly chat about political presentation. Parliament is sidelined too, since around 120 ministers, whips, and other appointees owe their salaries, pensions, and careers to the Prime Minister's patronage. And Downing Street pushes so much legislation through Parliament that MPs do not have enough time to read it, never mind debate it.

The civil service too is now completely politicized, stuffed fuller than it ever was with political appointees. It now takes its orders from party officials rather than elected ministers. It no longer announces public information objectively, but now spins the news to make the ruling party look good, and leaks it selectively to help the government's media supporters and punish its critics. MPs now discover what's going on from the Sunday papers, rather than from their order papers.

Patronage and sleaze
We were promised an end to Tory sleaze. But New Labour sleaze has proved far worse. Cherie Blair was perfectly willing to ignore the rules against profiting from office and cash in with world tours promoting her books on Downing Street life. The Blairs were delighted to sponge free holidays in the Mediterranean yachts or palatial Caribbean homes of the rich and famous.

Indeed, as its membership plummeted, the Labour Party became increasingly obsessed with cultivating wealthy people. Honours and appointments were exchanged for million-pound donations. Public policy was adjusted to suit the convenience of large donors. Financial support, both private and party, was accepted from people like Geoffrey Robinson and Richard Desmond, whose business affairs were under official investigation at the time.

Party donations have been booked as loans to keep them secret from the public standards watchdogs. Ministers took loans, donations, and even free homes without declaring them. MPs abuse public money to buy, furnish, and profit from second homes, and to put family members on the payroll. They harassed and vilified the officials who were appointed to investigate such abuses. The list goes on. It is hardly the promised 'end of sleaze'.

The decline of justice

But it is the end of justice. Even the legal system has been subverted to serve the ruling party's interests. Ministers once respected judges, but now they openly criticize them for being 'weak' or for rulings they disagree with.

Police and public officials can fine us on the spot, without the involvement of any courts. The protection of trial by jury has been abandoned in many cases, on grounds of 'efficiency'. We can now be tried twice for the same offence. In some cases, we have to prove our innocence, rather than prosecutors having to prove our guilt. Our assets can be seized even if it is merely suspected, not proved, that we got them illegally.

The police now arrest, caution and prosecute people solely to meet targets, rather than to keep the peace. They can now arrest us for any offence, however minor. And when they do, we can be held for four weeks without charge – though the government wants the power to hold us for seven weeks.

Meanwhile, the anti-terrorism legislation is used by local authorities to spy on whether we are using our recycling bins correctly and by the police to pick up harmless critics of the government. With the authorities being prepared to abuse the law in such ways, and with no trustworthy legal process to protect us, it is plain that justice in Britain now exists only in name.

The surveillance state

No part of our human activity escapes the watchful eye of the surveillance state. Britain has a quarter of the world's CCTV cameras, the largest number of any country. They don't cut crime, but they are another tool that the police and officials can use to fine us for minor offences. Cameras to police London's road congestion charge, or in the growing numbers of average speed control areas, photograph every car going past. Our movements are no longer private.

Meanwhile, we are all on the database. If you're arrested for even a minor offence, or indeed by mistake, your DNA will be taken and added to the database along with over five million other people's. Soon you will have to pay for an ID card that will be linked to a database with information on all of us.

The worrying thing is that this information will be accessible to countless junior public officials – as our medical records and other personal details already are. The state has robbed us of any right to privacy. Not that our data is secure anyway: the state manages to lose files containing millions of our names, dates of birth, and bank account details on a fairly regular basis.

The nanny state

The authorities say they need this information to protect us. So anyone who comes within sight of a child – even just parents helping out on school trips – must now be checked by the Criminal Records Bureau. So they don't bother.

Meanwhile, to protect our safety, village Christmas party organizers have to put nut warnings on their mince pies, can't serve you a glass of wine without a permit, or let you sing carols without an entertainment licence.

Nothing is off the nanny state's agenda. From smoking to drinking to eating chocolate oranges, they tell us how to live – and make us do so if we show reluctance. And they employ entire professions of five-a-day officers (to make us eat more fruit), walking officers (to make us take more exercise), real nappy officers (to encourage recycling), and quangos and tsars to defend us from every imagined vice to which human flesh might succumb.

Struggling to find touch

Plainly, our politicians and our officials have completely lost touch with the real world in which the rest of us live. Having scrapped the old state institutions as elitist or outdated, they now have no way to gauge the mood of the nation or to get things done in ways that respond to local conditions. To find out what the public want, they commission opinion polls, which lead them towards populist policies without much thought of principle. To respond, they can only issue blanket regulations from the centre, which turn out to be simply absurd when applied to local circumstances like the village party.

Their centralized decision-making system cannot handle difference and diversity, which is why politicians are always struggling to define Britishness – and urging us all to be a part of it. Their lives would be so much easier if we were all one big, happy, homogeneous community, drinking warm beer and wrapping ourselves in the flag. Then they could talk directly with all of us, and have one rule for us all. But that's pretty hard in a country where several million people don't even want to be called 'British' at all.

The Millennium Dome was the summit of this forlorn hope. It was supposed to sum up who we were at this historic moment; but by cutting out anything politically incorrect, divisive, gritty, divergent, challenging, non-conformist, conflicting, tribal, bloody, or simply curmudgeonly, it ended up portraying British society as a sort of saccharine mush.

Public services

The new rulers told us that public services would be rebuilt. So where has that additional £1.2 trillion plus in taxes actually *gone*?

Much of it has gone into public sector salaries. Family doctors now earn over £100,000 a year, and they don't even have to work nights or weekends to get it. Money has gone into the old-style extensive hospital sector – which is also very expensive – rather than on delivering services near to where we live.

That is no comfort to a patient with cancer or heart disease, where Britain's survival rates lag behind almost all the other rich countries. Our access to life-saving drugs is worse than elsewhere. One in eight of us have to wait over a year for treatment. And 10,000 of us die in hospital each year from infections like the superbug Clostridium difficile.

In education, spending has risen by more than half. New teachers have been recruited, but the real growth is in (the less qualified) classroom assistants.

Exam results continue to improve steadily upward. But the upward trend began before 1997, and there is no sign that the extra billions have made any difference at all. But employers are increasingly sceptical about the value of all the A and A* grades that the schools now produce, while universities use their own entrance exam because they don't trust A-Levels at all. They are right. On international tests where schools can't cram kids for the exam, our results are actually slipping down the league tables. A third of A-grade candidates failed Cambridge University's own admission test for maths in 2009.

Police numbers have also risen on the back of the tax avalanche, but again the greatest growth has been in administrative, civilian, and 'community support' staff rather than front-line officers. The police spend 40 per cent of their time on paperwork: London's police spend more on administration than they do investigating robberies.

Burglary has fallen, but only because longer prison sentences keep burglars off the street. Drug use is up, and violent crime is up. Meanwhile, our prisons are so overcrowded that there is neither time nor space to try to reform criminals. Most people who appear before our courts have been there before.

Our welfare system has grown too, and become even more dysfunctional in the process. Thanks to Gordon Brown's incredibly complex tax credit system, two-fifths of us now receive some form of state welfare benefit. Means testing has expanded – not been reduced, as we were promised. The pension credit makes it irrational to a quarter of us to save for retirement, because we just lose benefits if we do.

High taxes levied on low incomes mean that few people have much incentive to move off benefits and into work. And the rules support single-parent families rather than couples. Indeed, the benefit rates actually encourage couples to split up – often with terrible effects on the children, who are more likely to get taken into care, involved in crime, and become victims of addiction and educational failure. It is hardly a welfare system that we can be proud of.

Public boom, private bust
High levels of debt don't help struggling families either.

Personal debt in Britain is higher than it has ever been – the highest in the world, and much higher than when Will Hutton was complaining about it in 1995. Government debt is much higher too. It is scheduled to reach 57 per cent of national output by 2012 as Britain borrows to see itself through the financial crisis.

But Britain's high rates of public debt didn't start there. Gordon Brown promised us an end to boom and bust, but in fact he created both. His 'prudent' rules on debt and deficits in fact allowed both to expand hugely. A mighty surge in public spending – without being tied to reform in the public services – was paid for by massive increases in both borrowing and taxation. Private pension funds were raided to boost generous public sector pensions and salaries; stealth taxes multiplied; charges for passports, council services, and official documents were all ratcheted up. And public borrowing always turned out to be far higher than Gordon Brown's uninformative Budget speeches suggested.

Meanwhile the Bank of England struggled to keep price increases at 2 per cent when in reality – due to cheap Chinese imports and large-scale immigration-prices should probably have been falling. It was a wild, borrowing – led binge, and now we are suffering the hangover. The boom has turned to bust.

Any talk of financial prudence is now jettisoned. Years of reluctant, faltering effort to simplify taxes have now gone, with new tax rates and fiddling changes in allowances, all designed to shift the cost onto the rich. New Labour, with its supposed financial prudence and support for wealth creation, is dead.

Goodbye, Cruel Britannia

It is disappointing that an administration that showed real plausibility as a financially solid, radical and reforming administration has achieved so little and made worse so much. We were promised Cool Britannia and a People's Government, but instead we got boom and bust, injustice, surveillance, regulation, stealth taxes, interference, sleaze, lies, hoodies, and binge-drinking ladettes.

But perhaps the most dispiriting aspect of the state we're in is that it has become our master, and is no longer our servant. The politicians tell us how to behave, even in our own homes. The police are incentivized to stop, arrest, caution, spot-fine, or prosecute us, rather than to keep the peace. Tax inspectors are incentivized to screw as much as possible out of us – under threat of imprisonment – rather than to reach a fair and just settlement. Our whole relationship with the state has become adversarial, rather than collaborative. The state has lost our trust and our respect.

The rot does indeed start at the top. And that is where we need to start if we are to cure it. We need to establish new legal restraints on our rulers if we are to protect ourselves from their excesses. For unless it is restrained, political and official power turns – and has turned – at frightening speed into the abuse of power.

We need checks and balances that prevent our political leaders, their unelected advisers, and their police and officials pushing us around just as they please. And in particular, we need to devolve power downwards – not to parliaments and assemblies of yet more politicians, but to the people from whom it should ultimately derive. Only this will allow Britain to recover its pride and position again, repair our broken democracy, and regenerate a society free of the pious bullying that we have been subjected to in recent times.

2

ROTTEN GOVERNMENT

Decisiveness versus democracy

In September 2008, when world financial markets were in meltdown, the US Treasury Secretary Hank Paulson quickly devised a $750 billion emergency package to restore confidence. Uncle Sam would take over the banks' bad debts, so that investors could focus on the future once more. But Congress had to agree. And it took two solid weeks to get that agreement, even with Paulson going (literally) on bended knee to Congress, a great deal of arm-twisting from the President, and a lot of horse-trading from all sides.

In Britain, by contrast, a bank bail-out of equal size was decided over a late-night curry in Downing Street on Monday, announced on Tuesday, presented to Parliament on Wednesday, debated for just 90 minutes on Thursday, and signed into law on Friday.

Gordon Brown said it showed his government's superior ability to act decisively. In fact, it shows that America still retains some semblance of democratic debate, while we don't. In Britain, the Prime Minister and colleagues in Downing Street decide what is good for us and then it's nodded through Parliament. It's hardly democracy: it's a centralist autocracy.

Where did centralization start?

For centuries, prime ministers' power has been limited not just by the whim of the electorate, but by Parliament, the law, the civil service, local authorities, and even Cabinet colleagues. Now that has changed. There are almost no limits on prime ministers and the small clique of party apparatchiks that run things from 10 Downing Street.

In this, Margaret Thatcher was New Labour's model. She centralized decision-making, taking powers to force local authorities to sell their council houses, for example. And her tough leadership style, praised by Peter Mandelson in *The Blair Revolution,* saw off most Cabinet and civil-service opposition.

The Blair government would not let state institutions stand in their way either. They entered Downing Street with a 22-strong team of political advisers – over the years, that number grew fourfold – and didn't even bother to read the civil-service briefing provided for all incoming administrations. They were the People's Government: they knew exactly what had to be done on behalf of the People, and they would take whatever power was needed to do it. Anything that thwarted them would be pushed aside.

But that meant pushing aside state institutions that have important functions. The civil service, the Cabinet, Parliament, the judiciary – the tensions between them all help to make sure that policies are conceived soundly and tested against a wide range of views; that laws are fairly executed; and that governments cannot just do what they damn well please.

Mrs Thatcher took central control in the attempt to disperse power from the state to the people. New Labour suffered no such liberalism. Its leaders grew up in the 1960s, when state centralism was in vogue. Some – Peter Mandelson, Charlie Whelan, John Reid – joined the Communist Party of Great Britain. Others wrote in *Marxism Today.* Many learnt the importance of strong party organization from university Leninists, even if they opposed them. David Miliband's father was a prominent Marxian political theorist. And so it goes on.

The end of Cabinet government

There was an old joke about Mrs Thatcher, that at a Cabinet dinner she ordered fillet steak. 'And what about the vegetables?' asked the waiter. 'Oh,' she replied. 'They'll have fillet steak too.' There was a basis of truth in it. I attended a private lunch in Downing Street in 1990, where several Cabinet ministers were present. She plainly had little time for their views, and thought them weak. She openly humiliated the Deputy Prime Minister, Sir Geoffrey Howe. I wondered how such weighty politicians could put up with it. But of course they didn't: within weeks, Howe denounced her in the House of Commons and precipitated a leadership election, which she lost.

There were no such problems in Blair's Downing Street. Cabinet ministers had no pretence to status or independence. The Cabinet wrangling about Europe that froze John Major's Cabinet was fresh in their minds. They knew they were just cogs in the New Labour Project. Party strategists would make the important decisions, not them. They would be told the 'line to take' in public, and clear their speeches, interviews, even lunches, with Alastair Campbell's press office.

Gordon Brown's key policy of handing interest-rate policy over to the Bank of England was decided before the Cabinet even met. Even then, Cabinet meetings were brief-just an hour a week-and mostly about presentation, not policy. With no opportunity for debate, ministers just signed off each other's proposals without much scrutiny. Where they did have opinions-a majority thought the Millennium Dome should be abandoned before it turned into the inevitable fiasco-Blair pressed on anyway.

Decision-making fell to an inner Cabinet, and to a vast array of committees (59 Cabinet committees, 44 ministerial committees, and 5 working groups, at one stage). They would be chaired by Blair, Brown or Mandelson-or even by unelected advisers like Campbell. It was all very informal, in the New Labour style: issues were discussed on the sofa, without bothering to take minutes.

But only a few people can fit onto a sofa. True, Cabinet government produced arguments and deadlocks, but at least it ensured that policies were thoroughly discussed, and objections noted. Sofa government is based on little information or debate; and when those policies turn to disaster, nobody can check who actually agreed what. It hardly makes for good government.

The demise of Parliament

Another obstacle to good government is ministers' careers. Business executives know it can take them five years to get to grips with a job, but ministers rarely last more than two. Between 1999 and 2007, John Reid served as Secretary of State for Scotland, Northern Ireland, health, defence, and home affairs, as well as being leader of the Commons and minister without portfolio.

So to shine in any job, ministers have to move quickly. Their status depends on working up Bills and steering them through Parliament. The best policy might be to do nothing, but ministerial careers, salaries and pensions don't advance like that. Ministers have to push through their solutions, like ID cards and child databases, even where there is no problem.

This rush of activity is why twenty or more major bills are pushed through Parliament each year-many of them designed to clean up the mess left by the last. But Parliament cannot handle this volume of traffic. Ever more debates have to be cut short. The 'was once a shocking rarity, used only apologetically. New Labour used it more times during their first five years than it had been used in the thirty years since the War.

But Downing Street strategists have no time for the traditional role of Parliament – scrutinizing legislation from many points of view, and holding the Executive to account. So Parliament has been sidelined along with the Cabinet. Tony Blair voted in only a tenth of Commons votes, which shows his opinion of the place. While he did agree to appear before the heads of Commons committees, he also cut Prime Minister's Questions from twice a week to once – and at a time chosen to suit, not Parliament, but the lunchtime news agenda.

Government by press conference

Gordon Brown not only took his key Bank of England decision without reference to the Cabinet; he also announced it at a press conference, without reference to Parliament. The rule that major announcements should be made in Parliament has been torn up. Parliament is no longer the nation's democratic clearing-house: Downing Street prefers to leak and spin government news in a more controlled way than it can when 635 MPs and the entire lobby media get it all at once.

Betty Boothroyd, as Speaker of the House of Commons, rebuked ministers time and again for this, but to no avail. Parliament now doesn't debate proposals: it simply reacts to decisions announced to the weekend media.

But MPs have been willing victims. Few have much outside income, now that City board appointments have been tightened up. Their careers and incomes depend wholly upon them becoming ministers. So they keep Downing Street sweet. And their luxurious new offices in Portcullis House mean they are no longer so cheek-by-jowl in the bars and lobbies where plots to thwart overbearing ministers might be hatched.

Parliament's weakness means more bad ideas go through into law. Ministers often don't even turn up for debates on their own legislation, so there is no chance for MPs to influence them. Sometimes, MPs don't even get an opportunity to discuss seriously important issues. For example, the details on murder sentences in David Blunkett's criminal justice legislation were added only at the report stage as an amendment, without even being debated.

Ministers push through so much legislation that there is hardly enough time for MPs to read it, never mind scrutinize it. Even ministers don't seem to read their own legislation or understand its implications. David Blunkett expressed shock when Lord Woolf announced big cuts in prison sentences, despite the fact that his own law permitted it. And the Home Office minister Mike O'Brien assured the world that his 2003 Licensing Act would not impose petty bureaucracy on pubs and hotels, nor drive live music out of local venues. In fact it has done both, as everyone who had read the legislation knew it must.

Civil service neutered

Another longstop against executive tyranny now brought to heel is the civil service. Again, it didn't start with New Labour. Mrs Thatcher's Cabinet Secretary Lord Armstrong was famously 'economical with the truth' on her behalf during the 1986 *Spycatcher* trial. His successor Robin Butler approved government funds to help Conservative Chancellor Norman Lamont evict Miss Whiplash from a rented flat, even though the embarrassment was personal rather than a matter of state.

Margaret Thatcher thought the civil service at best slowed things down and at worst were unhelpful; but she found useful their experience and meticulous attention to detail, and just bullied them at the margins. Blair's team, however, seized control of the whole civil service structure. His Chief of Staff, Jonathan Powell, though a party official, was given unprecedented official powers to boss around the bureaucrats – as was his Press Secretary Alistair Campbell.

Unelected party advisers intervened in the promotion of civil servants. The almost complete turnover in the corps of government information officers under Alastair Campbell is testimony to that. Party nominees sidelined officials and took charge of administration as well as policy: the Number 10 Policy Unit under David Miliband became an executive team, not just a think-tank. Apparatchiks pushed into areas normally thought to demand impartiality, like the honours system. They re-wrote government press releases to mislead journalists. They passed the blame for ministers' mistakes onto officials. In no time at all, the civil service went from watchdog to lapdog.

Mrs Thatcher was right about civil servants' plodding nature. But the civil service also ensured that state power was not used corruptly for party gain, scrutinized policy proposals to ensure their robustness, made certain that Bills were properly drafted, and ensured that politicians' decisions were legal.

Now, they don't even get invited onto the sofa. They have been swept away, just as the safeguards of Cabinet and Parliament have been swept away. This lack of restraint leaves Downing Street free to 'act decisively' in pretty much any way it wants. But it also exposes them to the results of their own hubris – as the 'lordships for loans' scandal spectacularly showed.

Constitutional muddles

It all explains why so much legislation either promotes party interests, or is a complete mess. The constitutional changes of the last decade are an example of both.

Old Labour's key constitutional demand was to abolish the House of Lords, with its undemocratic, built-in Conservative majority. For decades, there were three times as many

Conservative peers as there were Labour ones. The 1983 Labour Manifesto promised to sweep the Lords away: but that became known as the 'longest suicide note in history' as Mrs Thatcher stormed to a second landslide victory.

A decade later, a more moderate Labour leader, John Smith, proposed a more principled approach. The Lords would not be abolished, merely reformed: but there would be important constitutional changes elsewhere – devolution to the regions, adopting the European Convention on Human Rights, electoral reform, and a Freedom of Information Act.

Tony Blair inherited this package, but showed little interest in it. The Liberal Democrat leader Paddy Ashdown spoke of how Blair's eyes would glaze over during constitutional talks.

Instead, the package became entirely tactical. House of Lords reform would demolish a Conservative bastion. Elected mayors would keep key cities under Labour control. Party funding reform would expose the Conservatives' rich backers. Devolution would undermine the Scottish and Welsh nationalists. English regional assemblies would bottle up the Conservatives in the South East and drain local power from the Liberal Democrats. A coherent reform package was turned into a ragbag of random, opportunistic, self-serving, partisan measures, which pass for our constitution today.

The devolution disaster

Devolution is an example. The Scottish National Party, led by the clever and dynamic Alex Salmond, was taking seats in Scotland – Labour's heartland. Blair reckoned that while Scotland's voters were very happy to give Labour and the Conservatives a bloody nose, they did not really want independence: they enjoyed far too many English subsidies. So New Labour would take the wind out of the SNP's wails by giving Scots nearly all they wanted – more self-determination, without losing England's money. They made the same calculation for Wales, where Plaid Cymru was also threatening Labour.

No thought was given to the consequences of these odd arrangements. Nobody answered the question posed by West Lothian MP Tam Dayell: how could it be right that he, a Scottish MP, could vote on the running of schools and hospitals in England, but not those in his own constituency?

But the plans went ahead regardless. Grand new homes were built for the Scottish Parliament and the Welsh Assembly. The Assembly building in Cardiff Bay ended up costing £67 million, over five times the original budget. It was par for the course: after all, the House of Commons, built 150 years ago, ended up three times over budget and 24 years late. But the Scottish Parliament building surpassed even this, costing £414 million against initial estimates of £40 million. Nobody even seemed worried that it was designed by a Catalan architect who had obviously never known rain.

Today, though, Scots are unsure that they get good value from the £600,000 they spend annually on each Member of the Scottish Parliament. And devolution is biting Downing Street back too. The Westminster-dominated Labour Party is resented as a sort of colonial administration. The SNP picked up even more seats, and now controls the new Parliament.

Then Home Secretary John Prescott was keen to push forward with the whole plan for regional assemblies in England, and build up new strongholds for Labour. Since the motivation was party advantage rather than good government, the idea was to start in the North East of England, where Labour support was strongest. But the referendum there in 2004 was roundly defeated with a 78 per cent No vote: electors thought they had enough government already, and couldn't stand the thought of getting yet another layer of it. So plans for regional assemblies were shelved, making Scottish and Welsh devolution look even odder.

House of Lords reform

Another upheaval with no constitutional vision is House of Lords reform. The first idea was to remove the hereditary peers and carry on. But that would turn the House of Lords into Britain's biggest quango, its members all hand picked by the Prime Minister, not a body with any legitimate claim to represent the public.

So various proposals for electing peers were mooted. The 2001 White Paper suggested a modest 20 per cent being elected – Downing Street saw no reason to dilute the Prime Minister's power overmuch. Things stuck there for six years. But as the Blair administration stumbled on, more people began to see good reasons why its power should be diluted. The 2007 White Paper grudgingly suggested upping the proportion of elected members to 50 per cent; but then the Commons voted for either 80 per cent or 100 per cent. Downing Street went quiet again, presumably hoping that this unseemly enthusiasm for democracy might gradually fade away.

Meanwhile the hereditary peers were indeed removed. Or most were: the Conservative Leader in the Lords, Viscount Cranborne – whose family have been running intrigues since the Tudors – conspired for himself and 91 others to remain in place for a while.

But unfortunately for Downing Street, the loss of the hereditaries made the House of Lords feel more legitimate than before, and more entitled to stand up against the House of Commons. So Downing Street has found the Lords blocking its legislation, like the flagship Prevention of Terrorism Bill in 2005, and threatening to block much more. In 2008 the Lords sank another flagship measure – to allow the police to hold terrorist suspects for 42 days without charge.

How Downing Street must wish that it could revisit the 1983 Manifesto again and just scrap the lot of them and get on with governing the country in its own way! But when they try, they often mess up spectacularly. A classic example was the Constitutional Reform Bill 2005, which would abolish the office of Lord Chancellor. The annual TV pictures of a grown man in wig and black tights bowing to the Queen at the State Opening of Parliament and then retreating backwards from the Throne were more than New Labour modernizers could bear. Sadly they overlooked the fact that dozens of laws mention the office and hinge on its existence. After red faces all round, the office was retained, but given to a minister in the Commons, where black tights are less favoured.

Electoral reforms
Another part of the John Smith package that Tony Blair inherited was electoral reform. For a while the Liberal Democrats believed they might actually get their one key demand – proportional representation at elections. Tony Blair and the former Liberal Democrat leader Paddy Ashdown talked about the issue before the 1997 election. But it curiously disappeared off Blair's agenda after his landslide victory.

Nevertheless, even New Labour strategists could not believe their luck would last forever, and sooner or later they might need the Liberal Democrats. Whatever its effect on the country, proportional representation would produce an almost permanent Lib-Lab coalition: they would not have to worry about the Conservatives any more. So the 2001 Labour Manifesto promised a review of the electoral system, and the Liberal Democrats patiently waited for Blair to make good that promise. But waiting for Blair, as Paddy Ashdown later remarked, was like waiting for Godot.

Downing Street did deliver on promises to make voting

easier. It was presented as reform in the public interest, but party interest was strong too. Conservative voters tend to be older, and older people are more likely to vote. So anything that makes voting easier, like easier postal voting, benefits Labour.

In fact, easier postal voting benefited them rather too much. In 2005, Judge Richard Mawrey quashed the results of two Birmingham council elections because hundred of postal-ballot signatures had been forged. Activists had simply applied for votes by post, got them sent to a convenient address, and filled them in.

Modernizing government

Such scandals happened despite the Political Parties, Elections and Referendums Act 2000 – a law designed to showcase how New Labour principle had replaced Conservative sleaze. It required political bodies to register large donations. To the distress of charitable think tanks, its first draft would have classed them as political bodies too, though it specifically excluded the overtly leftist Fabian Society – causing Westminster insiders to wonder just how carefully this law had been written.

Subsequent events confirmed its shortcomings. It did not require the parties to declare loans, even if there was little sign of them ever being repaid. And most of the £17.94 million raised for the 2005 election campaign came through this method. The names of £1 million supporters could be concealed, even as the Prime Minister was recommending them for honours. Indeed, they were even concealed from the Party Treasurer Jack Dromey. The scandal when this news broke forced the government to bring in a new 2006 measure to outlaw unregistered loans too.

The Freedom of Information Act was another bold proposal in the 1997 Labour Manifesto, heralding the era of open government. But openness had to wait for three years until the Act was passed in 2000, by which time ministers were having reservations about it. The openness that seemed such a good idea in opposition did not seem so good in government.

So the Act was hedged around with exemptions, and departments were given five years to 'prepare' for the legislation before it came into effect in 2005. The shredders must have been running red hot. Even now, journalists who use the Act to obtain departmental information complain about the sheer time and effort that it takes to make ministers comply with the simplest requests. And some suspect that the Act simply encourages more sofa government-decisions being taken without notes or minutes, leaving no paper trail to be found.

Farewell, Frau Battenberg
You can love or loathe the Queen. But the monarchy is supposed to represent the whole nation, which of course no politician ever can. That is why monarchs never allow themselves to get drawn into party politics. But that makes them easy prey, unable to strike back, when the politicians want to subvert the institution of monarchy for their own purposes.

It started with the death of Diana. Tony Blair upstaged all the royals with his 'People's Princess' eulogy: dark coat, faltering speech, he seemed at one with the nation. It upstaged the opposition leader John Major too – his press aide Fiona Gunn rang to wake him when the news broke, but he thought it inappropriate for a party leader to make speeches on it. Blair had no such qualms.

He muscled in on the Queen Mother's funeral too, demanding to read a lesson. A state funeral is no place for a politician, but it was great political positioning. He even tried to upstage the Queen at the State Opening of Parliament, where the whole point is to demonstrate that government is there to serve the whole nation, not just one set of political interests.

But New Labour identifies itself with the nation. That is why Jack Straw once referred to Blair as the 'Head of State', while the Number 10 website talked of the Queen enjoying audiences with Tony Blair, rather than vice versa. Blair also talked of 'my' armed forces. But we should all be worried when politicians start to believe that the whole might of the state exists to serve their own ends.

The extremely big tent

Meanwhile various celebrities have been brought in to make it look as if all the nation's big names share in the New Labour enterprise. When Greg Dyke and John Birt both came into the 'big tent', it seemed as if even the BBC itself was part of the Project. Actors, entrepreneurs, doctors, chefs – Lloyd Grossman on hospital dinners, Jamie Oliver on school lunches – have all been recruited.

But pretty soon they all find that the big tent is just a talking-tent, designed for show. Those inside never get to take any real decisions. They are invited in only to make the government look cool.

No: if you can't be bothered to stand for election but still want to make decisions, you need to get yourself on a quango. We now have endless numbers of policy Tsars, working parties, policy forums, commissions, reviews, panels, and action teams. There is the Social Exclusion Unit, the Women's Unit, the Freedom of Information Unit, the Anti-Drugs Co-ordination Unit, the Forward Strategy Unit, the Prime Minister's Delivery Unit, the Office of Public Sector Reform, the Office of the Third Sector (the what?), and many, many more.

Politicians like quangos. They can dump any problem on a quango and then just forget it. They can refer any complaint to a quango and say it's not their fault. And the more quangos you have, the fewer complaints you get, because nobody is quite sure who is in charge anyway.

Between 1997 and the end of 2004, New Labour created 113 new quangos, before it stopped counting – the figures are now almost impossible to dig out. The cost is huge: the salaries of quango bosses cost over £100 million, while the Regional Development Agencies, just to take one set of quangos, employ 2,500 staff at a cost of £2 billion a year. And many quangos actually have the power to issue fines and put people out of business – despite the fact that nobody has ever elected a single member of them. That is the scale of the democratic deficit which today's government has created.

Inflammation at the Treasury

At the Treasury-formerly HM Treasury, but who needs Her Majesty? – Gordon Brown sidelined officials, working solely with a handful of advisers such as Ed Balls (which might explain the costly, cumbersome projects such as tax credits).

Brown's Treasury was not just about spending and cost control. It became the driver of change. Since he was giving out the money, he wanted to control how it was spent. So he imposed targets on every bit of the public sector – specifying what NHS waiting times, school results, levels of street crime, or immigration numbers they had to produce for his cash. Of course, people soon found ways round them – hospital trolleys were re-classified as beds, and corridors as wards, so the targets were met. But eventually the weight of these central controls became overwhelming. Doctors, teachers and police officers still complain that they spend more time dealing with the paperwork than doing the job.

Brown initiated various policy reviews – 42 of them in all – on civil-service efficiency, housing, health, transport – seemingly in competition to what Blair's own Strategy Unit,

Delivery Unit, and Efficiency Programme were doing. The promised 'joined up government' didn't even join up Number 10 with Number 11. It was a diarchy, a competition between Blair and Brown; but ultimately, Brown decided what happened, because he controlled the money.

The rotten state of government today

But even the micro-managing Gordon Brown cannot actually run the leviathan that he and his system have created. For a time, the Duke of Wellington ran his entire government by visiting each ministry in his coach every morning, before retiring to his club for lunch. Now, the centre cannot keep track of all the public bodies it has created or the programmes it must manage. With no delegation to the civil service, Cabinet, Parliament, or local people, Downing Street simply does not have the time to check every policy detail.

That is why so many things end in disaster. Downing Street intervenes constantly, but not to any effect. Public services have multiple objectives that can't all be specified, targeted and monitored by the centre. Centralism just produces one-size-fits-all policies that don't fit local circumstances.

A typical result was when churches discovered that the new Licensing Bill would require them to apply for permission to sing hymns. True, this was reversed: but how silly a system is it that produces such absurdities in the first place?

Government by media

Downing Street's power has the media in thrall. After the July 2005 London bombings, with Parliament in recess, Tony Blair went on television to announce a 'twelve point plan' for dealing with terrorism. He hadn't bothered to tell the Home Secretary, and many of his points turned out to be impractical, illegal or already law, but the media were captured and the days' headlines were bought.

Likewise, Downing Street bends to media campaigns. When Foot and Mouth Disease struck a farm in Devon, the cattle in neighbouring farms, though healthy, were slaughtered too, under the regulations. Somehow a pure white calf – which the papers called Phoenix – escaped the cull, and was found alive among a heap of dead animals five days later. It provided great pictures, and Phoenix became a national celebrity. The Daily Mirror launched a 'Save Phoenix' campaign.

A Downing Street spokesman appeared to say that the rules would be changed so that animals in neighbouring farms would not automatically be culled when Foot and Mouth broke out. The photogenic Phoenix would be saved.

It was pure government by media. The vets had not been consulted, nor even the Agriculture Secretary Nick Brown, who learnt it from the Ten o'Clock News. Nor did it stop four million other animals being slaughtered. Still, the law can't stand in the way of a good story.

In the 24-hour news world, things move fast. Politicians have to be quick with instant responses, and instant solutions. After the 1996 school shootings in Dunblane, the politicians' instant response was to ban all handguns. It didn't occur to them that UK national shooting teams would then have to practice in Norway (it took ten years for the ban to be relaxed for a handful of Olympic shooters), nor that a handgun ban meant that only bad guys would then have access to them. And indeed the ban made no difference: handgun crime continued to increase. When two innocent bystanders were killed in Birmingham during a shoot-out between drugs gangs, the Home Secretary's first official response was to blame violent rap music.

It was hardly getting to the heart of the problem. But such is the intellectual incoherence of government by media, where the message is the policy. There is no vision or principle: if it doesn't play on the TV chat shows, it gets ditched.

But if the test is what works right now, nothing works in the long term. By trying to please everyone, you end up pleasing nobody. You get lost in trivial posturing – abolishing the Lord Chancellor, banning foxhunting. But it achieves nothing: we still have a Lord Chancellor and foxhunting is still going strong.

The dodgy dossier

Iraq is a classic example. An invasion was on the cards in April 2002, when Tony Blair visited George Bush in Texas, and took legal opinion on whether a war was justified. It was not clear whether Saddam Hussein really possessed weapons of mass destruction, but by July 2002, Downing Street considered war inevitable.

So the intelligence facts had to be distorted to fit the policy. A small clique took all the decisions – Number 10 liaised directly with the White House; the Foreign Office and the ambassadors were frozen out. Gordon Brown too.

To justify war to the media, Downing Street concocted the famous 'dossiers' of September 2002 and February 2003, outlining the supposed threat. Some parts came from intelligence sources; but much of the second was recycled from *Jane's Intelligence Review* and a graduate thesis based on decade-old reports, complete with the same spelling mistakes. They were published in the normal way, by leaks to a Sunday newspaper.

On Radio 4 the journalist Andrew Gilligan said that Downing Street had ordered the September dossier to be 'sexed up'. Alistair Campbell dismissed it as fantasy, before launching a massive mole hunt to find the source of this disclosure. The net closed in on senior civil servant David Kelly, who committed suicide under the strain. Only then did anyone bother to involve the head of the civil service, Cabinet Secretary Andrew Turnbull. It showed that this affair was all about party politics, not national policy.

Nobody can check the truth of Campbell's claim that the September dossier was not 'sexed up' for the media, because the decisions were made on the sofa, without minutes. An inquiry decided Downing Street was not to blame, and BBC executives were fired. But most commentators thought it all a whitewash.

Our rotten political state
The dodgy dossier affair shows just how far government, and the institutions of the state, have been corrupted to serve purely party interests. The Cabinet, Parliament, the civil service, even the monarchy have been pushed aside by a small, poorly informed, unelected clique that puts presentation above principle.

Because they indentify the state's interests as their own, this ruling clique feels perfectly entitled to change the constitution, override the rule of law, and extinguish both liberties and even lives to achieve their purposes. They have no clear process for taking decisions, leaving nobody accountable for what is decided. They try to control and command from the centre a government that they have made too big to control and command at all.

A system of checks and balances has been turned into a central autocracy. But while power corrupts, it is also very pleasant. It is unlikely that politicians of any other party would choose to restore the constitutional limits on their action.

It's a rotten state of affairs, and the amazing thing is that our politicians can still believe – and convince us too – that it is all in the public interest. But then the technology of spin and self-deceit are some of the most remarkable creations of this new, close-knit political clan that really believes itself to represent the whole People and to be the People's Government.

3

SPIN

Letting the Sun in

Cherie Blair famously said that she wouldn't have the *Sun* in the house. But that did not stop her husband cosying up to its proprietor, Rupert Murdoch.

It was quite a turn-around. In the 1980s, Labour and the trade unions had boycotted Murdoch's News International titles after a bitter workforce dispute over his introduction of new production technology. There would be no Sun in Transport House, any more than in Cherie's. And few kind words about Labour would appear in the *Sun*.

But the *Sun* is Britain's largest-selling daily paper. Its readers are exactly those working-class voters that Margaret Thatcher wooed away from the Labour Party and which New Labour had to woo back. They could hardly expect to make the *Sun* support them; but perhaps they could soften its hatred. ('If Kinnock wins today,' it said of Blair's predecessor on Election Day 1992, 'will the last person to leave Britain please turn out the lights?')

Blair first met Rupert Murdoch in 1994, and put his considerable charm to work on him. A year later, he flew to Queensland to outline the New Labour case to Murdoch's executives at a News International senior management conference. The gruelling 48 hours he spent flying there and back was a considerable investment of time and energy for a party leader, and Murdoch appreciated that effort. By 1997 Blair had convinced Murdoch that a Labour government would not hit News International with new employment and media laws, and that it would hold off from joining the Euro-one of Murdoch's bugbears.

The New Labour hierarchy must have wept in delight when, three months before the 1997 election, the *Sun* changed sides and supported them.

But New Labour had become consumed by its own culture of spin, where long-term vision and principles were sacrificed for favourable daily headlines. Eventually the owner of the *Sun* would lose patience and his newspaper would come back to bite them.

The spin machine

The Party started as they meant to go on. They spun as New Labour in opposition, and they would spin as New Labour in government. They correctly realized that the world had changed. An effective soundbite, or going on Richard and Judy, won over more floating voters than any number of worthy policy reports. Increased newspaper competition meant that journalists now wanted scoops and exclusives, not general press releases. And the new 24-hour news channels wanted constant announcements and initiatives to feed their hungry schedules.

New Labour in opposition exploited such things brilliantly. A sophisticated computer filing system allowed them to give journalists instant rebuttal to any Conservative statement. The defections of Conservative activists were held and timed to perfection for maximum media impact. They fed the media constant scorn against Conservative sleaze, and showily twisted the knife further by not opposing the independent anti-sleaze candidate, Martin Bell, in Tatton.

In terms of setting the news agenda, responding to issues,

framing their policies positively, and making sure they looked good and inspired confidence, they were far ahead of the Conservatives. Their slick presentation was key to their electoral landslide in 1997. But this same obsession with presentation, and the seeming willingness to sacrifice truth for its sake, has come to make the public question whether they can actually trust a word that politicians say.

The media approach

New Labour's spin machine was organized, professional-and political. Organizationally, it was highly centralized, with the Downing Street Press Secretary Alastair Campbell at the hub. He was the sultan of spin. His office managed all media traffic, framed all policy presentations, handled all public announcements, and scheduled all interviews and appearances. No deviation was tolerated: even Gordon Brown's press secretary, Charlie Whelan, was forced out because of his tendency to brief journalists independently.

Campbell was the first Downing Street press secretary to attend Cabinet meetings. Everyone, including the head of the Downing Street Policy Unit, David Miliband, was junior to him-something unimaginable in previous governments, even in the time of Mrs Thatcher's formidable press secretary, Bernard Ingham. By 2001, Campbell was even kicking the Chief Whip out of his traditional home at 12 Downing Street to make room for his spin-doctors.

Professionally, Campbell's sultanate was equally uncompromising. His new Strategic Communications Unit coordinated all government announcements on a daily 'grid' designed to avoid conflicts, maximize their impact, and dominate the daily news agenda. Former journalists-like Campbell himself-were hired into the government information service, on the grounds that they would understand the media far better than any career civil servant.

Within eighteen months, nearly all the civil-service information officers had gone. They were replaced by a new generation with much greater loyalty to the New Labour message-and more willing to be more proactive in presenting it. The government press machine became not just more organized and more professional: it became more politicized too.

The privatization of public information

Previously, Downing Street press secretaries had always been civil servants. Even Bernard Ingham was chosen for Mrs Thatcher by the civil service. Ingham was fiercely loyal to his boss, but kept an appropriate distance from her party: he never went to Conservative conferences.

By contrast, Campbell was first and foremost a New Labour partisan. But remarkably, he was given powers over the civil service too. It was a revolution.

And now, a once-impartial civil service is a willing partner in cutting out the House of Commons and working out how best to leak government news to friendly journalists for the benefit of the ruling party. They seek to get extensive and favourable coverage for the good news, hide the bad news under more interesting items, and give ministers time to spin each story before opposition politicians can respond. Trading public information for party advantage is now second nature to them.

Meanwhile, official government reports now look more like glossy manifestos than businesslike and impartial presentations of public information. They come in large, showy formats, often with more photographs than text, with upbeat, full-page messages from the Prime Minister, and full-colour spreads to show an active, dynamic government at work.

The Foreign Office's first annual report on human rights

was a classic of the genre. Of its 50 pages, five were full-page colour spreads. There were photos of a smiling Prime Minister, a smiling Foreign Secretary. Even a picture of the Queen-who is supposed to be above politics – was included in order to support the message that the whole country should feel good about the progress its busy leaders were making on human rights.

The brand's the thing

Departments themselves have been re-branded to get the ruling party's message across. From my office in Westminster I watch a seemingly constant procession of signwriters plying their trade on the other side of the road as the Department of Education and the Department of Trade and Industry go through regular transformations. After each Cabinet re-shuffle, the old signs are taken down and temporary new ones are put up. Then a little later, those come down and up go the permanent signs in stainless steel or enamel, with some spanking-new departmental logo.

Thus Mrs Thatcher's old Department of Education and Science became simply the Department for Education under John Major, with the Skills bit shoved up the road to Trade and Industry. Then it became the Department for Education and Employment. Then the Department for Education and Skills, just to show how work-oriented it was; and of course for sounds much more pro-active than of. Now it is the Department for Children, Schools and Families, and bits of it have been hived off into a new Department for Innovation, Universities and Skills.

Children, Families, Innovation, Skills... the whole point of this re-branding is to make us think that our government is really on top of the things that matter.

Meanwhile, the old Department of Trade and Industry was

dubbed The Department for Enterprise, as New Labour reminded businesspeople just how new it had become. And now it hits all their bases – pro-business, anti-red-tape – as the Department for Business and Regulatory Reform. Just don't ask who created all the regulation that the department is now committed to reform.

It all costs a fortune. There is extensive opinion polling to find out what names will resonate with the public; new logo designs don't come cheap, either, and the government no doubt pays over the odds. But they judge it worth every penny of our money to explain how busily our rulers are working on our behalf.

Nor does it stop there. Those of us who suffer the various departments' awful services are now 'customers'. Too bad that we didn't have the ability to choose some other provider, as real customers of competitive private businesses do. It all amounts to nothing: just the creation of a subliminal message.

The Cabinet message

Even Cabinet members are chosen to send a message about the government's positioning, rather than to get the best people into the key jobs. When Gordon Brown became Prime Minister in 2007 he wanted to distance himself from the Blair administration. The words 'new' and 'change' were everywhere. So we got the first female Home Secretary, Jacqui Smith, and a fresh-faced Foreign Secretary in the shape of David Miliband.

It's all a long way from John Major's time, when he selected his Cabinet and then realized that it didn't contain any women. That kind of political incorrectness could never happen today. The message is the priority. If ministers actually prove to be up to the job, that is regarded as a bonus.

No wonder that ministers are so reluctant to debate. It started from the first day of the New Labour administration:

ministers would go on programmes such as the BBC's Newsnight, but only for a one-on-one interview with the presenter. The camera would then swing to the other side of the table, where two opposition MPs would battle it out as the minister slipped away. The idea was to show ministers on a higher level than these mere, bickering politicians.

Subverting the press

The sudden politicization of the Downing Street press office was felt particularly strongly by the journalists who cover Westminster – known as 'the lobby' after the Parliamentary lobbies where they traditionally hung around to buttonhole MPs. At the regular press briefings, Campbell took pleasure in humiliating those journalists who asked awkward questions, and they could be pretty sure that they wouldn't get many of those choice snippets of advance information – like the date of the next election, or what celebrities would be in the next honours list – that would give them a scoop and advance their careers.

Perhaps most astonishingly for an official government spokesman, Campbell would actually try to get journalists sacked if they ventured off-message. One political correspondent was in his editor's office when Campbell phoned (it was his favourite communication method, both discreet and deniable). He demanded that the correspondent should be fired, threatening to freeze the paper out of exclusives if he wasn't. But the editor was a confident individual, and called the bluff: he simply leaned back in his chair and put Campbell's call on speakerphone so that the whole office could hear the rant. The correspondent kept his job.

But others didn't. Newspapers were indeed frozen out until their line softened or their political correspondents were moved to other work. Even the firebrand Daily Express seemed to turn itself into a Europhile paper when policy demanded it. Too often, journalists would not even bother to read ministerial statements: they simply reproduced the 'line to take' from Downing Street. That was much safer than getting on the wrong side of a formidable spin machine.

I always wondered why the press took so long to turn against an administration that they knew simply lied to them, sometimes with only the thinnest attempt at concealment. Journalists told me time and again that they did not trust a word from any minister. But of course the reason why they give in to this bullying is that they depend on the hand of government to feed them. New technology has made the media much more competitive, and journalists spend more time at their computers, watching news feeds and filing stories and blogs, and less time in the Westminster bars hunting out stories.

So the journalists are after scoops, and the politicians are after coverage. It is a mutually beneficial arrangement. But it is corrupt. Journalists pretend to be objective but in fact are the willing messengers of those who feed them with stories, in a mutual conspiracy against the public.

Unseemly bedfellows
The fit between journalism and politics has never been closer. Being a journalist is a stepping stone to becoming a politician, as Michael Gove or Boris Johnson demonstrate. And journalism has provided a nice retirement job for politicians such as Michael Portillo, Roy Hattersley, and David Mellor.

The closeness of this partnership between the press and the politicians became obvious a few years ago when a copy of the Downing Street media 'grid' was leaked. The schedule specifically included campaigns that the *Sun* intended to run some days later. Rather than merely report government initiatives, the paper was making itself a part of their promotion.

In other cases too, potentially controversial government announcements have been given exclusively to a newspaper in return for a series of favourable pieces. To the insider's eye, it is obvious that all the articles and features must have been prepared long in advance – that is, in connivance with the political spinners.

Even businesses get drawn into these conspiracies. An example is the 2008 proposal to ban plastic supermarket bags: one day it was trailed in the Daily Mail, the next day Marks & Spencer said they would gladly comply, and on the third, Gordon Brown announced it as policy. In real life, things don't happen so fast: it must have been sold as a package at the start.

Insider dealing

Government information can be very valuable, which is why more care should be taken with it. In the financial markets, insider information has been outlawed, because people can make fortunes from a tip-off – such as the size of the profit or loss that a company is about to announce – at the expense of the shareholders to whom that information rightly belongs. City regulators would never allow companies to sell their financial information to different parts of the market at different times.

But in the political market, that is exactly what happens. Information that rightly belongs to the public is traded, not usually for money, but for power. It's a form of insider dealing that enables politicians to puff themselves up and deflate their enemies.

Even the civil servants gain, if they can trade information in ways that please their political bosses. The system undermines their traditional objectivity. Instead of providing information fairly to everyone at once, the whole government information machine has become insider dealers in it. If they worked in the

City, rather than Westminster, they would all go to jail.

Blair himself disclosed the following day's unemployment figures in order to help get a friendlier reception at the Trades Union Congress – though such economic figures are commercially sensitive. But his ultimate cheek was telling the *Sun* the date of the 2001 election before even consulting the Queen. The leak was timed to coincide with a speech Blair was giving at St. Olave's girls' school assembly. The hymns, stained glass, and uplifting sentiment ('I want to win not just your vote, but your heart and mind') were a perfect start to a campaign – even if the girls themselves, being too young to vote, were a little confused.

The subversion manual

Instead, both civil servants and government ministers have turned the insider trading of public information into a science.

One technique is of course to leak upcoming announcements to friendly journalists who will give them good coverage. It also helps to get the journalists on side and keep them there. A similar technique is to give favoured journalists inside access to senior politicians – such as in-depth interviews that other media are denied. For example, Alastair Campbell arranged for the *Sun* to have exclusive world stories and interviews with Tony Blair immediately before the 1997 election. The favour might well have helped swing the paper behind Blair's party.

However, it can be equally useful to leak a positive story or give an exclusive interview to a paper that is not generally reckoned to be on side. Since they get such scoops so rarely, they are more likely to play it big, gushing their gratitude across several pages. Such large and favourable coverage in turn causes other media, and the public, to comment on how even this normally hostile paper seems to be supporting the latest government initiative; and that in turn makes them more supportive too.

Front-page exclusives, of course, are gold dust not only to the newspaper which runs them, but to the spin-doctors who mastermind them. Such prominence – which of course can be bought easily enough – makes the story seem that much more important. As such, it gets mentioned and reviewed on that day's television and radio news. Although the story was broken by a competitor, other papers are then obliged to mention it too, in a widening, deepening spiral of spin.

And yet the politicians are furious when public servants use the same techniques against them. In 2006 the new head of the army, General Sir Richard Dannatt, played the media brilliantly with his complaint that British soldiers who risked death in Afghanistan and Iraq were paid about half the minimum wage, and his advice that Britain should quit Iraq. It was hugely effective spin on behalf of the army. Of course, the government hated such presumption, and in 2008 Gordon Brown blocked Sir Richard's expected promotion to Chief of the Defence Staff.

Sources close to the Prime Minister

In fact, Gordon Brown is just as proficient at the arts of spin as those he criticizes for practising them. Despite his much-vaunted 'war on spin' as Prime Minister, the cost of Whitehall spin-doctors has trebled since 1997, to £5.9 million. And with that has come a huge rise in the number of unattributable briefings – another useful technique for spin-doctors.

Journalists need scoops, but cannot always get anyone to corroborate their most sensational stories on the record. People are often glad to tip off a journalist, but not to have their name attached to the subsequent report. So journalists rely more and more on anonymous sources. When you see the phrase 'sources close to the Cabinet said yesterday' you can be pretty sure that this anonymous tip-off came directly from a Cabinet minister. When you see 'sources close to the Prime Minister' you can be pretty sure that it came, maybe not from him – he's busy, after all – but certainly from the Downing Street press office.

Members of the general public are now quite used to see the most explosive stories coming from anonymous sources who give anonymous quotes. But this technique of building stories around unattributed quotes is highly corrosive. The less scrupulous journalists – some cynics might say that's all of them – are no longer averse to simply making up quotes that their sources might well have said, had they been asked the question and volunteered an answer.

American newspapers are much less willing to run unattributed quotes in a story, and some do not allow it at all. While the technique can sometimes help to ferret out the truth, it is also lazy and corrupt.

And it allows those with power to conceal their actions. The Downing Street media machine can and does brief journalists against ministers who are critical of some part of government policy, without those ministers knowing whom to strike back at when the story appears.

Hoist with their own spin

But that's spin-business: those who live by the soundbite die by the soundbite. And soundbites have come back to sink their teeth even into the master of the business, Tony Blair.

Spin-conscious politicians know that it isn't the handful of people in a studio audience who count, nor even the hundreds in a conference hall. It is the impression you make on the millions watching on television. Even so, there are limits to how far you can take those in the room for granted.

In 2002, Tony Blair chose to assert the 'traditional values' of his administration to 10,000 Women's Institute delegates in the

Wembley Arena. They were having none of it. A series of recent sleaze stories had given the lie to his assertions. And his glowing account of the National Health Service was just too much. Many WI members were closely involved in hospital work, and they knew what a dismal state the NHS was really in.

As Blair started reeling off a list of his government's supposed achievements, he received that rarest of rebukes from such a traditionally courteous audience – a slow handclap. Many delegates got up and left, complaining that the Prime Minister was trying to turn their non-political gathering into a party political broadcast for the benefit of the television cameras. The Chair had to call for order. Blair himself looked uncomfortable, ditched his further intended remarks on the NHS, and finished up quickly.

It was a public-relations disaster. And all the more so because it contrasted so very starkly with the highly cultivated image of effortless competence and control that 'Teflon Tony' normally exuded. The story that the newspapers reported next day was not the government's traditional values and record of achievement in the NHS. The headlines were about Blair's spectacular misreading of a mainstream, middle-class audience.

Government by media trail

We have been treated to other hilarious embarrassments too, thanks to ministers' technique of using the media to trail ideas. When they are not sure what to do, but want some quick impact, they float some proposal in the press somewhere – preferably on an unattributed basis – and see whether it finds any resonance among the general public. The news media are of course willing participants in this.

The technique is also used to soften up the public for something that might be thought difficult or disagreeable – like Gordon Brown trailing his proposed ban on free plastic supermarket bags.

In the absence of any ideology or principle, finding out what the public might go for is vital – hence the fixation with opinion polls. But doing it by trailing quarter-baked ideas so publicly can cause some red faces.

The reddest came as a result of Tony Blair's suggestion of marching young offenders off to cashpoints so as to extract spot fines from them. Most, of course, would not have cash cards anyway. And the idea of midnight courts was introduced with great fanfare before it was quickly and quietly forgotten after a less than enthusiastic reception from both the public and those who run the justice system. The idea of 'three strikes and you're out' for burglary was also dropped after everyone realized it was so daft. And as for the proposal of 9pm child curfews – which made a good soundbite, but which were utterly illiberal – few local authorities even bothered to take up the government's suggestion.

This bizarre spin culture provides excellent material for the parodies of Bremner, Bird & Fortune. But many members of the public don't find it so funny. And nor do politicians themselves. In 2002, Labour MP Clare Short told reporters that the government was basically good, but its presentation was 'crummy and lousy'. In 2003 the Speaker of the House of Commons, Glasgow MP Michael Martin, described government spin-doctors as an 'absolute nuisance'; Alastair Campbell 'got up his nose'; and Tony Blair's press aides were 'sweat-rags' (after a Clydeside saying that you should speak to the engineer and not the sweat-rag).

Too clever for everyone's good

In 2007, fifteen British sailors were captured by Iran, accused of spying, and then eventually set free by Iran's President Ahmadinejhad in a grand public gesture designed to contrast

Britain's military action in Iraq with his own humanity and grace. Spin, it seems, is used by politicians the world over.

The only woman in the group, Leading Seaman Faye Turney, was not just a sailor, but a wife and mother. The Ministry of Defence calculated that her human-interest story could help deflect attention from the humiliation that the affair had heaped on the armed forces. In a remarkable reversal of strict military rules that prevent service people from selling their stories, they allowed Faye to appear on ITV's Tonight With Trevor Macdonald and sell her story to the *Sun* for £100,000.

Some of the money she would receive was earmarked for navy families. But the strategy unravelled when other members of the group who had been through exactly the same ordeal complained that the rules had not been waived for them and that it was unfair that only one of them would benefit. The public thought so too: a petition was circulated, calling for whoever authorized the sale of Faye's story to be sacked. Although Downing Street flatly blamed the MoD for the unpopular decision, former army chiefs asserted publicly that a decision of such public and political importance must have gone through Downing Street. It looked like yet another case of the government's spin-doctors being too clever for their own good.

And ours. After years of bitter experience, few of us trust a word that politicians say. We know that they twist statistics and reports and events in order to serve their message and help keep them in power. Just a fifth (22 per cent) of people polled by the Commons sleaze watchdog said they thought ministers tell the truth.

That is why, when the government insisted there was no evidence to back claims that the MMR vaccine (against, mumps, measles and rubella) might produce autism in children, parents simply refused to believe them. Many parents opted to

have their children given the three vaccines in separate inocula-
tions. Others refused to have their children inoculated at all,
despite the fact that the real dangers from these diseases far
exceeded the supposed dangers that the scare was based on.
The public's simple refusal to believe the stories that politicians
spin them actually put the health of their families at risk.

A new generation of spin

And now there is a new generation of spinners in Downing
Street, no less skilled than the last. When at the Treasury,
Gordon Brown clearly understood the importance of spin. He
employed a twelve-strong team of political advisers to help him
at it. And he was content for his short-lived spokesman, Charlie
Whelan, to release highly misleading figures about the
Conservative administration's financial legacy – a ploy that was
exposed soon enough, but which served to erode the Treasury's
traditional reputation for accuracy and objectivity.

But other parts of Brown's spinning took longer to unravel.
His Budget speeches were triumphs of opacity, expounding
only the good news and leaving the bad to be discovered, if at
all, some hundreds of pages deep into the doorstop Red Book.

His July 1997 budget, for example, announced some
supposedly technical changes to dividend credits. It took the
press weeks to work out that this amounted to a huge tax on
the country's pension funds – and the savers who depended on
them for their retirement.

Brown's 1998 budget speech similarly glossed over changes
that turned out to be major stealth taxes. By 1999, the press was
holding back its instant praise for his glib promises. By the time
of his fifth and sixth budgets, they weren't taking anything at
face value any more. Instead they were warning that whatever
he had said at the Commons dispatch box, the real tax
bombshells should only be known after the economists had

picked through the small print of the Red Book.

By the 2005 election, the Sun – which New Labour had spent so much effort on in 1997 – was beginning to lose patience with the party's dissembling. It had 'got to deliver', said the paper, if it wanted their support. In the event, they got the paper's support – signalled by red smoke coming from a chimney on its London offices. But they cannot hope for the same support again.

Future spinners
The Conservatives, meanwhile, have begun to play the spin game themselves. In a spectacular opening show of their green credentials, their new leader, David Cameron, had himself filmed driving a team of Huskies across a Norwegian glacier. He too cuddled up on the talk-show sofas. And he reached out to Labour voters with an exclusive personal interview in the *Guardian* – which, as his spin-doctors had planned, the paper featured with enormous prominence.

Unlike governments, opposition parties may well have a perfect right to favour some journalists over others, and to leak out news about their personalities and their policies in ways that bring them the maximum positive impact. It is, after all, their information, not the state's.

The situation is – or should be – quite different for governments, since much of the information they deal with is properly the public's information. Yet, just as state institutions have been bent to serve party interests, so has information itself. The economic figures, budget presentations, the contents of the next Queen's Speech, even intelligence information, have all been sold and spun for party advantage.

Would David Cameron end this corruption if he were elected Prime Minister? Or, understanding its enormous value to a party in power, would he continue the same culture, even

while trying to convince us that he had scrapped it? It is hard
to know, and even harder to be confident. Perhaps the rot has
spread too deeply, and too widely, across the whole of the
political clan.

4

ROTTEN POLITICIANS

Burying bad news

It shook the world. On 11 September 2001, nineteen Islamic terrorists with links to al-Qaeda hijacked four commercial passenger airliners, crashing one into the Pentagon, and two into the twin towers of New York's World Trade Centre. In minutes, over 3,000 innocent people were dead.

I learnt of this appalling crime at around 13.45 London time, just before the second aircraft struck its New York target. I was on my way to the BBC to talk about the expected nationalization of the rail infrastructure company, Railtrack. The producer called me in great agitation, to say the schedules had all been cleared to cover this atrocity, which he urged me to watch live on television.

He was one of many who telephoned me, just as I telephoned many others. By the time the Pentagon was struck, at 14.37 London time, almost everyone in Westminster must have been watching the awful events unfold. But it was at 14.55 London time that Stephen Byers's special adviser, Jo Moore, sent an email to the press office of her department that read:

It's now a very good day to get out anything we want to bury. Councillors' expenses?

The Department did indeed announce, next day, some minor changes to the system of local councillors' allowances.

But the papers were full of other things.

The political clan

A month later, though, the 'good day to bury bad news' email finally leaked out. It rightly provoked a wave of disgust among commentators and the public. It showed just how low the political clan would stoop to deceive the public.

It was not something that could be passed off as a bad joke, instantly regretted. We all knew that it was entirely typical of how the political clan work: a total obsession with presentation, a callous disregard for anyone outside their political world, the confusion of public and party interests, and the conceit that they could get away with it. But this time, it was a conceit too far. There were loud calls, from the papers and the public, for Jo Moore's resignation.

They didn't get it. The political clan stick together. They never resign, unless their whole survival is threatened. After a week of stonewalling, we got the nearest thing they have to an apology. Before a specially invited camera crew, Jo Moore said sorry: to the Secretary of State, to the department, and to the government. It took just seconds. She answered no questions.

As she turned, the camera caught a smirk, as if she were congratulating herself on another successful bit of spin. Only later did we all realize that, while she had apologized profusely to all her class comrades, she had offered no words of apology at all to those who had lost friends and relatives in those harrowing events.

The career path

Jo Moore's career too was entirely typical. A political activist, she worked as a local-government press officer in London, then for the Labour Party. After a short time at a lobbying firm, she became a spin doctor in the Department of Trade – one of those political jobs paid for by public money.

The political clan are mostly just like this: metropolitan and middle class university activists, who get their training in think tanks and trade unions. They get jobs in politics, fight a 'hopeless' parliamentary seat, then a 'safe' one that gets them in to the House of Commons. There, they dutifully oblige the whips, and hope to be rewarded with a foot on the ministerial career ladder, which is their route to the uplands of higher pay, perks, and pensions.

They know nothing about the hardships of the real world, or anything outside the recession-proof world of politics. Few have ever actually run anything before they are put in charge of government departments with thousands of civil servants. It is no surprise that they mess up so spectacularly: the Millennium Dome, the over-budget IT programmes, a Home Office 'not fit for purpose'.

A disconnected clan

Because their world is so far from ours, the political clan struggle to connect with us in any authentic way. They bone up on football and reality TV, adopt Estuary English, and use symbols to show how they are really like us – Harold Wilson's HP sauce, perhaps, or Tony Blair's family-photo coffee mug. It's all fake, but through these techniques they hope to communicate directly with us, the People, without their carefully contrived messages being distorted by a sceptical media.

When real people do get in the way of a good message, they are swept aside – like 94-year-old Rose Addis, who was admitted to hospital after a fall but was left two days in her own blood-spattered clothes. It was a story the spin doctors had to kill, especially since it came on top of other scandals such as the case of Mavis Skeet, who died when her cancer became inoperable because her surgery had been cancelled so many times.

So a 'swift rebuttal' plan swung into place, with a hospital spokesman (and Labour supporter) implying that Rose was a racist who had refused help from the non-white staff, rather than the problem being any fault of the NHS. Patient confidentiality was abandoned as politicians on all sides rushed to use the details of this sad case for their own party advantage.

Politics and plutocrats
But while they are happy to brush aside ordinary people, the political clan are very keen to be seen with the rich and famous, and accept their favours. The Blairs cadged countless free holidays off them, staying at Sir Cliff Richard's spread in Barbados, Silvio Berlusconi's villa in Sardinia, Sir Elton John's place in Portugal, and Sir Ian McKellen's house in France. British Airways even upgraded them to first class when they spent New Year with Bee Gees singer Robin Gibb and his wife Swina at their Miami mansion.

It is not just the reflected glow of their celebrity. These 'friends' are much safer than the real-life flatmates or colleagues who might embarrass them. Such as Tony Blair's old boss Lord 'Derry' Irvine, who within weeks of becoming Lord Chancellor spent £650,000 of public money on decorating his official apartments in Westminster, including £59,000 on wallpaper at £400 a roll.

Government spinners said it was all part of a planned Palace of Westminster makeover – which was a lie. Although the place probably was looking a little drab: the Conservatives never dared to change a light bulb for fear that Labour would condemn them as profligate.

Just before the 1997 election, I visited the official home of a senior minister. It was a magnificent, historic building, but inside it was a mess: worn carpets, grubby wallpaper, scuffed furniture and ghastly 1970s fittings. I asked why he didn't have the place restored to its original glory – after all, it was used for official functions, and its many visitors must also be pained to see a historic house in such a dowdy condition. He said frankly that he did not dare spend any money on it, because the opposition's spin machine would immediately accuse him of using public money to feather his own nest. Of course, within weeks of his Labour successor taking over after the election, the whole place was given a complete period makeover. The Conservatives weren't always clean, but at least they were never quite so shameless.

Lord Irvine embarrassed his old employee again when he retired as Lord Chancellor in June 2003 with a taxpayer-funded pension package worth £1,900,000. It was rather more than the pension funding that the government allows ordinary citizens to accumulate before they are hit by punitive rates of taxation. And not bad for just six years in the job.

Official home comforts

The top politicians love their official homes. Only a series of misfortunes winkled the Deputy Prime Minister, John Prescott, out of his 21-room grace-and-favour country house, Dorneywood. There was his affair with his secretary Tracey Temple; then he was photographed there playing croquet when he should have been running the country during Tony Blair's absence in Washington.

It was all very bad public relations. Prescott was stripped of his department, but allowed to keep his title and, remarkably, his £133,000 ministerial salary.

Dorneywood is one of many grace-and-favour homes that are in the gift of the Prime Minister – though, like the Prime Minister's country house, Chequers, it is run by a charitable trust at no cost to taxpayers. There are top-floor flats in 10 and 11 Downing Street. The Northern Ireland Secretary lives in the eighteenth-century Hillsborough Castle, and Scotland's First Minister in a Georgian mansion in Edinburgh's Charlotte Square.

Chevening, a 3,500-acre estate in Kent, is normally occupied by the Foreign Secretary, as is Number 1 Carlton Gardens in Westminster. The Home Secretary has another house in nearby Belgravia. The Speaker of the House of Commons and the Lord Chancellor both occupy fabulous apartments in the Palace of Westminster. And there are three grace-and-favour apartments in Whitehall's Admiralty House, in one of which, from 2002, John Prescott entertained his secretary. (He also had a London flat provided by his trade union, which he forgot to mention to the Parliamentary sleaze watchdog.)

Perhaps ministers need special homes if they face security threats, or need somewhere to meet foreign dignitaries. But it is an obvious source of corruption when the Prime Minister has patronage over homes worth millions. It is just another of those levers that Downing Street can use to keep ministers under the thumb. And democracy suffers when ministers are so cut off from the real world, gliding in their chauffeur-driven cars between their departments, occasional appearances in Parliament, and their taxpayer-funded official mansions.

Resigning matters

Along with the salary, the perks, the flunkies and the pensions, the chauffeur-driven car is what ministers prize most. It's so much better than hacking it on the bus with the rest of us sweaty mortals. No wonder they never resign.

The Conservative Chancellor Norman Lamont didn't resign, even after Britain's humiliating exit from the European Exchange Rate Mechanism in 1992. Nor did the Home

Secretary Michael Howard, despite a spate of prison breakouts that made his department look almost comically careless.

Lesser members of the clan are expendable, though. Jo Moore finally went in February 2002 when her department chose the day of Princess Margaret's funeral to publish some unflattering railway statistics. A leaked email from her boss, the former BBC journalist Martin Sixsmith, was (inaccurately) reported as saying 'Princess Margaret is being buried [on Friday]. I will absolutely not allow anything else to be.' The public hilarity left Moore unable to be taken seriously again.

But ministers resign only when the spin-doctors can't control the story any more. One such was Trade and Industry Secretary Peter Mandelson, who forgot to mention, either to his building society or to the House of Commons, that his new home in London's Notting Hill was bought with the help of a £373,000 loan from millionaire MP Geoffrey Robinson – whose business affairs were coincidentally being investigated by Mandelson's department.

But the political clan protects its own, and Mandelson soon came back, as Northern Ireland Secretary. He was sunk a second time by reports that he had telephoned the Home Office on behalf of Srichand Hinduja, a major sponsor of the Millennium Dome project, who was seeking a British passport – but was being investigated by the Indian government. It was another public-relations catastrophe, and Mandelson resigned a second time.

After a spell as EU Trade Commissioner, though, he returned to the Cabinet for a third time in 2008, as Business Secretary. It caused many to wonder: do these people have no shame?

Perhaps they don't. David Blunkett also resigned twice after public-relations calamities. While Home Secretary, he had an affair with Spectator publisher Kimberly Quinn. It ended acrimoniously in August 2004 and Blunkett took Quinn to court to determine the paternity of her unborn child. Meanwhile, there were reports that he had tried to expedite a residence visa for Quinn's Filipina nanny; and had given her a taxpayer-funded railway pass. He was forced out – yet still held on to his grace-and-favour Belgravia home.

Back again as Work and Pensions Secretary, it emerged that Blunkett had shares in a company called DNA Bioscience – which provided paternity tests to the Child Support Agency, part of his department. He argued that the shares were held in trust so he had no conflict of interest. But he ignored three letters from the Advisory Committee on Business Appointments urging him to contact them, and he failed to consult them on two other paid jobs that he had held.

Regardless of the rights or wrongs of any of this, why don't ministers see the gulf they create between their lifestyles and ours? Most people are a world away from £373,000 loans, friendships with Indian billionaires, affairs with rich publishers, and personal shareholdings. Why don't they steer clear of them? But in the cocooned world of a minister, you think you can do anything.

Double standards

And the double standards are astonishing. John Prescott got away with having sex in the office, something which would bring a swift sacking to any ordinary person in a private business. Or a public servant for that matter: in 2008, PC Gary Bayldon, 48, was jailed for four months for having sex while on duty (though he left his radio on so he could answer calls). But ministers seem above the rules.

Another example of double standards was Foreign Secretary Robin Cook, who promised us an 'ethical' foreign policy. But his domestic ethics were flimsier: he was having an extramarital affair with a staffer, Gaynor Regan. As Cook and his wife awaited a plane at Heathrow Airport, New Labour spin-doctor Alastair Campbell called to say that the story was about to break and he must make a choice. He chose to keep his job and to leave his wife: it was divorce by press secretary.

Rumour had it that Downing Street went further, trying to bury the story by suggesting to the press that MI5 was investigating a senior Conservative. It seems perfectly possible, given the grief that ministers' sex-lives cause the spin-doctors. In October 1998, the former Welsh Secretary, Ron Davies, resigned as First Secretary of the new Welsh Assembly after being mugged by a man he met on Clapham Common, a gay pick-up area in London. Alastair Campbell supplied the spin: it had been 'a moment of madness'.

But Culture Secretary Tessa Jowell kept her job after signing a £350,000 mortgage deal that enabled her husband to bring to the UK a wodge of cash that Italian investigators thought might be a bribe from the Italian Prime Minister Silvio Berlusconi. Instead, it was her husband who went: the couple separated shortly afterwards. Again, it all makes people wonder what kind of a world these politicians are living in.

Trouble with money

To ministers, money is just as hazardous as sex. John Prescott (again) famously accepted ranch hospitality and a cowboy outfit from Philip Anschutz. At the time, his department was reviewing bids, one from Anschutz, to build a new super-casino. The Chairman of the Committee on Standards in Public Life, Sir Alistair Graham, judged it as 'clearly in breach of the ministerial code' that is meant to stop ministers accepting favours.

Then there was steel magnate Lakshmi Mittal's £2 million gift to the Labour Party. Blair subsequently wrote to the

Romanian Prime Minister recommending Mittal's firm – something many people thought an abuse of office, since it wasn't even a British company he was supporting. But he did the same again for Rupert Murdoch, calling Italy's Prime Minister Romano Prodi to help him buy an Italian newspaper there.

Labour's secretive third-largest donor, David Abrahams, channelled donations through friends and employees, apparently without some even knowing. Peter Hain failed to register a £103,000 campaign donation from a 'think tank' that seemingly did a lot of accounting and not much thinking.

The list goes on and on. But why do political parties get themselves in such messes? Largely, it's because the rest of us have stopped supporting them, and they need rich donors. Few of us are bothering to vote for these sleaze-bags-Labour won the 2005 election with fewer votes than the Conservatives lost with in 1997. Only 22 per cent of us actually voted for this government. And fewer of us are prepared to join the politicians' rotten organizations. Party managers have had to look for funds elsewhere.

But it is corrosive. People are bound to question whether public policy is being distorted to please party backers. A blanket ban on tobacco advertising that was proposed in 1997 was bad news for Formula One, headed by Labour's million-pound donor Bernie Ecclestone. But the sport was specifically exempted after he made representations to Tony Blair (It took years of Freedom of Information requests to confirm the details.) The U-turn was so eye-popping that it forced Blair onto BBC TV's On the Record to proclaim himself 'a pretty straight sort of guy', and the Labour Party repaid the £1 million.

Soon afterwards there was a £125,000 donation from porn publisher Richard Desmond, made days after the Department of Trade found him a fit and proper person to take over Express Newspapers, and just a week before new rules would have forced the donation to be declared ahead of the June 2001 election.

All perfectly legal: but doesn't it seem obvious that politicians should aim to keep their financial dealings so far above suspicion that nobody even questions them? The remarkable thing is how often they don't.

Loans for lordships

The loans for lordships scandal is a prime example. Tony Blair created more peers than any previous Prime Minister. And many of them subsequently turned out to be £1m donors to his Party, a fact that was concealed from the Whitehall panel who scrutinize honours recommendations.

There have been strict rules against selling public honours since 1925, though it has always happened. Most politicians are too clever to mention both sides of the bargain in the same breath. But Scotland Yard investigated when Des Smith – a member of a quango charged with finding sponsors for the flagship city academies programme – allegedly told a reporter that such donors typically received honours.

Scotland Yard's questioning lasted thirteen months, and took 6,000 pages of evidence – even, in a historic first, from the Prime Minister. Downing Street briefed viciously against Assistant Commissioner John Yates, who led the inquiry. The House of Commons Public Administration Committee interfered too. And the Attorney General did not stand back from the case, despite the obvious conflict between his roles as a legal officer and a party politician.

When the party in power isn't selling honours, it can dispense them to political advantage too. After Peter Temple-Morris MP left the Conservatives and joined Labour, he was rewarded with a peerage. It was thought the sort of thing that might encourage others to do the same. And if press barons are made into real ones, it might encourage more favourable reporting too.

Parliamentary scams

Even the Conservatives criticized Yates – but then the political clan stick together. They all have their rackets to preserve. Such as parliamentary allowances.

MPs might claim to be poorly paid on £64,766 – twice the average wage – but they have Britain's most generous pension plan. Food and drink in the House of Commons are subsidized. There is a gym and other facilities. They also have a £93,854 staff allowance, which many MPs spend on their spouses and family members. The 2008 prize for this went to Derek Conway, who paid his sons £40,000 from his staff budget, even though they were full-time students.

London MPs also get an extra £2,812, and all are entitled to money for IT, worth about £5,000, office expenses of £22,193, and up to £23,083 towards the cost of a second home. Furniture is allowed too, as detailed on the official 'John Lewis list', showing what domestic comforts our lawmakers can claim at public expense. Maintenance bills are also allowed, as are claims for food up to £400 a month (with no receipts being required). MPs also enjoy unlimited free travel in the UK and free parking at the airport. They can claim taxi fares, and a 40p per mile car allowance. They even get 20p a mile for cycling.

In 2008, though, MPs sought to demonstrate their self – restraint by voting themselves a pay rise of just 1.9 per cent (backdated, naturally). But the package also included a £10,000 rise in allowances, so most parliamentary families would not have to tighten their belts too much.

MPs went to huge efforts to conceal all this. They resisted

scrutiny under the Freedom of Information Act, saying it would harm their confidential dealings with constituents. The Speaker even went to court to stop MPs' second-home addresses being published, citing security concerns. But the main concern was their institutional racketeering being exposed.

But of course it did come back to haunt them – and indeed incriminate them. The original deal stitched up by MPs was that all these expenses would be a matter between them and the House of Commons authorities. Their receipts (if they needed to show receipts) would never be exposed to the light of day. Unfortunately, the Freedom of Information Act changed all that. The Commons authorities spent tens of thousands of pounds of taxpayers' money in the courts trying to resist the exposure, but eventually lost. Then they set about 'redacting' the receipts – blanking out details that supposedly threatened MPs' security, but which in fact concealed the full extent of their institutional corruption. Or it would have done, if the Daily Telegraph had not got to the receipts first. It was the most searing political scandal since Profumo. Almost all MPs had put in claims that were at least questionable, and some had put in claims so outrageous that they were forced to stand down in advance of the next election.

Among the ingenious devices that would have been concealed by the 'redaction' process was 'flipping'. MPs would claim their second home allowance to do up one property, then claim it was their main home and use the next year's allowance to do up another. Several spent thousands on a property and then sold it at a profit. MPs would tell the House of Commons that one property was their second home in order to get the allowance to spend on it, but then tell the tax authorities that it was their main home in order to avoid paying capital gains tax on its sale. Some would use their expenses to order furniture that was intended for a second home but was delivered to their first home. Many MPs claimed the maximum amount of their food and living expenses, without showing any receipts. The list went on and on. The MPs who were exposed claimed, correctly, that they were only doing things that were allowed under the rules. But of course it was MPs themselves who created these rotten rules in the first place, and for the precise purpose of deceiving the public.

Taxpayers subsidize the parties
In another vast and deliberate confusion of public and private interests, taxpayers have even been made to subsidize the political parties themselves. It's called Short Money, after the former MP Edward Short who invented it, and it gives the Conservatives £4.8 million, the Liberal Democrats another £1.75m, and other parties around £500,000.

Sinn Fein doesn't qualify because as republicans they refuse to take their seats, but a separate subsidy scheme covers them. The Lords have their own scheme too – Cranborne Money – which dispenses £773,000 to opposition parties.

But not even this is enough for our political parties. Sir Hayden Phillips, who chaired inter-party talks on funding, proposed that this taxpayer subsidy to the parties should be increased up to £23 million!

The confusion of public, private and party
When John Major's wife Norma wrote a book on Chequers in 1996, she was careful to donate any proceeds to charity. But the current generation of politicians and their families seem much more confused between their money and the public's.

In 2005, the code that prevents ministers cashing in from their jobs did not stop Cherie Blair from making a world tour to promote her own book on Downing Street life, The

Goldfish Bowl. In Washington alone, she pocketed £30,000 for a speech at which she was billed as the 'First Lady of Downing Street'. And she was introduced by UK ambassador Sir David Manning, even though it was a purely private visit: the public-private confusion seems to have penetrated the diplomatic corps too.

In the same year, Mrs Blair raised eyebrows for her charity speaking tour of Australia, where the £102,000 expenses paid to her and her agent left just £6,690 for the charity. Another engagement in Melbourne raised just £6,774 for charity but cost £17,000 for the speaker.

It's a wonder the Australians had her back after her 2003 Supermarket Sweep. While visiting the famous Global International store in Melbourne, she was invited to choose 'a few gifts' and left with 68 items worth £2,000.

It's a wonder that Britain had her back, for that matter, after we discovered that her dealings with convicted fraudster Peter Foster, who had helped her get money off a nice pair of Bristol flats, were rather more extensive than Downing Street first admitted.

The corruption of business
The American bank robber, Willie Sutton, was once asked why he robbed banks. 'That's where the money is,' he replied. But today, the money is in government.

Having large parts of the government's work contracted out to private business is probably much more efficient than leaving everything to civil servants. But it has given politicians yet more patronage, and corrupted the private sector too.

I go to innumerable meetings in the plush parliamentary committee rooms of the £231 million Portcullis House, where even the fig trees in the atrium cost £150,000. There you see business people, or their paid lobbyists, saying: 'Well, minister, this scheme would work much better if you just gave it this small tweak' – a tweak which invariably would put more public money their way. They never say: 'Minister, this scheme stinks and you should scrap it,' even if they know that to be true. Their snouts are too deep in the trough.

Lobbying and donations do pay off: not because contracts are awarded corruptly (though some are) but because they get you noticed and give you a chance to put your case for some business. The accountants Arthur Andersen were sued by the Thatcher government, and frozen out of government work, over their auditing of DeLorean, a carmaker that went bust in 1981, taking millions in taxpayers' cash with it. But the firm made friends with the opposition, and provided them with expertise and credibility. Within months of the 1997 election, the case had been settled and the firm was back bidding for government business, including (serves them right) the Dome.

And at the end of long and distinguished career in the public service, politicians (not to mention their advisers) can look forward to a comfortable retirement in the House of Lords, or on the payroll of the various consulting firms that pick up government contracts, or both. After leaving government, the former health minister Lord Warner became an adviser to Deloitte, and is now an adviser to PA Consulting. Transport Tsar Lord Birt became adviser to Capgemini in 2006. Downing Street adviser Michael Barber became Sir Michael and is now a partner at McKinsey. And various other special advisers have also found themselves such jobs. After pious New Labour criticism of Conservative ex-ministers stepping into jobs with firms that they or their departments had given government contracts, ministers at least now have to take 'gardening leave' before they can walk through the revolving door. But piety in opposition does not extend to piety in government, it seems. It is hard to know which becomes more corrupted by this revolving door: politics, or business.

Certainly, politics and business have jointly found one neat way to shunt support to political parties without it seeming to be a donation, and that is to take a stall at the party conferences. Conferences are more like trade fairs these days. The Labour Party once boasted that its own was 'the largest political exhibition in Europe'. Everyone took stands – not just businesses, but trade unions, pensioner bodies, pressure groups, newspapers, and broadcasters. And these stands cost a fair bit of money.

A lot of which is our money. Now that the Conservatives are looking like a party of government again, their exhibition trade is picking up too. Among those exhibiting in 2008 were various regional development agencies, a smattering of city councils, the Environment Agency, the British Council, Network Rail, the Heritage Lottery Fund, the Arts Council, and hundreds more. Once again, the political clan is buying friends and favours with our money.

It's a great source of party funds, of course, especially when you are in power – or are likely to be in power soon. Conservative conferences between 1996 and 2006 were dismal, forlorn affairs. Lobbyists couldn't see the point of bothering. Now of course the lobbyists, not to mention all those taxpayer-financed quangos, are falling over themselves to be there.

The dominance of politics

Power begets fortune. Politicians depend heavily on the ministerial salaries, the pensions, the official homes, the quango appointments, the campaign support, and the wining and dining that all comes with office. That is why Gordon Brown stepped into Tony Blair's shoes without any vote, even within the Labour Party. Many of Brown's colleagues had serious doubts about him; but they thought it much better to keep silent than risk their power, perks, and position with a potentially divisive election.

Usually, the only MPs who are prepared to speak out against the politicians' conspiracy against the public are those who are wealthy enough not to rely on the perks of office. For the rest, the bigger that government grows, the better; and the same is true for the wider political clan of advisers, commentators, quango members, and lobbyists. The bigger the business of government grows, the better it pays. Politics becomes less about principle, less of an opportunity to make a difference to people, and more of a career – a career with rather good fringe benefits.

And anyway, principle doesn't get you elected. As fewer and fewer of us bother to vote, elections are decided by a small number of floating voters in a small number of marginal seats. The votes of about 2 per cent of the population are the only ones that make a difference. These are the ones that the party machines must understand and get on their side. They do detailed opinion research to find out what this vital subset of society thinks. If they are worried about crime, the politicians will get tougher on crime. If they are concerned about healthcare, the politicians will promise more spending on the NHS. If they don't like their party's past, the politicians will disown it.

If you ever wonder why politicians and everyone involved in the industry of politics seem so distant from the general public, this is the reason. Their focus is not on the general public, but on the narrow interests that will win elections. And once elected, they lose themselves in the perquisites and processes of government. The bigger it is, the more lost they become.

Prime ministers soon become more cut off than most. People speak of the Downing Street 'bunker': and just getting a prime minister the two hundred yards from there to the

House of Commons is a major security exercise. Those of us who work in Westminster are well used to being swept aside by the squadron of police outriders and bullet-proof cars as Gordon Brown's motorcade roars by.

Unfit for office

Our government politicians have created a rotten state that serves them well but serves us badly. Distant from the general public, untouched by the realities and hardships of the real world, and motivated by office and ambition rather than principle, they become absorbed within their own creation. And the rules of that unreal world are not the same rules that govern the rest of us.

Or so they think. With so many people hanging on their every word, jostling even to get into their presence, never telling them they are wrong, doing everything they demand, and praising their every move, it is perhaps not surprising that they come to think of themselves as infallible and indestructible.

They forget to list gifts from businesspeople whom they later recommend for an honour. They take loans when they can't take donations. They spend less time getting on top of their red ministerial boxes than they do getting on top of their secretaries. They never admit mistakes. They never resign, except when public relations disasters overwhelm them.

The reason they feature so often on the front page of the News of the World is that they have pushed aside all of the restraints that would keep them off it. But do they care? Or do they just think that the rules don't apply to them, that they can brazen it out, or conceal the details from us?

Politicians need restraints, just like the rest of us. They recognize that they need to have anti-sleaze laws and anti-sleaze watchdogs to keep our trust. But it's a great irritation to them when these watchdogs are actually dogged on sleaze. As Sir

Alastair Graham, Chairman of the Committee on Standards in Public Life, was forced out by Tony Blair, he expressed regret that he was unable to convince the government of the need for ethics, saying its record on public trust was 'wholly, completely and unforgivably negative.'

'I think it is demonstrated by opinion polls,' he said later, 'that the public think this Government is as sleazy as the last.' The remarkable thing is that he sounded surprised.

5

INJUSTICE

When friends become terrorists

I could hardly contain my shame as I watched the dignified figure of Geir Haarde in front of the television cameras. He was summoning up every atom of self-restraint as he described what Britain's government had done to him and his people. As Prime Minister of Iceland, he was the leader of one of the world's most cultured and peaceful nations – a much better and more genuine friend to Britain than most of its EU partners. But the British government, using the full weight of its law, was treating this proud people as terrorists.

It was October 2008. The world's financial markets were in free-fall, and banks were going bust. One of them was Iceland's Landsbanki, with which 300,000 British residents (including me) held accounts through its Icesave subsidiary. The Icelandic government would be responsible for paying compensation to these account holders. Geir Haarde admitted that his small country was in deep financial embarrassment, but that he was working to find a satisfactory solution to the problem. But instead he was struck a triple blow by Gordon Brown's clunking fist. The British government seized Icelandic assets. And not just the assets of Icesave, but those of Iceland's last solvent bank, Kaupthing – which collapsed as a result, leaving Iceland even more financially embarrassed. But the final blow was that this hugely hostile, bullying action against a tiny and friendly country was all done under anti-terrorist legislation. No wonder Geir Haarde could scarcely contain his rage and disappointment.

The Anti-Terrorism, Crime and Security Act 2001 that Britain used against its Icelandic friends was a response to the 9/11 attacks. It went through Parliament in record time, receiving the Royal Assent in December. Whether most MPs even had the time to read the measure, never mind reflect on it, is an open question. But its provisions are staggeringly broad, and – unfortunately for Iceland, as it turned out – allow the Treasury to freeze assets if they fear 'action to the detriment of the UK economy', or even a threat to the property of a single UK national.

More abuses of terrorist law

Indeed, the astonishing scale of the powers that our weak and willing Parliament have handed over to the police and the executive is best illustrated by their abuses.

Take the case of Sally Cameron, 34, held under the Terrorism Act 2000 for walking on a cycle path through the harbour in Dundee. 'One day,' she told The Times, 'I was told by a guard on the gate that I couldn't use the route any more because it was solely a cycle path and he said, if I was caught doing it again, I'd be arrested…. The next thing I knew, the harbour master had driven up behind me with a megaphone, saying, 'You're trespassing, please turn back.' It was totally ridiculous. I started laughing and kept on walking. Cyclists going back were also laughing…. But then two police cars roared up behind me and cut me off, like a scene from Starsky and Hutch, and officers told me I was being arrested under the Terrorism Act.'

She wasn't the only innocent victim of this clunking

legislation. An eleven-year-old girl was stopped and required to empty her pockets; a cricketer was stopped and questioned about why he was carrying a cricket bat; and it was used against peaceful protesters outside an arms fair in London's Docklands.

The Terrorism Act allowed the government to nominate places where the police could use stop-and-search powers. MPs discussing the proposals might have thought this would be limited to particular times and places where the risk of terrorism might be severe. But no: ministers instantly declared the whole of London a stop-and-search area. It still is. Tens of thousands of people are stopped and questioned each year under this legislation.

But while these powers haven't actually caught any terrorists, they have proved to be a very convenient way of shutting up anti-government protestors.

Perhaps the most celebrated case was that of Walter Wolfgang. He was 82 years old, a Jew who had fled the Nazis, and was now a Labour activist and peace campaigner. But when he dared to heckle a speech by the Home Secretary Jack Straw at the 2005 Labour Conference, he was hustled out and arrested under the Terrorism Act. Disagreeing with a government minister, it seems, is now a terrorist offence. Which I guess makes me a terrorist, and you guilty of handling terrorist material.

It was just as well for Walter that he was now British. For the Anti-Terrorism, Crime and Security Act 2001 allowed the Home Secretary to detain foreign nationals indefinitely without charge or trial. Under it, nine refugees were held without charge in Belmarsh prison – contrary to the government's promise that the law would be used only when conventional prosecution had failed. The Law Lords eventually ruled that it was also contrary to human rights. That did not phase the government, which brought in an even tougher law, the Prevention of Terrorism

Act 2005, allowing the Home Secretary to keep anyone – UK or foreign – under indefinite house arrest instead. Prompted by the 7 July London bombings, the measure was frog-marched through Parliament even quicker than the 2001 Act, with large parts of it not even drafted when it was presented to Parliament. (It didn't do much good anyway – a third of those held under house arrest simply escaped and are still at large.)

War is peace

But then war is peace. Politicians know that if they can convince us that we are likely to be bombed, gassed, or poisoned by terrorists, we will quite willingly grant them any powers they want in order to deal with the threat. Nice for them: but those powers can be greatly abused.

In 2003, police raided a flat in North London and proclaimed that they had found a factory for producing ricin, the deadly poison used to kill Bulgarian dissident Georgi Markov on Waterloo Bridge in 1978. Tests showed it wasn't, but that didn't stop Tony Blair telling us that the 'danger is present and real'. Nor did it prevent the Home Secretary prejudicing the subsequent trial by saying 'Al-Qaeda is on our doorstep'. There was no ricin, and the suspects were found not guilty. But they were re-arrested and held under indefinite house arrest. Court decisions don't seem to mean much to our politicians these days.

Of course, the terrorism threat is real, as the London bombings of 7 July 2005 made clear. But in response, we seem to have given our government powers to track us anywhere, stop and search us in the street, arrest us for any imagined offence, imprison us for peaceful protest, hold us without charge for 28 days (though they'd like it to be 42), extradite us to the United States without evidence, ban us for being members of even non-violent organizations that they don't

happen to like, export us to other EU countries to stand trial
for things that aren't even a crime here, take and file our DNA
samples before we've been convicted, charged or even
cautioned for any offence – and much more as well. In the
name of defending our liberties against terrorism, we seem to
have lost them. Even those who were injured in the 7 July
bombings say they are dismayed.

Free speech and protest
Our traditional value of free speech is one of these losses. The
Serious Organized Crime and Police Act 2005 was billed as
setting up a Serious Organized Crime Agency, a sort of British
FBI that could take on the mafia. So its powers are strong. But
while ministers were at it, they thought they would clean up an
eyesore on their own doorstep.

Peace campaigner Brian Haw had been camping out in
Parliament Square with various posters criticizing the Iraq war.
It was indeed an unsightly spectacle, and as a local, I too was
embarrassed at a key tourist spot being despoiled – and
annoyed at part of my public space being permanently
occupied by a private individual. For some reason ministers
could not remove the demonstration under existing law, but
they came up with a cunning plan. They would sneak into the
Bill a ban on demonstrations within one kilometre of
Parliament – claiming it as another anti-terrorism measure.

It was a sledgehammer to crack a nut, but even then it
missed him. The courts ruled that since Brian Haw's resident
protest had been going before the Act was passed, it did not
apply to him, only to future protesters.

But lots of other people got crushed, right enough. Like the
36-year-old management accountant Steve Jago, who in 2006
staged a one-man protest outside Downing Street. He was
carrying a placard bearing the quote from 1984, 'In a time of

universal deceit, telling the truth is a revolutionary act.' A sensible response might have been just to tell him to go home, but no, Jago was arrested and charged under the Serious Organized Crime and Police Act. He was found to have a number of copies of a Vanity Fair article entitled 'Blair's Big Brother Legacy'. These were confiscated, and he was told that, as 'politically motivated material', they would be used in evidence against him. But if the British authorities can maintain that an American fashion and culture magazine is terrorist material, then nobody who visits a dentist's waiting room is safe.

Then the vegan chef Maya Evans, 25, was convicted of breaching the Act for standing at the Cenotaph in Whitehall and reading the names of 97 British soldiers killed in Iraq. This small and dignified protest was considered a terrorist threat so profound that 14 police officers and two police cars swooped in to arrest her. She was fined and now has a criminal record.

The 80-year-old anti-war campaigner John Catt was stopped under the Terrorism Act – outside the same 2005 Labour Conference that Walter Wolfgang was being thrown out of. As someone who joined the Communist Party of Great Britain in 1946 and never missed a Vietnam War march, the police may well have had their eye on him, but he'd never been convicted of anything. The excuse for stopping him under the Terrorism Act was that he was wearing an 'offensive' T-shirt which said George Bush and Tony Blair should be tried for war crimes.

Causing offence to members of the government now seems to be a crime – and these days, you can be arrested for any transgression. Charlotte Denis, 20, was arrested at the 2005 Midlands Game Fair for wearing a 'Bollocks to Blair' T-shirt. She was told it might offend someone, so had to be removed. She refused because she had only a bra on underneath, so she was nicked.

You might have thought that the police would want to avoid the public ridicule that this incident landed them in. But just a year later Leicestershire trader Tony Wright, 60, was handed an £80 fixed penalty fine for causing 'harassment, alarm and distress' by selling the same T-shirts at the Royal Norfolk Show.

Goodbye to the rule of law

And when we do get recorded as terrorists because some official doesn't like our T-shirt or because our name happens to match some botched entry in a police computer, what safeguards to we have? Not many, because all our ancient legal rights are being systematically subverted or abolished in the name of efficient government and the pursuit of crime.

Take habeas corpus. The Terrorism Act 2006 allows police to hold anyone for 28 days without charge on suspicion of being involved in – or even encouraging – terrorism. It used to be that suspects had to be charged or released within 24 hours, and detention without charge was a time-limited response to some emergency. Now it has become a permanent feature of our legal system.

In the Counter Terrorism Act 2008, the government wanted to hold people without charge up to 42 days. They used a great deal of bribery and bullying to get the measure through the House of Commons. But the House of Lords-one of the few limits on arbitrary central government that still occasionally works – struck that down. Immediately, the Home Secretary Jacqui Smith truculently announced that a new 42-day law was already written and printed, and would be introduced just the very first time an excuse arose.

The same Act removes another legal protection, the right to silence. It was on its last legs anyway. Juries are already told that if a suspect chooses to say nothing, it might indicate their guilt. (Then again, it might just indicate that they don't trust the police an inch in distorting what they do say, or tricking them to make some injudicious or incriminating remark.)

Thin end of the tyranny wedge
Terrorism is a very good excuse for when our leaders think it would be useful to replace the rule of law with the rule of politicians. But other serious crimes can provide the thin end of that wedge too.

Most members of the public still suppose that people are presumed innocent until proven guilty. But that is no longer true in serious fraud cases, where the accused may now have to show that they acted legitimately, rather than the state having to prove the opposite. In humble industrial tribunals too, the burden of proof falls on the employers.

Most people would also assume that someone can't be punished until they have been convicted. Again, this is no longer true in the case of suspected drug dealers, whose property can be confiscated if officials suspect that it came from drug profits, even if this cannot be proved.

The double jeopardy rule, that you can't be tried twice for the same crime, was designed to stop the harassment of alleged victims. But now that has gone too. Where compelling evidence arises – like DNA – serious cases can be re-tried.

Even trial by jury has been suspended. Serious fraud cases are thought to be too complicated and too long to entrust to juries. (Though perhaps if our prosecutors were paid by results rather than by the hour, they might be shorter and simpler.) And there are proposals to 'streamline' the justice system by shunting various sorts of jury cases down to magistrates' courts.

Many people will agree with these changes as a way of making sure that those who have committed the most serious crimes do not get away with it. But then who decides what crimes are 'serious'? If daring to heckle the Home Secretary can get you arrested as a terrorist, how can any of us feel safe? If you have confidence in politicians, you might see little reason to restrain them. But the politicians have given us very little evidence that such confidence is justified. They need to be restrained, under the rule of law.

Attacks on the judiciary

Sometimes the justice system does stand in the way of politicians. It prevents them from acting in ways that are actually illegal, and exposes the weaknesses of their ill-drafted laws. Naturally, they don't welcome this. At one time, ministers never criticized the courts. Now any unwelcome court decision triggers one of their tirades against 'weak' judges, and a promise to bring in even 'tougher' laws or suspend even more of our legal rights.

They really believe that they, not the courts, are the standard of what should happen in Britain. After all, they, not the courts, have been elected. Only they can catch the mood of the nation. And the mood of the nation should prevail.

They do not see that the legal protections that have been built up over the centuries are there for a good reason. That these things too express the mood of the nation – a nation that got sick of autocrats using their unlimited powers to harass, arrest, imprison, torture and execute people who just happened to disagree with them on politics or religion. These safeguards may prevent the public's will being done at particular moments; but in the longer term they preserve the sort of freedom and justice that we all want to live under.

Spot fines replace justice

But who needs courts anyway? Over the last decade there has been a massive growth in extra-judicial measures like fixed-penalty notices – spot fines. It is simplicity itself. Police officers see – or think they see – someone discarding an apple core. They issue the person with a spot fine for littering. Indeed, it doesn't even need to be police officers – without any public debate on the matter, the police have given the power to levy spot fines to a total of 1,406 officials, from litter wardens to dog-catchers.

Most people find it easier to pay the fine rather than challenge the decision, which would mean going to court, which is time-consuming and costly. But it allows the police to boast great success in catching and punishing villains. Police commanders can get up to £15,000 in performance bonuses, and performance depends partly on how many people are given spot fines, charged, or cautioned. Officers are expected to achieve a certain number of these things each month. So they pick easy targets. In London, for example – a city where violent street crime has exploded – three officers wasted half the night by holding a 19-year-old student for five hours before cautioning him for holding open the door of a lift in an Underground station. The police are incentivized to arrest the wrong people – harmless, minor offenders rather than real thugs committing serious crimes – and that's exactly what they do.

Now fixed penalty notices have been extended to assault, threatening behaviour, obstructing the police and many more things that would previously have been dealt with by the courts. But spot fines are so much easier for police and officials: that is why there are now so many of them. Whether you can call it justice is a different matter.

ASBOs and respect

Anti-Social Behaviour Orders also undermine our legal protections. They can see you put into jail without the involvement of any jury.

The idea of ASBOs is to enforce acceptable norms of behaviour. And of course it is the police and local bureaucrats who decide what those acceptable norms are. It's summary justice – the powers of judge and jury are given to officials, to make you behave as they see fit. And it's not only to stop people playing loud music through the night or threatening neighbours with violence. Officials can and do deem almost anything anti-social. ASBOs have been used against a 13-year-old using the word 'grass', a 16-year-old wearing a single golf glove, and an 87-year-old being sarcastic to neighbours.

Break the ASBO and you go to jail. Just the 'balance of probability' will do – a standard of evidence thought unacceptable in criminal trials. But you may be lucky: ASBOs are ineffective, around half are breached, and the police don't really have enough time to prosecute everyone.

The whole system seems to have been dreamed up in some focus group in which everyone complained about noisy neighbours or kids in hoodies hanging around the bus stop. More bellyaching than justice.

And it gets worse. We have Super-ASBOs for people the police believe are criminal but can't prove it; Violent Offender Orders to restrain people whose background suggests they might be future criminals; and even Baby-ASBOs for the under-10s. Soon we'll be serving prison sentences on kids still in the womb.

Extradition

Our government is so keen to promote the international war on terror that they signed a treaty allowing British citizens to be extradited to America on the basis of no evidence at all. Three British bankers were hauled off, not for any terrorist offence, but for an alleged fraud, even though the crime of which they were accused took place in the UK. Under American law it's possible to throw 'racketeering' charges at just about anyone who forgets to leave a restaurant tip, so the NatWest Three, as they were called, petitioned the Serious Fraud Office to prosecute them in the UK so as to show up the lack of evidence and stop the extradition. They did not succeed, and the extradition went ahead. As predicted, the Three plea-bargained, admitting smaller charges in order to avoid the prospect of thirty years in the slammer for being Al Capones.

The European Arrest Warrant is a similar scheme, which Britain signed up to in the wake of 9/11. It means that any EU country can extradite us to stand trial there – even if what we were doing wasn't actually a crime in Britain. Since most continental countries have a legal system even more rotten than ours, this has serious implications. Some can hold you for months or even years without charge while investigations continue. Not even prima facie evidence is needed. When Jonathan Hiles, 18, was fatally injured in a Zakynthos nightclub incident, the Greek government had British student Andrew Symeou arrested under an EAW, even though Symeou says he wasn't even there at the time. There is no evidence that would allow British courts to prosecute this case, and yet we were expected to export Symeou to Greece, where he could spend months in prison without charge.

Even more remarkable is the case of Australian teacher Gerald Toben, who was arrested in Britain under a warrant issued by the Austrian authorities, on the charge of holocaust denial – which isn't even a crime here, nor in Australia. When Prince Harry goes to fancy-dress parties wearing a Nazi uniform, he could get into serious trouble.

Home office unfit for purpose
Here at home, the government's celebrated 'tough on crime,

'tough on the causes of crime' pledge led to huge increases in police spending, up from £8.5 billion in 1996-7 to £18.8 billion in 2008-09. Police staff numbers are up by 56,590 since 1997, we're told: though only 14,000 of those are actually front-line officers, the rest being community support officers and administrative staff. The number of front-line constables actually fell by 1,460 between 2006 and 2007, though a lot more of our police seem to have been promoted to superintendents and chief inspectors.

Community support officers – there are 16,507 of them – are not all that much cheaper than front-line police. And they are less effective, as we discovered when two of them refused to jump into a pond in Wigan to save drowning 10-year-old Jordon Lyon, because they had not been trained in water safety.

Meanwhile, the police officers' job has become a lot easier, because almost everything is now a criminal offence. At least 3,609 new offences have been created since 1997, as you will discover if you impersonate a traffic warden or try to sell a squirrel. And official powers just multiply. The anti-social behaviour unit has a budget of £25 million, and in addition to ASBOs we now have crack house closure orders, dispersal orders, disorder notices, parenting contracts...

Then there's the government's neighbourhood policing programme. New York has a few more police than we do in London. But there are twice as many on the street. And the fact that we've shut 516 police stations seems at odds with neighbourhood policing. As does the fact that recruitment is still done centrally rather than in the neighbourhoods – which rather defeats the object.

Failure to defeat crime
Our police and justice system is the most expensive in the world, but what do we get for it? A 2005 international crime

survey found Britain top of the EU charts for car theft, assaults, and burglary, and second for theft and pickpocketing.

The government claims that crime is falling. But it depends which crime figures you believe. Many people who are victims of crime don't bother reporting it on the grounds that the police won't do anything anyway. So there is a gap between what people tell pollsters and what they tell the police. And yes, crime reported to the police has fallen a little. But the fall started long before 1997. Meanwhile the British Crime Survey finds that people's real experience of crime, as reported to pollsters, is that street robberies, violence, gun crime and knife incidents have soared.

Ah, says the Home Office, the number of offences brought to justice has risen: we are better at actually catching and punishing criminals. Maybe. But nearly half these punished offences are minor incidents that are dealt with by spot fines. We aren't catching gangs who wield guns and knives, we are catching street traders who sell apples by the pound and their customers who drop a core in the gutter. Meanwhile the number of court convictions, reflecting the prosecution of more serious crimes, has actually fallen.

And of those people who do end up in the slammer, too many are children, or young adults. After a 50 per cent rise in the number of teenagers in custody, the numbers have eased a bit, but there are still 11,500 under-21s in Britain's prisons. All the figures show that young offenders are more likely to become repeat offenders if they go to jail – the 'crime college' problem – so why do we do it? Again, it's because kids are a lot easier for the police to catch and deal with.

Burglary has fallen, but that has nothing to do with police performance. Burglary has become harder because it's such a scourge that we all now fit alarms – in the EU, only Ireland has more. And longer jail sentences are simply keeping burglars out of circulation. On the other hand, only half the 281 people sentenced for having a gun in 2006 got even the minimum jail sentence, which might explain why gun offences went up, to around 18,000 – which does not even count the incidents where guns are brandished but not fired. True, gun offences have fallen since that peak – but then knife crime has become more prevalent.

Failure to reform
The jails have given up trying to educate and reform our criminals. We just keep them out of circulation. Unfortunately that means the prison service is stretched well beyond its capacity. The 25,000 'extra prison places' that ministers boast about are just more prisoners being crammed into the same cells. Staff numbers haven't kept pace, so less is done to help criminals to rehabilitate.

That leads to reoffending, which costs taxpayers around £11-£15 billion (nobody is quite sure). Of the 306,600 people sentenced for indictable crimes in 2007, 88 per cent – 269,806 of them – had past convictions. Some 31 per cent of them had up to four convictions, 20 per cent of them between five and nine convictions, and a shocking 37 per cent had ten or more previous convictions. Does that make you feel safe?

But our forces of law and order have a couple of cunning plans. The first is to release prisoners early, with a tag. Some 42,000 prisoners were released early in 2008. Sounds like a quick way to cut prison numbers, but many offenders simply remove the tags, often the tags don't work in the buildings where they live, and about a quarter of people on tags reoffend within weeks. At the end of 2008, some 623 early-release prisoners, accused of 845 new crimes were still at large. So our law officers have a second cunning plan. They pay foreign prisoners £3,000 to go home. At a stroke, we reduce prison overcrowding.

Possibly. Foreigners cause Home Secretaries a lot of bother. They like to pander to the public's baser instincts and look tough on illegal immigrants and foreign criminals. But their practical efforts look more like the Keystone Cops. Until 2002 the rule that foreign prisoners could be deported was rarely enforced. Then there was a big media fuss and teams were dispatched to deport more. Then the attention focused on getting rid of failed asylum seekers. So ambitious targets were set with great fanfare – then quietly dropped when found unachieveable. Today, the Home Office hasn't the faintest clue how many foreigners are living in Britain illegally – it doesn't even know how many foreign students there are studying at our universities.

Charles Clarke had to resign as Home Secretary in 2006, when it was disclosed that 1,023 foreign prisoners had been freed from jail without being deported, and lost track of. It wasn't his first offence. His replacement John Reid declared the whole department 'unfit for purpose'. A disappointing verdict, given the billions of taxpayer money lavished on the place: Home Office spending has risen by 73 per cent in real terms since 1997. Why hasn't it bought results?

Police partiality

The police remain the least accountable public service, all the more so as their powers expand. Sir Robert Peel used to say that we were all law enforcement officers: the only difference was that his 'bobbies' did it full time.

But today's police have lost any sympathy and support that the general public might have had for them. They know that if they intervene in some disturbance, or report some offence, they are more likely to be charged with something themselves. It's an easy way of meeting their arrest targets.

The police are no longer impartial. They comment to the media on cases even before they are tried. They leak the names of celebrities they arrest, which can ruin them, even if (like Pete Townshend, arrested on child pornography allegations) they are never subsequently charged. Pretty soon we will be like the United States, where even mild-mannered business people are led away in handcuffs by armed police. It's not remotely necessary, but it makes great television footage that suggests that the police are clamping down on people who must be really dangerous (or they wouldn't have to be handcuffed, would they?).

Now the Association of Chief Police Officers is lobbying for the creation of a dedicated 3,000-strong counter-terrorism border force. No doubt this will back up Customs & Excise officers when they decide, quite arbitrarily, that you've brought back too much alcohol and cigarettes for your personal consumption and impound it – and your vehicle. (Though you can buy it back at the next auction.) This isn't justice: it's harassment and theft.

The real threat to our liberty

In ten years, our politicians have used the threat of crime and terrorism to do what two world wars couldn't. Free speech has gone, habeas corpus has gone, we're being spied on, inspected, controlled, censored, bugged, put on a database, spot-fined, dispossessed, imprisoned without trial – all for the benefit of government leaders who care more about getting headlines than they do about us.

It's not obvious that the current terrorism threat is worse than that which the IRA posed in much of the last forty years. After all, the IRA mortar bombed Downing Street, destroyed a hotel where the Prime Minister and the Cabinet were staying, brought down office buildings in the City of London, and killed or maimed thousands of people, including innocent civilians. But whenever British governments tried to meet that threat by curbing liberties – internment, trials without juries – the policy backfired sorely.

Throughout the height of the troubles, people could still travel between Britain and Ireland without passports. Today we're told we shouldn't be able to walk down the street without an ID card.

It is natural that government should want to frighten us. It helps convince us that we really need them, and that they are worth all the money we spend on them. It makes their perks and privileges, their waste and inefficiency, seem minor. And all this activity is good for advancing ministerial careers.

It is natural too that police and officials should welcome all the new 'tough' powers they are voted. They make it easier to check, brigade, and control us. And the more offences they can pick us up for, the higher their arrest and conviction numbers, and the more they too can justify their existence as our protectors.

Preying on our fear is a game that neither politicians nor officials can win. Every 'tough' measure makes us more and more alarmed that we are living in a country so infested with evil that we really do need these draconian laws. To reassure us, they propose even 'tougher' controls. But that just makes us more alarmed still.

And so it goes on. In the process, our liberty spirals into a black hole. We have not been giving up our rights and freedoms hesitantly, but anxiously, gratefully, and urgently. It has happened so rapidly that most of us do not even realize that we no longer live in a liberal country. We live in a country where freedom exists only in name.

6

SNOOPERS

The licensing Gestapo

An Englishman's home is his castle, so they say. Not any more. There are now 1,043 powers that allow state officials of various sorts to enter your home, make searches or do whatever else they think themselves entitled to do. Obstruct them, and you could face a fine of £5,000.

Four out of ten of these entry powers have been introduced in the last twelve years. They include the right to come in to see if your pot plants have pests or don't have a 'plant passport'; to check if your hedge is too high; photograph and seize your rubbish; confiscate your fridge if it doesn't have the correct energy rating; and 1,039 other reasons. Including the power to burst in and check your TV licence.

Picture this: the blades of the helicopter beat as it hovers over a city of computer components. A police siren sounds, changing pitch as it speeds to some crime scene. We hear a big dog barking. Then comes the authorities' message: 'Your town, your street, your home. It's all in our database.' The official voice is calm and threatening: 'It's impossible to hide.' There is a knock on the door. Our palms sweat. Everything fades to black.

No, it's not some nightmare from the days of Cold War Russia. It's an Orwellian advertisement from the BBC telling us to pay our licence fee. It's pure state thuggery. In just 40 seconds, this sinister advertisement shows how far we have become the slaves of the database state, instead of its masters. You thought we lived in a free society? In a free society, no government could tell its citizens, with such quiet condescension and with no hint of embarrassment: 'We are spying on you. We know all about you. Just watch your step.'

Previous advertisements in this Gestapo genre showed a family laughing at some TV comedy programme. Comes the voice-over: 'If you have a TV licence, you're laughing.' Outside, a van draws up. Black leather boots crunch up the path, the family still oblivious. The voice continues: 'If not...' A gloved hand presses the bell. Suddenly, the family stops laughing, their faces gripped by sheer dread.

It's time we citizens stood up against this state-sponsored trespass and intimidation, particularly now that anti-terror legislation is being used to spy on whether our dogs are fouling the pavement and that we're closing our wheelie-bin properly. And it's time we told Gordon Brown that we don't much like 'our town, our street, our home' being in his database – particularly in view of the regularity with which his civil servants lose our information in the mail or forget it on the train.

Surveillance and privacy

Our octogenarian troublemaker John Catt was stopped a second time under the Terrorism Act as he and his daughter Linda drove through London to visit his son. They were threatened with arrest if they refused to answer police questions. Their car had been spotted by the CCTV cameras installed around the City of London after the IRA's 1993 Baltic Exchange bombing. It was tagged on the Police National Computer database for the simple reason that Catt had previously been stopped for wearing his 'offensive' T-shirt.

At one level, it's good to know that the police keep tabs on dangerous characters. It's also frightening to think that someone stopped because of their choice of T-shirt should evermore be tagged as a potential Osama Bin Laden.

It's alarming, too, that while the police busied themselves threatening John Catt, they seemed powerless to stop the extremist Muslim cleric Abu Hamza encouraging his followers to kill non-believers. And what is most staggering of all is the extent to which we as ordinary members of the public are kept under surveillance.

It's commonly reported that there are 4.2 million closed-circuit television cameras in the UK. But that was the estimate back in 2005. Since then everyone seems to have given up counting. Of course, many are private installations, on private premises, though the police have no trouble getting these recordings on demand. The same is true of our mobile phone records, which can track our movements anywhere in the country: indeed, number recognition software can track where you are right now.

Meanwhile, motorways are being equipped not just with speed cameras, which photograph cars that are going too fast, but average speed cameras, which by necessity have to record the number plates of all passing cars, whatever their current speed. And in London, in addition to the City of London's own ring of Leicas, there are the cameras that enforce the congestion charge by snapping the cars that enter the zone and comparing their numbers against central records.

The public actually like CCTV, because they feel it makes them safer. It doesn't. More people in Britain admit to being victims of crime than almost anywhere in the world, and yet we have far more CCTV cameras than anywhere else in the world. Even government figures can't show that cameras prevent crime – except in car parks.

Spying made simpler

And cameras are getting smarter. Middlesbrough was the first place to introduce CCTV cameras with loudspeakers, so that the police could not only watch what you do but also tell you to stop it and go home. Shoreditch in London actually made money selling its surveillance tapes – a clear invasion of the privacy for any of us who happen to be pictured on them. And Merseyside proposed mounting CCTV cameras on a blimp, just to make sure that they caught everyone.

Now there is facial recognition software so that cameras can trace your precise movements without any human beings having to spend their time on it. There is even behavioural recognition software that can detect whether we are acting suspiciously. Wearing a suspect T-shirt, perhaps. There are cameras in police cars and now on police helmets. Even X-ray CCTV.

This all helps officials keep track on us, even if it doesn't help cut crime, outside of car parks. It doesn't even do much to help prosecute crime, since most of the images that are recorded are of insufficient quality or security, or breach the Human Rights Act or the Data Protection Act, and so would be inadmissible in court. But it does help the forces of law, order and decency to get their performance figures up by prosecuting soft targets. Like Babiker Fadol, who was fined £50 (under a 120-year-old by-law) for putting his feet up on a train seat, after being caught by Merseyrail security officials with their head-mounted recording equipment.

I am sure that Britain would be a much better place if our security officials just smiled politely and asked us to show consideration for others by taking our feet off the seats, rather than slapping a fixed penalty fine on us or marching us off to court. But – as we're all discovering when our anti-war underwear is snapped on X-ray CCTV and we're driven off to the slammer to be held for three weeks without charge – give these people power over us, and the incentive to use it, and they won't hesitate.

No place of sanctuary

A while back I took some American relatives round Ely Cathedral. The Cathedral asks for a donation from non-worshippers to go in, which seems fair, and I was asked if I would like it to qualify for gift aid. I readily agreed: better that my tax should support this fine old building rather than the Chancellor. I gave my postcode and house number, and instantly my name and those of my family flashed up on the teller's screen. The Americans were shocked that we Brits should be so minutely catalogued and easily accessible. Given the incongruity of this high-tech system in an eleventh-century stone vaulted cathedral, I was rather surprised too.

This isn't the half of it, though. On the way to Ely we passed through an average speed check system. Our car was photographed at the beginning and the end, and our registration number logged by number-recognition software – as were everyone else's. So there again, the authorities knew exactly where we all were, and when. (Officially, the information is kept on record for two years, but who knows how long it is kept in reality?) And we would not have escaped scrutiny by going on the train or by bus, because they all have surveillance cameras too. If we had walked, we would probably have shown up on at least a score of the millions of CCTV cameras around Britain.

Log on to Google Earth and you will see the extraordinary detail that satellite imaging can achieve. When I look at the spy-in-the-sky pictures of my house, I see you can't quite count the number of hairs on the dog's back, but it's close. We're not safe from satellite surveillance, either.

But skulking round Ely's hedgerows in wide-brimmed hats

would not have preserved our anonymity, because our mobile phone records would have revealed exactly where we were. Even when switched off, their signals are detected by phone masts, and kept on record, in case the police subsequently demand them.

The police also have the power to bug telephone calls on behalf of 800 different bodies, including NHS trusts and, of course, all those councils who are so distressed that we might be fly-tipping rubbish. And soon you won't be able simply to buy a phone and a pay-as-you-go SIM card and hope to remain incognito. In October 2008 the then Home Secretary Jacqui Smith proposed that people should have to produce passports in order to buy a phone, so that state officials would know exactly who is responsible for any phone signal they happen to intercept. (But since whoever drafted the Identity Act forgot to make holding a fake passport illegal, you could maybe get hold of one of the 10,000 fake passports that are circulating and use one of them to buy your phone.) Ms Smith wanted to track all our phone and internet traffic, too.

The database state

What makes our descent into a surveillance state-and now a database state – so worrying is that you can't trust the people who run it. And with the data that is collected on us getting more and more intrusive and more and more personal, that is hugely dangerous.

The Criminal Justice Act 2003 allows police to take DNA samples of anyone they pick up for an arrestable offence – without their consent. And since the Serious Organized Crime and Police Act made all offences arrestable (from the terrorist atrocity of wearing the wrong T-shirt right down to throwing an apple core), and since the police are keen to meet their arrest targets (yes, they really do have arrest targets), that adds up to a lot of people. The database currently holds at least 5.2 million samples: that's about 8 per cent of the UK population, the highest of any country in the world.

Of the 722,464 DNA samples collected in 2006-07, roughly half, some 350,000 were taken from children under 15. One sample came from a seven-month-old baby girl, though it was taken with her mother's consent as a victim of crime.

And once you're on the DNA database, guilty or no, the police would rather like to keep you there. In October 2008 lawyers from Liberty finally won a six-month fight with Avon & Somerset police to have the DNA of an innocent thirteen-year-old boy removed, after he had been falsely accused of writing graffiti. But it took some effort.

Indeed, the authorities' efforts to hang on to the DNA of perfectly innocent people have been so outrageous that in December 2008 the European Court at last ruled that the samples from about 800,000 people who have not been convicted of anything should be removed from the database. There was much police grumbling at this, but little action by way of compliance. Having spent £300 million on this database (roughly the cost of 10,000 police officers), they are reluctant to part with any of its contents. However, the Home Office reluctantly agreed to remove the samples of people arrested, but not convicted, for minor offences – but only after a keeping them for six years (and twelve years in the case people arrested, but not convicted, for serious crimes). Given the enthusiasm with which the police pursue their arrest targets, that still means that hundreds of thousands of perfectly innocent people will still have their DNA kept on police files.

The only people who are able to keep themselves off the database seem to be terrorists: the Prevention of Terrorism Act 2005 was so badly drafted that it prevented police from taking DNA or fingerprints of suspects held under house arrest on anti-terrorism control orders.

Now DNA is very intimate material. It can be used to identify your parents and other relatives, indicated your distant ancestry, and even give a clue about your life expectancy. It's not the sort of thing that anyone would really want to entrust police officers with, forever, just because they once cautioned you about dropping litter or wearing a humorous T-shirt.

Identity crisis

The Identity Cards Act 2006 provides, as its name suggests, for a system of national ID cards. But more importantly, it sets up a National Identity Register, a database that will hold finger-prints, a digital facial scan, an iris scan, and the current and past places of residence addresses of all of us. Plus anything else that ministers come up with – there's plenty of space on the database.

Other countries that have ID cards don't demand so much information, and the United States, everyone's Number One terrorist target, doesn't have them at all. But Britain's authorities won't be able to resist collecting more and more information on it. Wartime ID cards were expanded for non-security purposes by Clement Atlee's postwar government – until police abuses got so bad that his successor Winston Churchill killed ID cards off.

People don't understand quite how intrusive all this is – though they might do, when they are sent a summons to turn up and be scanned. Or when they get fined £1,000 for forgetting to send the authorities their change of address.

Those fines will come in useful for the Home Office, which figures that the scheme will cost £5.6 billion to run for ten years. But an early study by the London School of Economics (LSE) suggested that the costs could be as much as £12 billion or even £18 billion. The government tried to prevent the publication of this report and harassed the author's associates. But knowing what we know about government IT projects, it's a pretty good guess which figures prove to be most accurate. (The LSE has subsequently declined to update the study because of the 'secrecy and contradictions' it has found within the project.)

The government may even make a pound or two selling our information on to private companies (those that lobby government, say) – perhaps with the excuse that it will help them process all those checks on us that modern life and official regulations make necessary. Gordon Brown was quite willing to buy stolen Liechtenstein bank information in order to track down tax-dodgers, so I don't think he will have any qualms about selling the personal details of 60 million of us to the highest bidder.

Ministers say we won't be forced to carry our ID cards. So what would be the use of them? We're told they will help us protect ourselves against identify fraud – of which there are about 70,000 cases a year. They are more likely to do the opposite. If your credit card is compromised, some of your money might be stolen; if your ID information is compromised, your whole financial and personal life is stolen.

The system is certainly unlikely to rescue us from terrorism of fraud. The London bombers did not attempt to conceal their identities. MI5 was tracking the 2005 London bomber Mohammad Sidique Khan for weeks before they decided he wasn't a threat, and gave up. Meanwhile, 95 per cent of benefit fraudsters don't lie about their identities – only their circumstances.

It's already frightening how much information our rulers demand we make public, where fraudsters could find it. Official records such as planning applications, for example, combine your address and signature and are available to anyone online.

Officialdom is already exposing us to fraud on a grand scale.

Not even our children are safe. The ContactPoint database system (£224 million to set up, five months late, and £44 million a year to run) lists the name, address, and date of birth of every child in England, plus contact details for their parents and schools. The government's aim is to create 'joined up' health, education and social services for young people. Since the data on our children would be accessible by many agencies and individuals, the government's advisers Deloitte and Touche judged there was a 'significant risk' of it falling into inappropriate hands. This is hardly comforting to parents.

Is your data safe in their hands?

We simply can't trust Gordon Brown and his colleagues to look after the vast batches of data they now demand from us and squirrel away in their files. In November 2007, HM Revenue & Customs (HMRC) lost disks containing information on 25 million parents – information including their bank account details, dates of birth, and bank accounts. And it's not as if this carelessness with our details is a one-off. That was just one of 2,100 security breaches at HMRC in that year.

Meanwhile, a laptop stolen from a Black Country hospital in 2007 contained the intimate medical records of 5,123 patients. Around 4,000 NHS smartcards, which enable NHS doctors and administrators to gain access to patient records, went missing too. Even these are relatively minor breaches. The NHS admits that data on around 1.7 million patients had been lost in a variety of ways – dumped in a skip, put on a disk that went missing, left in the pub, or filched from lockers.

In fact, civil-service laptops with our data on them go missing all the time. Every agency – Revenue & Customs, Citizens Advice Bureaux, local authorities, the Navy (which lost one containing the passport, National Insurance, and bank numbers of 600,000 recruits) – in every part of the country – Bolton, Sutton Maidstone, Essex, Hertfordshire, Norfolk, Gloucester – is losing them.

In 2006 the police managed to get three laptops containing the pay and pension details of over 15,000 Metropolitan Police officers nicked. Police in Devon and Cornwall simply threw out a computer disk containing the names, addresses, phone numbers and ranks of their employees. Losing computer disks, or just putting them into a skip, seem to be the favourite way in which state authorities put us all at risk of identity fraud and worse. Another 4,000 medical and personal records were on a USB stick that was accidentally dropped by a member of staff. Well, USB sticks are small.

In 2007 the Medical Training Application Service accidentally revealed data on hundreds of junior doctors, including their religion, police records and sexual orientation. The details of 40,000 benefit claimants were lost by social services. And an NHS Trust in East London lost CD cases holding the names and addresses of 160,000 children. This is all getting scary.

Files on 20,000 people – including their bank account numbers and health details, phone numbers and addresses, date of birth, pay slips, bank forms and interview records – that Haringey Council had stamped 'confidential' came to light in a building used by squatters. British drivers were also astonished to learn that their data was stored and even sold abroad – a fact that came to light when a data-storage facility in Iowa lost the details of 3 million learner drivers.

This sorry catalogue shows that our data just isn't safe in their hands. And with ID cards, things are going to get much worse. After all, an ID database won't be much use unless officials can check it: so you can be sure that some or all of the details on 60 million of us – details which are intimate and private, or which could be used by fraudsters for identity theft

– will be accessible to thousands of minor officials. They'll be copying it, losing it in the post, forgetting it at the pub, putting it in a skip, getting it stolen, putting it up on MySpace, selling it to the News of the World, or flogging it to who knows what flaky country.

Abuse and error

The fact that officials hold so much sensitive information on us means that, even if they don't just lose it, they can easily abuse it. Like the police officers caught ogling female airport passengers; others using cameras to look in to private houses; and those who posted on the internet CCTV footage of innocent couples canoodling. It seems we can't trust our guardians at all.

Then there were the NHS junior doctors and nurses found accessing the medical records of a number of celebrity patients at their hospital. Soon, under the government's Transforming IT programme, the information held by education, health, social services, and other officials will all be combined. So junior doctors will probably be able to look up our criminal records and school reports too. And maybe get aerial photographs of our homes from the Whitehall central valuation database while they're at it.

HMRC officials tried to explain their 25-million record loss by saying that it was just the action of some junior employee who had copied the files. So you mean that junior employees can copy 25 million files without managers even knowing about it? Let's face it, this state data leviathan is out of control.

And the personal information that countless junior bureaucrats are so cavalier with is valuable. One civilian police worker passed records on to private detectives who then sold it to the newspapers. DVLA staff passed on to animal rights activists the names and addresses of the owners of vehicles driving into a guinea-pig farm. And so on.

Not only are our lives and safety compromised by the deliberate action of even quite junior state employees. Simple error is rife in government IT systems too.

The DVLA (again) admits that over 800,000 of its vehicle records are incorrect and nearly 8 million driver records are wrong. The Police Inspectorate believes that more than a fifth of the entries in the Police National Computer contain errors. Some 13,000 people turned out to be wrongly labelled as criminals by the Criminal Records Bureau (CRB), causing many to lose their jobs. The entry on Amanda Hodgson, 36, a law-abiding mother who applied to be a welfare assistant at her local primary school, said she was a heroin addict with convictions for assault and battery going back eighteen years. Officials told her that the only way to clear her name was to have her finger-prints taken and wait for these to be checked against every unsolved crime in the country.

That's the same sort of confusion that inconvenienced hundreds of travellers in January 2005, when America turned back a BA flight to New York in mid-Atlantic, when they discovered that one of the passengers' name matched that of a terrorist suspect (though of course, it was a mere coincidence).

And the mistakes continue. In the year to August 2009 alone, the CRB wrongly reported some 1,570 people as criminals when they were innocent, or as guilty of a more serious offence than they actually committed, or (most worrying) as having a clean record when in fact they did not.

Sharing misinformation
The Prüm treaty compounds the felony. It promotes data sharing between EU countries and Gordon Brown took the lead in the discussions on it (despite spinning another story entirely to the media). So now we will have other EU countries

presuming that we are vicious criminals because the entries on some government computer are in error, or because our DNA is still on the register since the time we last dropped an apple core.

One of the people whose DNA records must have been winging their way around Europe is Darren Nixon, 28, from Stoke-on-Trent. He was arrested, fingerprinted, photographed and DNA-swabbed for the crime of listening to his MP3 player while waiting for a bus home from work. A passer-by phoned the police, thinking that his MP3 might be gun. Police tracked his bus journey using CCTV (of course) and when he got off the bus he was surrounded by armed police, bundled into a van, and hauled off to the cells.

Though perfectly innocent, the police fully intended to keep his DNA stored on the database, in perpetuity, along with all the convicted rapists and murderers. Hopefully the European Court decision will now force them to erase it. Nevertheless – assuming they actually entered his data correctly – they will keep a computer record that he was arrested on suspicion of a firearms offence. So every time there is a crime of violence in Stoke-on-Trent from now on, his name will pop up on the computer and he may well be interviewed as a potential suspect. No doubt they'll send armed officers to pick him up: you can't be too careful with dangerous iPod-toting gangsters.

Nobody would object to the police and security forces in Europe sharing information on people who were wanted for really serious offences. But when any of us can end up permanently recorded on a police computer as the result of a simple mistake, it's an intrusive injustice. It's not just the Stoke on Trent constabulary you have to worry about: now that we share everything your data could pop up on the screens of investigators anywhere in Europe. You could find yourself being picked up under a European Arrest Warrant, hauled off to a Greek jail without any evidence being presented, and kept there for the best part of a year, just because someone at a bus stop couldn't tell your iPod from an Uzi.

Computer says no competence

And we might all have more confidence that Gordon Brown and his friends could actually manage our data if it wasn't so much like Little Britain round here. Is there actually anybody competent in charge of government IT projects? This government has spent more than £70 billion on consultants and new IT systems, but do any of them actually work?

Even the flagship Identity Register is two years behind schedule, and won't now be rolled out until 2011 or 2012 – conveniently after the next election. The Conservatives say they will cancel it, but even they want ID cards for foreigners living here. It won't be long before they find the thought of ID cards for everyone rather useful and will try to sell it to us as a really great scheme that will shower amazing benefits on each and every one of us.

But government's handling of IT projects is invariably hopeless. The Child Support Agency was set up in 1993 to reclaim child maintenance from absent fathers. After years of complaints that it wasn't up to the job, IT experts EDS were given £539 million to fix it. Eventually the government ordered it to be broken up and scrapped. Meanwhile the Department of Work and Pensions cancelled a new benefit processing system after spending £106 million on it. It was one of many cases where reassuring statements in Parliament did not actually reflect the mess-up that was going on.

Then there was the Libra computer system for magistrates' courts, which cost nearly four times its original £146 million estimate and was years late. Instead of the courts simplifying their working methods to make IT solutions practicable, they tried to fit the IT round their over-complicated processes. The Criminal Records Bureau – those nice people who check whether parents are fit to help serve school dinners or go on field trips – also got into an IT stew. Though most applications for criminal records checks came on paper forms, their new system couldn't capture the data off paper, and was overwhelmed.

The Scope system to link up MI5, the Ministry of Defence and other security services also came up against the huge complexity in how state agencies work. The first part of it is up and running, albeit two years late. Other parts have been scrapped. We don't know the whole story because that is 'secret'. But we do know that the cost to the Government's communication headquarters of simply moving IT kit from one building to another was £300 million, or fifteen times what the GCHQ board originally estimated.

The Rural Payments agency, whose computer system cost £37.4 million, succeeded only in pushing farmers into bankruptcy because of its late payments of money under the Common Agricultural Policy. New systems at the Passport Agency in 1999 slowed the processing of passports from 10 days to 50 days because staff weren't properly trained for it. On an even grander scale, the Ministry of Defence Information Infrastructure cost over three times its £2.3 billion estimate, and was hugely delayed because officials grossly underestimated the snags in rolling it out.

The real cost of failure

Government IT incompetence costs us all money – not just in terms of waste, cancellations and delays, but in real losses from fraud. When DWAP personnel files went missing, fraudsters scammed the tax credit system for millions.

Or take the short-lived Individual Learning Accounts

programme. It was another headline-grabbing but quarter-baked idea, which became a fraudster's charter thanks to poor design and IT management. The 1997 election hype was that ILAs would stimulate adult education by giving tax incentives to employers. But in the event, tens of millions of pounds ended up going to fraudulent organizations which registered online as 'learning providers'. Shouldn't ministers and MPs have got to grips with the potential risks a bit better before allowing such a crazy system to go live?

And government IT failures don't just damage your pocket, they damage your health too. The grandmother of all IT projects is the National Health Service IT programme. You might think that, as the biggest IT programme in the world, it would be managed by the world's best and highest-paid IT professionals. In fact it is the usual cadre of civil servants, paid peanuts in relation to the size of what they are managing and, as usual, out of their depth.

Key suppliers pulled out because they think the NHS IT system and its management are so hopeless. Along the way, appointments and treatments have been delayed and records lost. And what was announced as a £2.3 billion plan to speed up NHS record keeping is now heading for a budget of anywhere between £12 billion and £20 billion – the government is has until now been reluctant to agree to a review that might reveal the exact cost – and seemingly endless delays. With around 1.4 million people working in the NHS, I reckon that's enough to give every doctor, nurse, administrator and cleaner their own web-enabled laptop – and still have enough left over to buy them each twenty more to leave on the train.

The price of privacy
In view of the waste, I would have preferred it if the NHS had just put my medical records on a memory stick – and everyone

else's on theirs — and told us it would be really helpful if we could carry them around, because then the doctors could check exactly what medicines we're on if we get knocked over by a car and are rushed to hospital. I would certainly feel safer looking after my own information than letting state employees keep hold of it.

We just can't trust Gordon Brown's rotten state with our information. They cannot collect it, manage it, nor protect it competently or correctly. They lose it and abuse it, they ship it out to countries with even less respect for data privacy than we have, sell it on to private firms, and use it to snoop on us, spread embarrassing facts about us, or blackmail us. And they make it easy for fraudsters to do much the same.

Nor do Brown and his colleagues even very bothered about such abuse. To them, having joined-up information on us, information that can be accessed and cross-referenced by every agency of the state, is extremely good. It makes government easier to run, because every bit of it has all our details. It means they can make sure that even the smallest transgression is spotted, punished and fined. It makes it easier to see if their targets are being delivered. And it dishonestly creates the impression how seriously they are taking the war against terrorism, crime and anti-social behaviour.

So once again, we have sobbed with gratitude as our freedom, and our privacy, disappear down the black hole of the bureaucratic mind and into the hands of people whose motives and whose competence we cannot trust.

7

NANNIES

Each weekday, I visit the fruit stall in the Westminster street market. I might ask the stallholder for half a pound of grapes or maybe a punnet of raspberries. And she breaks the law by selling them to me. For the law now demands that fruit should be sold in metric measures. Pounds and punnets won't do.

But that's not what her customers want. They never ask for metric measures. They always ask for pounds and punnets. So every day, she breaks the law many times – even though this market is right in the shadow of New Scotland Yard.

But there's little chance of the Metropolitan Police stopping our harmless and mutually agreeable trade. Ministers have told police and trading standards officers not to bother enforcing the law. On the six occasions where traders were prosecuted for using imperial measures, the public outcry was just too great.

Metric measures came in when Britain joined the Common Market (now the European Union) in 1973, but they started to be enforced only when tighter legislation was introduced in 2000. That led to the first 'metric martyr' prosecution, of Steve Thoburn, a Sunderland market trader. His case, and three others, went to the Court of Appeal, where the convictions were upheld.

The public was outraged, and the authorities decided to go easy on the issue. Even Brussels got the message. In 2007,

Gunther Verheugen, the EU trade commissioner, said: 'Pounds and ounces are in no way under threat from Brussels and never will be.'

That news obviously did not filter down to officials of Hackney council, who seized the imperial scales of market trader Janet Devers, 64, and charged her with twelve separate offences under weights and measures regulations. The prosecution left her with £5,000 in costs, a criminal record, and a lasting entry in the police computer. Again, the public were outraged.

Why do we have such pettifogging rules? If people want to buy and sell ale by the firkin or cloth by the ell, why shouldn't they? And why should nannying officials feel it important to prosecute such minor breeches of a law that should not exist?

Number and cost of regulations

Each year, the state requires us to fill out more than a billion forms. And each year, the government passes twenty or more major laws. It also approves around 3,500 regulations, amounting to around 75,000 pages of rules, with another 25,000 pages of explanation.

Nobody can possibly keep up with this torrent of red tape. It imposes huge costs on businesses and public services, but all attempts to stem the flow have failed abysmally. We're drowning in red tape. Meanwhile, we seem to be increasingly risk-averse: the fear of litigation makes us glad for the safety of regulations. And the regulators themselves love to invent more and more new rules because it's what keeps them in work.

But it's descended into farce. The absurdity of some rules – like the warnings on peanut packets that say 'May contain nuts' – have made health and safety rules a laughing stock. But it's no laughing matter: regulation is killing important parts of our social lives, from pubs to village fetes. And when our children are told not to play football in the playground in case someone gets hurt, it is robbing them of their childhood too.

The burdens on business

The UK's new Department of Business, Enterprise and Regulatory Reform isn't living up to its name – certainly not the 'Reform' bit. In 2009 the British Chambers of Commerce reported that the cost of regulation on businesses rose by more than £10 billion over the year before, to a staggering £76.8 billion.

That's more than six times the 2001 figure, and the Chambers' annual Burdens Barometer shows how the costs mount up. There's data protection rules, groundworks regulations, working time regulations, student loan bureaucracy, part-time worker initiatives and flexible working schemes, the stakeholder and occupational pensions system, age and sex discrimination rules, disability law, maternity and paternity rules, buildings regulations, rules on the use of animal by-products, water use and environmental regulations, statutory dismissal procedures, new financial accounting rules, corporate responsibility requirements, working at height codes, and many, many others. The barometer is rising.

Yet these regulations are brought in without thought to the consequences. The 2005 Control of Noise at Work Regulations aimed to protect workers on construction sites or in noisy factories. But some bright spark pointed out that the crowd noise at Old Trafford, Anfield and Craven Cottage often exceeds the 90-decibel limit. Wouldn't players have to wear earmuffs? And wouldn't orchestras playing the 1812 Overture have to do the same?

There were red faces all round, and the arts and entertainment industries were given two years' grace to find a solution to their problem. Of course, it's not really their problem, it's the regulator's problem; but nobody expects the regulators to admit their mistake and come up with something better. So concert halls will have to spend thousands working out what to do and putting some solution in place.

Costs like these are being foisted on people all over the place, just because some bureaucrat miles away from the action thinks that some particular rule or standard would be nice to have. The Care Standards Act 2000, for example, has forced the closure of hundreds of care homes whose layout doesn't match its pedantic standards. It specifies at least eight single rooms to each double – which may not even be right for the mix of customers that a care home has. It specifies that rooms should be 14.1 square metres – so if your grandmother's room in a care home is only 14.0 square metres she has to move, or be shunted back into an NHS ward where she has absolutely no room at all.

Under the Childcare Act 2006, providers of crèches and nurseries have to register and follow a set of 'education' guidelines. They run to 148 pages. All the staff need criminal records checks, naturally – you can't just leave your kids with people you trust. It all raises costs and makes childcare unaffordable. The same thing happened with the 2000 regulations on houses in multiple occupancy. Facing a 32-page form and £1,000 registration fee, many landlords sold off their properties rather than letting them out. So young parents now can't afford childcare and can't even rent a room. Who benefits from that, exactly?

And so it goes on. Nursing homes don't allow you to bring in home-made birthday cakes for your granny's friends because that breaches the food hygiene rules. Small hotels are closing their bars because the cost and effort of their licence now wipes out any profit they might have made. Restaurants have to apply for an entertainment licence before they can have a violinist serenading the tables on Valentine's Day.

Burdens on public bodies
Public bodies are burdened by much the same regulations as are businesses. So soldiers learning to play the bagpipes are limited to 24 minutes of practice a day, while Grantham PE teacher Terry Plumb, who leads pupils on rock climbing and moun-taineering trips, had to sign a form to say that he could safely get up and down a ladder.

Regulators hate ladders. You would think firefighters would be pretty skilled with them, but if you ask the fire brigade to help you fit a fire alarm, they won't be able to use your stepladder to get up to the ceiling. That contravenes the working at height regulations. Don't even suggest that they might stand on a chair. Just put the alarm back in its box and hope you don't have a fire.

Some fire stations stop firefighters from sliding down the pole to get to a fire more quickly, in case they hurt themselves. Others have felt obliged to give crews special training on how to use the reclining chairs they nap on between call-outs.

Kirkby Lonsdale contractors were prevented from using ladders to change street light bulbs. A church in Beccles had to spend £1,300 to hire scaffolding in order to change the light bulbs. And residents of Balerno waited a year for graffiti to be removed from the village sign because Edinburgh City Council ruled it too risky for staff to shin up a ladder with a mop and bucket: although the eight-foot sign is on the pavement and not very high, under safety regulations they would have to stop the traffic on the busy Lanark Road to clean it.

It's not surprising that when faced such stupidity, people take things into their own hands. Since the council never lowered the kerb outside homes in Haverigg, Cumbria, residents cleverly built small asphalt ramps at the edge of the kerb in order to get their cars up the drive. But the council came along and ripped them out, in case someone tripped over them.

The discrimination scam

Councils and other public bodies have to collect ethnic information on the people they deal with. It's supposed to prevent them discriminating against different groups. So when you call the police to say that your shed has been broken into, they are keener to ask you which of five ethnic and seventeen sub-ethnic groups you belong to, than to come round and have a look at the damage. It's on the basis of information like this that the Lake District National Park was forced to stop running guided walking tours, because most of the people who wanted to go on them were white, middle-class, and middle-aged. Another local pleasure killed off by daft regulation.

When I was raising money to build a statue of the economist Adam Smith in Edinburgh, I thought the project worthy of support from the National Lottery Heritage Fund. So I sent off for an application form. Page 1 was something like: 'Tell us about your organization. Would you say its staff are mostly white/mixed race/Asian or Asian British/Black or Black British/Chinese or Other Ethnic Groups?' Page 2 was: 'Tell us who this project is meant to help. Are they mostly white/mixed race/Asian or Asian British/Black or Black British/Chinese or Other Ethnic Groups?'

Since a statue is meant for the benefit of anybody who walks by, I couldn't answer the second question. As for the first, I don't think that most of those who do pass by the statue over the next thousand years or so would give a hoot. That's why I can't remember the questions precisely: I binned the form without even ticking a single box. It was obvious that the whole process of allocating lottery funds had been politicized, like many other state services. The original idea was to prevent dis-

crimination, but in fact it brings discrimination into services
where discrimination has no place. Why do none of these
official forms allow you to answer, simply, 'British', or 'none of
your damn business'?

I spent a time as a parent-governor of the local state
secondary that my children attended. One year we admitted a
disabled boy who could not get up the stairs. I suggested
adjusting the timetable so all his classes could be on the ground
floor, but this wouldn't do: under the disabled access
regulations, the whole building has to be accessible to everyone.
Re-timetabling would be discriminatory. So we ended up
spending £500,000 installing a lift for the use of one child, even
though the building was due to be demolished two years later.
It seemed typical of how the state wastes our money on the
blinkered pursuit of rules that are simply pointless or inappropriate to local circumstances.

The failure to cut red tape
The cost of over-regulation has been evident for years but
politicians' efforts to reduce the burden have all failed. The
Conservatives introduced a Deregulation Unit to abolish
unnecessary regulations and make the rest easier to comply
with – though it did neither. The incoming New Labour
government didn't like the presumption of 'Deregulation', and
thought that 'Unit' didn't sound proactive enough, so they
changed its name to the Better Regulation Task Force.

The change from 'Deregulation' to 'Better Regulation'
indicated that any chance of actually reducing the burden of
regulations had gone. Amid great fanfare the Task Force
cancelled 27 minor regulations on things such as selling
turpentine, but it let thousands of more serious ones come in.

The Regulatory Reform Act 2001 and the Regulatory
Reform Orders 2001 were billed as 'the regulation to scrap

regulations' but five years later the system was equally complex and even more burdensome. Then there was the Regulatory Impact Unit, which would do cost-benefit Regulatory Impact Statements before new regulations were implemented. But these simply became another box to be ticked before ministers did what they planned to do anyway. Now the Unit has been renamed the Better Regulation Executive just to confuse everyone further.

Another law, the Regulatory Reform Act 2006, promised to cut red tape where previous law had failed. But at the same time it allows the government to amend existing regulations as it pleases without any debate at all, which hardly seems to improve democratic accountability.

The Better Regulation Task Force became the Better Regulation Council, and has now morphed into the Risk and Regulation Advisory Council, which, we're told, will 'halt the march of the nanny state'. To show how serious this is, Gordon Brown has asked the new body to report directly to him on issues such as nut warnings on peanut packets and whether schools should ban conkers as too dangerous. But it probably means that the nanny state has actually just got bigger. Peanut packers will no doubt be handed another 5,000 pages of rules on when they do and don't have to say 'May contain nuts', and teachers will probably get another 200-page circular telling them what safety gear the kids have to wear to play conkers.

The Dutch system would be much more effective: for every new regulation that the government wants to bring in, an old one has to be thrown out. Though it would be better if we threw out ten. After all, we have plenty to spare.

Regulation by media
Politicians like regulation because it solves immediate problems. Pass a working at heights regulation and you can announce that

nobody will be injured falling off a ladder ever again. Unfortunately, this overlooks all the invisible victims. Your house might burn down because you can't get anyone to put in a smoke alarm, your village sign will be covered in graffiti for ever more, and you'll have to sit in the dark when you go to church. But nobody will notice these problems until later, and meanwhile the politicians and the regulators receive applause for making the lives of working people safer.

It leads to regulation driven by headlines rather than risks. Train travel is much safer than road travel. About 3,000 people die each year in traffic accidents, but in most years hardly anyone dies in train crashes. But a train crash in which scores of people are killed or injured is a much more dramatic news event than thousands of road accidents in which just one or two people perish. And so we end up spending vast sums to make the railways even safer still.

The Cullen Inquiry, set up after the 2000 Hatfield Crash, duly reported that better rail safety was needed – specifically, the £3.5 billion European Rail Traffic Management System, which prevents trains going through red signals. In reality, that would save just one life every 16 months, and it would slow down the network to such an extent that more people would decide to drive instead, leading to dozens more deaths on the roads. But that's how regulation is made.

Another example is the 2002 murders of two 10-year-old Soham girls by their school caretaker. This was a dreadful tragedy, but it hit the headlines precisely because it was so exceptional. And the response – to demand Criminal Records Checks for anyone who might come into contact with children, from bell ringers to school governors, parents volunteering to coach football or help on field trips – actually impairs the lives of children. Most people resent the cost, bother and indignity of having to be checked by the police. So schools can't get parents to volunteer to coach football or help with school activities: in 2008 we were short of 40,000 school governors. And it's worth remembering that the Soham murderer, Ian Huntley, was indeed vetted by the police, but so incompetently that his murky past was overlooked.

The litigation culture

The 'no win, no fee' litigation system means that victims of accidents have nothing to lose by trying to pass the blame onto their employers or others, and much to gain if they succeed. Their lawyers may say that the firm's insurers can easily afford to pay out. But in fact it is the business that suffers, because their insurance premiums go up when a claim is made. They might have to cut back on staff or raise their prices to compensate, so other workers and customers lose out. Charities too have suffered because of this.

In the case of public bodies, it is taxpayers who have to shell out. Our education authorities pay out about £2 million a year in compensation claims to pupils. A recent year's tally included £5,000 to one kid whose finger was hit by a cricket ball, £21,500 to another who suffered back strain in a drama lesson, £3,500 to one who broke an arm in the playground, £13,000 to one who tripped up, and even £6,000 to one who was injured while breaking in to the school one night. Yet this is all chicken feed compared to the £396 million paid out by the NHS in 2008-9 for clinical negligence claims, or the £713 million it expects to pay out in 2009-10.

Such liabilities make public bodies very twitchy. They start imposing new rules on what you can and can't do, in order to limit their risk of being sued. West Monkton Parish Council told its allotment holders they each needed £5 million worth of insurance cover in case a visitor has an accident on their patch of soil. At £375 a year, that's forty times what they pay in rent.

And Bill Malcolm, 61, who put a length of barbed wire around his allotment to protect it from thieves – he had lost £300 worth of tools in numerous break-ins to his shed – was ordered to remove it by council officials. They feared that if thieves cut themselves on his barbed wire, they could sue the council for their injuries.

The rights culture

Our rights culture makes it worse. The welfare state has given us rights such as unemployment pay, free healthcare, and state housing; but it imposes no pressure on us to seek work, stay healthy, or save up for somewhere to live.

With the adoption of the Human Rights Act, focus of law and policy is now entirely on rights rather than personal responsibilities. It encourages people to seek compensation when bad things happen to them, but not to take reasonable care to prevent bad things happening in the first place. And the more we compensate, the less we encourage people to take care.

School caretaker Anthony Gower-Smith successfully sued Hampshire County Council, claiming £50,000 for injuries he sustained when he fell off a stepladder trying to remove a card display from a wall at the school gym. Gower-Smith had been using stepladders for thirty years and in 2002 had ticked a box saying that he had been given safety training, but the judge ruled that the council was 75 per cent to blame for his 2004 accident because their training on how to use the ladder was not sufficiently 'memorable'.

Risks are an inevitable part of life, and the proper way to manage them is common sense: look at the potential risks, work out what risk is acceptable, and rely on those concerned to take reasonable precautions. You can't eliminate all risk: and it's the nanny state's attempt to do so that gets us hog-tied in the most absurd and counterproductive red tape.

Regulators themselves

One big source of absurd regulations is regulators themselves. If we had half the number of health and safety officers, we would have half the number of daft health and safety rules, and probably better health and safety. Do we really need fleets of local-authority 'Walking Officers' to get us walking? Or NHS 'Five a Day Coordinators' to tell us to eat more fruit and vegetables? Or local council 'Real Nappy Officers' to tell us that towelling nappies are environmentally friendlier? (Which they aren't: disposables take up very little landfill, and when you wash towelling nappies you use energy to boil the water and you tip bleach and detergent down the drain.)

The Equal Opportunities Commission – in another rebranding, it's now the Equalities and Human Rights Commission – looked into the causes of 'occupational segregation'. That's quango-speak for the fact that most bricklayers are men and most midwives are women. The EOC was looking for 'new and creative ways of cracking the problem'. Crackers.

And don't imagine that our gas, water, electricity and telephones, now all privatized, are no longer controlled by the state. Their regulators tell these companies in minute detail how to run their businesses. A few years ago, media stories about pensioners who couldn't afford electricity prompted a new regulation that utility companies couldn't disconnect customers who weren't paying. So now, everyone knows that if they don't pay their bill, nothing will happen, and growing numbers of people are indeed deciding not to bother.

When they were nationalized, our utilities used to be run for the convenience of their workers. Now they are run for the kudos of the politicians. It's a pity we can't roll back the regulation, bring in real competition, and have utilities that are run for the benefit of their customers.

No grasp of scale

The traditional Easter charity duck race in Lymm, Cheshire, was cancelled on health and safety grounds. Despite the event's long and incident-free history, council officials ordered organizers to close a nearby road to prevent overcrowding – but refused to pay the £3,000 cost, which made the fundraising event unviable. Meanwhile, organizers of the annual Christmas Party in the village hall at Embsay, near Skipton, were told that they needed a full risk assessment, and would have to put nut allergy warnings on the mince pies. To hold a village Gilbert & Sullivan evening in a local barn, you now need to get an entertainment licence, and to serve people a glass of wine at the interval you have to get an alcohol licence too. Neither is cheap or hassle-free.

But these blanket rules are now making many local activities unviable. Of course people whose business is staging large music events or running pubs should need a licence. And people organizing a village entertainment should do so responsibly. The trouble is that even minor, local activities that cause no trouble to anyone are being caught up in the full rigour of uncompromising laws. That weakens the social bonds between us, and robs us of our social and cultural lives.

Birmingham Council forced clowns in Zippo's circus to down trumpets because their three-minute sketch would require them to apply for a live music licence at every location they perform. Which is quite a few, since it's a travelling circus. Doing that would just be too costly and time-consuming. But Jacqui Kennedy, Birmingham's Director of Regulatory Services (!) was uncompromising: 'We do not condone unlicensed events,' she said.

Loss of amenity

Pettifogging regulation is robbing us of other amenities too. An NHS trust set about chopping down a 50-year-old tree in case its fallen berries caused someone to slip. Bristol spent £5,000 on trees – only to dig them up because it was discovered that children might be harmed if they ate the leaves (though only in vast quantities). Norfolk cut down twenty horse chestnut trees in case children injured people by throwing up sticks to get down the conkers.

To the distress of bereaved relatives, Worksop council encased gravestones with wooden buttresses in case they fell over. Hexham simply flattened them all.

Newquay had to cut its striking £20,000 fountain to a fifth of its height because health officials say it could spray bacteria on passers-by.

South-West Trains had to remove 28 trains because lettering on their station-indicator boards was only 32mm high, against a standard of 35mm. That of course caused more overcrowding on the other trains.

Local pubs are closing at the rate of three a week because of the smoking ban, but the government's latest plans would force them to hire bouncers to keep a check on numbers, pay for a 'mystery shopper' service to ensure standards are being met, and send all staff for special training. Happy hours would go, there would be no music any louder than a hairdryer, and every licensee would have to meet police and licensing authorities twice a year. That's 400,000 meetings, and 33,000 working days for police and publicans. It means the price of beer will be going up in pubs – the one place likely to promote responsible drinking.

If you can't afford pub prices and want to pick up a 30p can of supermarket lager you'll have another shock, because the

Home Office wants shops to have separate alcohol counters so as to keep an eye on people's consumption. So if you want a pie and a pint, you'll have to queue twice. It must be only a matter of time before this nannying regulation of alcohol turns into an outright ban, the way that tobacco seems to be heading. Then no doubt it will be crisps.

The loss of childhood
It's not just adult amenities that are threatened. Over-regulation is robbing kids of their childhood too. The Manchester Taxi Owners and Drivers Association scrapped their annual seaside outing for disadvantaged kids in 2005 when they discovered that each cab would need a risk assessment, each child would have to be accompanied by an adult, and each adult would need to be checked by the Criminal Records Bureau.

Many swimming pools now demand one-to-one supervision for children, so a single parent with two kids can't go, and the kids never learn to swim. Pools in Dorset don't help on that front either: they were told to stop lending inflatable armbands to kids in case someone gets an infection blowing one up. Blue Peter stopped using egg boxes in their construction projects in case they were infected with salmonella. Durham education chiefs banned sack races from a school sports day in case children fell and hurt themselves. Schoolyard football was stopped at Burnham Grammar School, to avoid anyone being hit by stray balls.

Kids are perfectly responsible human beings. But our regulation state never allows them to be responsible. They would learn a lot from falling over in a sack race, but they are never given the chance. Politicians have made us so alarmed about knife crime that we keep our kids well away from knives: so they never learn, under adult guidance, the use and dangers of knives. To give your kids a sip of wine occasionally is thought shocking, so they never learn from adults how to drink responsibility. We hate militarism, so our kids never join the Scouts or the Guides. The result? They hang around in street gangs, get hammered, and end up knifing each other.

In France, alcohol is much cheaper, but teenage binge drinking is almost unknown. They introduce kids to alcohol in the home, where adults can teach them its pleasures and its evils. We had it right when boys went to the Scouts and got penknives for Christmas. Under adult supervision they learnt to handle these potentially dangerous things. And talking of penknives, the Swiss Army teaches young adults how to use guns – with the result that guns are almost never used in crime there, despite the fact that all adults possess one.

We should be exposing our kids to more dangers, so they can learn how to manage the numerous and inevitable risks that life throws at them. Adults too need to be aware of and understand daily risks if they are to manage them safely: but our regulation system manages to achieve the opposite. It tries to regulate all risk away. And it admits no exceptions, so we cannot manage even the most minor issues in our own way. That is misguided, costly – and often counterproductive.

Counterproductive regulation

Much regulation – perhaps most – achieves the opposite of what it intends. Environmental rules on waste recycling mean that old cardboard can no longer be burnt to generate electricity. Starbucks was forced to waste 23 million litres of water a day because health and safety officials told them to keep the taps running in order to stop germs breeding in the pipes.

The landfill tax encourages illegal dumping, which costs even more to clean up. In 2008 Gareth Corkhill, a bus driver from Whitehaven, Cumbria, got a criminal record for leaving his bin lid open four inches. He refused to pay a £100 spot fine to council inspectors, saying 'It's only an £80 fine for fly-tipping. I would have been better off doing that.' In another case, Andy Tierney was fined £50 for disposing of junk mail in a litter bin on his way past. Apparently litter bins are not for 'household waste'. A Swansea man was fined £100 for having a single paper in his bottle box. And a 12-year-old, who left a bag of paper alongside a recycling bin because it was full, was sent a letter by the council threatening a fine. None of this overblown officialdom helps encourage responsibility, even in the most avid recyclers.

Meanwhile, Thameside police refused to chase motorcycle thieves because the crooks weren't wearing crash helmets. So if you want to commit the perfect Thameside crime, make your escape on a motorbike and don't wear a helmet.

Only officials are fit to act
The regulation state sees only those in authority as truly fit to decide what can happen. Individual action is outlawed or discouraged. Risk assessors considered removing fire extinguishers from Bournemouth apartment blocks, because the presence of extinguishers makes residents more likely to try to put a fire out by themselves, rather than see their property go up in flames while they wait for the experts to arrive. The presumption is that untutored householders cannot make reasonable decisions about their own safety.

But officials are incentivized to follow rules, even when it is absurd. Like the case of the mother who stopped her car to aid her child, who was choking in the back seat, and was promptly issued a parking ticket. Or Burnley binman Matthew Carter, who was told by Pendle council to stop wearing his bandana because the English flag on it might be considered offensive and racist. It wasn't to Mr Carter (who, incidentally, is black).

And officials are quite willing to use whatever powers they

possess in order to make sure the rules are followed, to the letter. They have put cameras in old drink cans to run down fly-tippers, and used surveillance and phone-tapping – allowed under anti-terrorist legislation – to make sure that parents from one school catchment area don't try to send their kids to another. The public outrage at this abuse of anti-terrorist legislation has led the government to instruct local authorities not to do it any more. The amazing thing is that such an instruction was ever necessary.

Control of our private lives

Give anyone in authority powers, though, and they will use them: and use them to prevent us doing whatever their constipated metropolitan attitudes believe is bad for us, whether or not it harms anyone else.

The government has already banned smoking even in private premises, but now it wants new rules to 'denormalize smoking': tobacco products would not be on display in shops, and pub cigarette machines would be banned. The porn mags can remain in full view, but cigars have to stay under the counter.

It won't affect smokers who are content with their usual brand and will just ask for it. But if they want to wean themselves off the weed and choose a less strong cigarette, they won't know what to ask for. And in any case, where this measure has been adopted elsewhere, for example Iceland and Ireland, it has had no effect at all on smoking rates. It's just gesture politics – public policy as propaganda.

Meanwhile, the large supermarkets and petrol stations will be able to afford the specialist counters and trained staff required by this regulation. Small shops – some already hit by the loss of their post office business – won't. They will lose tobacco trade, and all the purchases that people make when they are in buying cigarettes. Another local amenity gone, yet another invisible victim of regulation.

Government adviser Professor Julian LeGrand even suggested that smokers should have to get permits to allow them to buy tobacco. And now the debate has moved on to what we eat and drink. Council bosses in Rochdale gave thirteen chip shops shakers with fewer holes in an effort to cut down customers' intake of salt. The £42 million National Fruit Scheme came not only with free fruit for schoolchildren, but full instructions on how to eat a carrot.

It might all sound rather silly and petty. But when it comes with huge powers of surveillance, CCTV, databases, spot fines and powers to arrest people on any offence whatsoever, the line between nannying and oppression has become no wider than a cigarette paper. Not that you will be allowed to buy one of those.

8

ROTTEN ECONOMY

We were promised an end to boom and bust. But we got both. First, a huge boom built on the back of low interest rates, inflation and soaring house prices, record levels of public and private borrowing, and a massive public spending splurge in which hundreds of thousands of new public-sector jobs were created. Then, a huge bust, with high-street banks failing, businesses going broke, unemployment soaring, even more astonishing increases in government debt, followed by vast tax rises to pay for it.

Back in 1995, Will Hutton complained passionately about the amount that the government was borrowing to fill the gap between what it was spending and what it raised in taxation. But borrowing today is higher than at any point since the Second World War. In November 2008, the Chancellor Alastair Darling predicted that the government would owe more than a trillion pounds – £1,020,000,000,000. That's an amount equivalent to 57 per cent of Britain's annual output (Gross Domestic Product, or GDP). It's such an enormous debt that there is a real chance of the government not being able to repay it: rates for insurance against Britain defaulting quadrupled after the announcement.

Never had it so good?
This is dire, though you would never guess so from listening to

the Prime Minister (and former Chancellor), Gordon Brown. For him, years of prudent economic management have left Britain strong and well able to weather an economic crisis that originated elsewhere.

The crisis resulting from the financial meltdown may well have originated in America, but in reality, Britain is not in a strong position to weather it. And that is due to the government's own profligate policies. Brown spent and borrowed wildly during the boom years, leaving nothing saved to tide us through the bad. Our only hope now is to borrow yet more to get us through to better times.

Gordon Brown's supposedly 'prudent' rules of economic management were no such thing. They allowed government borrowing to soar. And somehow it always turned out higher than his Budget predictions.

Meanwhile the tax take rose more than 50 per cent in real terms in the decade after 1997, thanks partly to stealth taxes and higher charges for local and national government services. Britain's tax burden rose faster than any in Europe, and our public-sector spending rose as a proportion of GDP, against falls in other European countries. And low interest rates boosted house prices and set us off on a borrowing and spending spree.

It was a huge party, and it ended in a huge hangover. But we cannot simply blame America or global forces beyond our control. Britain's taxing, spending, and borrowing binge has made our financial headache a lot bigger.

And we seem to be making it worse with a hair of the dog, borrowing even more in an attempt to make the pain go away. But that extra public borrowing will have to be paid for by higher taxes – and perversely, the government aims to load most of that burden on the higher earners who create Britain's wealth. There is no more talk of 'prudence'. New Labour now looks much like the Old.

Origins of the financial crisis

The current crisis certainly originated in the United States. The Community Reinvestment Act 1977 attempted to give poor minorities a step onto the housing ladder by outlawing 'redlining' – the banks' practice of refusing mortgages to people living in poor districts. So lenders were forced to make what we now know as sub-prime loans.

These loans were indeed risky, and by 1984 the Savings & Loan sector was failing. The US government bailed them out, and forced many to merge. But in doing so, they had created lenders that were still issuing risky loans, but were too important to be allowed to fail.

In 1995 the anti-redlining laws were strengthened even further. Banks feared reprisal from the regulators unless they complied. They knew that their loan business was bad, so they diced and sliced it and sold it around the world as 'securities'. That just spread the infection to other countries, in particular to those like Britain with large financial sectors.

In 1987, stock markets crashed, on fears that some lenders could fail. The Federal Reserve, helped by the Bank of England, responded by flooding the world with money. It worked, and crisis was averted. But it made the authorities believe that they could abolish any downturn simply by throwing cash at it. They did it for the dotcom crash, and after 9/11 even more money was pumped in, with US interest rates being brought down from 6.25 per cent to just 1 per cent. With loans now six times cheaper, the demand for mortgages boomed, and American house prices soared. Much the same happened in Britain too.

Gordon Brown and the American authorities thought they had ended boom and bust and created a permanent boom. But it was a boom paid for on borrowed money – and inevitably followed by bust, economic dislocation, and indebtedness.

The Bank of England

By giving the Bank of England power to set interest rates, Gordon Brown had seemingly taken monetary policy out of politics. It was designed to show his prudent intentions: there would be no possibility of getting out of trouble by creating a boom on the back of cheap credit.

High interest rates work by making borrowing more expensive. So people borrow less, and have less to spend. And if people aren't spending so much, shops and service providers have to cut their prices. So higher interest rates tend to curb price rises, while lower rates accelerate them. And Gordon Brown told the Bank that its interest rate changes should aim to keep price rises at roughly 2 per cent per annum.

But price rises are not easy to measure, and Brown discarded the traditional Retail Price Index (RPI) for a new one, the Consumer Price Index (CPI). This had the political advantage of producing a lower number, so that inflation would look less high. But the CPI ignores housing costs, which are important in Britain. The result was that while house prices were soaring – UK house prices doubled in the five years before the 2008 crash, a far steeper rise than in France, Germany and our other near neighbours – the Bank was focused on other things, so its policy did not sufficiently rein back on borrowing.

Furthermore, Brown's 2 per cent target turned out to be too high. China and other emerging economies were flooding Britain with cheap imports: in reality, prices should have been falling, or at least rising more slowly. Meanwhile, the large influx of workers from Eastern Europe should have been keeping wages down too. By lowering interest rates enough to permit prices to grow at 2 per cent, the Bank was unwittingly making borrowing too cheap and stoking up a false boom.

Worse, from April 2007 onwards, the Bank wasn't even hitting its target, and prices rose over 3 per cent and kept on rising. In other words, the Bank was making the borrowing binge even greater. Brown's choice of price target, and the Bank's inability to meet it, were not saving us from boom and bust, but were creating a borrowing boom that would inevitably end up with a gigantic bust.

Financially embarrassed

Brown also passed the responsibility of regulating the banking sector from the Bank of England to a new regulator, the Financial Services Authority (FSA), based in London's Docklands. That was a big mistake. The Bank of England had a much better grasp of what was actually happening in the financial markets. They could see who was coming in to borrow from them, and how much. They could take action promptly, quietly telling over-stretched banks to mend their ways.

Indeed, the Bank suspected that there was a problem with one of Britain's biggest mortgage lenders, Northern Rock, in October 2006, long before it went bust, and told the FSA so. But the regulator didn't see the scale of the problem, or act decisively enough to end it. Eventually the Northern Rock's riskiness was publicly exposed. Thousands of people queued up to get their money out, and the government felt forced to bail it out. Having bailed out Britain's most reckless bank, it could hardly refuse help to Bradford & Bingley, Royal Bank of Scotland, and the others.

The episode was a particular embarrassment because Blair and Brown had been keen to promote Britain's place as a financial centre. With manufacturing jobs migrating to lower-cost countries, they saw Britain's future in services, and financial services in particular. They positioned London as a major capital market. Wealthy fund managers flooded in, attracted by tax rates lower than New York's, and a sympathetic regulatory regime. Booming financial institutions threw up yet more skyscrapers in Docklands.

Indeed, their pro-business talk generally was good – this was New Labour after all. In advance of the 1997 election, Blair and Brown got the confidence of business, convincing them there would be no old-style tax and spend policies. They even produced a Business Manifesto alongside the normal one. They would not give the trade unions back their privileges. They would not try to protect jobs, but would help to equip British workers to prosper in dynamic world markets. They would not be nationalizing British industry.

And yet here we are, in a Britain where the government is now the majority owner of one of the world's largest banks, and has shareholdings and board-level representation on several of the others. It's a world Old Labour scarcely dreamt of.

Job creation

The way that Blair and Brown talked before the 1997 election sounded like they had a strategy that would generate greater economic efficiency, growth, and fairness.

In fact, there was no discernable change in Britain's productivity, and economic growth was actually slightly lower in the Blair years than in the Major years. Growth in the Blair years beat the EU average, but the US and other English-speaking countries grew faster. Now, of course, our economy is actually shrinking, and faster than most. Meanwhile, the wide variations in prosperity between different parts of Britain remain just as wide as they were, seemingly untouched by all the billions that are spent on regional development.

Certainly, the private sector created new jobs during the

Blair years. But that had less to do with Gordon Brown's economic measures than with the lagged effect of Margaret Thatcher's trade union reforms, which made workplaces more flexible and efficient. But this trend has been reversed by the massive explosion in employee rights that have come from both domestic and European regulation, such as the new rules on working hours and paternity leave.

And roughly 80 per cent of the new jobs that the private sector created went to migrant workers. There were quarter of a million fewer British nationals in work in 2008 than there were in 1997. Most of the new migrant workers came from the Eastern European countries that became EU members in 2004. Britain, to its credit, was one of the few EU members that did not put curbs on their right to travel and work here as the rules required. In return, we got not just plumbers and builders, but nurses, doctors and other public employees.

The early death of prudence
Indeed, too much of the extra employment in the British economy came from additional public jobs rather than private ones. Public employment has grown more rapidly: but it is the private sector that has to create the wealth that the public sector spends.

This large growth in public spending may seem remarkable in the light of the economic rules that Gordon Brown very publicly imposed upon himself. Under the sustainable investment rule, he pledged to hold public debt to a 'stable and prudent' level over the economic cycle. And under the so-called golden rule, the government would borrow only to invest, not to fund current expenditure.

But the second rule all depends on what you mean by 'invest', and the first all depends on what you mean by 'debt'. Various government liabilities – public-sector pensions, nuclear decommissioning costs, Network Rail's borrowings, future payments for schools and hospitals built under the Private Finance Initiative – have been soaring, but are not counted. Indeed, Gordon Brown fought constant battles with the statisticians to keep these liabilities off the Treasury's books.

And public services are not like businesses, which (hopefully) deliver a long-term financial return on your investment. The money put in to public services aims to deliver benefit now: it is more like spending than investment. When Gordon Brown spoke of investment on education or health, he was really talking about spending on these things. And although his rules were presented as self-denial, this was sheer duplicity. The rules allowed public spending to increase at an unprecedented rate as a proportion of GDP.

Public spending
Public expenditure has risen by more than half since 1997. In 2008 it reached 37.8 per cent of GDP, which means that of every £100 we earn, the government spent £37.80 of it. By 2010 the government will be spending 40.6 per cent of GDP.

In money, that is £680 billion – over £11,000 for every man, woman and child in the country. But public spending is not spread equally, or even fairly. In Scotland, public spending now accounts for 70 per cent of income; in the North-East of England it is 80 per cent. And public spending goes to particular groups, like older people, who get state pensions and use the NHS rather more. But younger people, facing high taxes such as national insurance and stamp duty, are net payers.

But the huge rise in public spending has not bought a huge improvement in public services. Much of the extra money has been dissipated in higher salaries and pensions. A lot is simply wasted – £101 billion or £4,000 per family, according to estimates by the Taxpayers' Alliance.

When the corporate troubleshooter David James (a Conservative) came up with proposals to slash £35 billion of waste from the public budget, you would have thought the Mongol hordes had arrived, given the screams from the government. But Gordon Brown saw no difficulty in quietly slashing his own £30 billion of waste from the civil service following a review by Sir Peter Gershon. That suggests that there is a lot more waste waiting to be cut, and that the government should have got onto it a long time ago.

It is only now, with the government looking into the abyss of a trillion-pound public debt, that the government has been moved to sell off assets that the state owns, but doesn't need to. Why do we need a state bookmaker (the Tote), a state conference centre (the Queen Elizabeth II Centre), a weather forecaster (the Met Office), a mapmaker (Ordnance Survey), a timber company (the Forestry Commission), or for that matter a coin maker (the Royal Mint)? All these are up for grabs in the government's fire sale. But of course, the state commercial TV station (Channel 4) isn't – politicians fear the trouble that media personalities might make for them. Nor, it now seems, are they brave enough to privatize the mail carrier (Royal Mail) as several other countries have done.

In addition, much of what the government does could probably be done better by private agencies – running back-to-work schemes or managing incapacity benefits, for instance. A good deal of the rest could benefit from better management. Government procurement, for example, is notoriously poor: a third of public projects are not delivered within budget. And government IT projects are a disaster, wasting tens of billions.

The European Union also wastes a large chunk of the money we hand over to it (which has soared 60% to £6.4 billion, equivalent to £257 per household or 3p on the basic rate of income tax). There is administrative waste (like having the European Parliament spread between Strasbourg and Brussels); strategic waste (building roads and tourist attractions that nobody uses); planning dysfunctions (like the bridge between Romania and Moldova, which has no road connection on one side); frills (all the PR telling us how wonderful the EU is); duplication (national bodies being reproduced at EU level); fraud (carousel exporting and importing of livestock, sometimes imaginary livestock, because you get subsidies each time); policy burdens (the social chapter, gold plating); policy consequences (all those dead fish dumped back in the sea because the boat is over-quota); and subsidies (like the Common Agricultural Policy, and subsidies for silkworm eggs, if you can believe that).

The tax burden

To fund the government's extravagant and wasteful expenditure, taxes have risen by a shocking 51 per cent since 1997 – and that's in real terms, adjusted for inflation. Earnings have risen too, but not as fast; so a greater proportion of what we earn now goes in taxes. We work five months of the year, from January 1 to June 2, solely to meet the demands of the tax collectors. That is a whole week more slave labour than when Gordon Brown became Chancellor in 1997. Over the next couple of years, with our incomes falling and the tax collectors even more desperate, we will have to put in even more time for the government's benefit.

And the greatest burden falls on the poorest. The bottom fifth of the population pay the highest proportion of their income in taxes. When people move from welfare into work, they start paying taxes and losing benefits, giving them an effective tax rate that in many cases is 70 per cent and which can reach 90 per cent. People in part-time work face extremely high rates if they move to full-time work, which is a hugely perverse incentive. Students just starting work face the new burden of student loan repayments. And of course poorer people are hit far more by the burden of VAT and excise taxes on alcohol and tobacco, which wealthier people can more easily afford. You might imagine that the rich pay most taxes: but the reality is that those on below-average incomes stump up most of the tax that the Treasury rakes in.

But not only are taxes higher and less fair: under Gordon Brown they have been made more complicated too. The tax code has trebled in size. Tax is so complicated that 40 per cent of companies' corporation tax returns contain errors. The tax credits and pension credits systems are so complicated that large amounts of benefit go unclaimed. And the system is getting even more complicated. In April 2009, the Chancellor announced a new income tax rate of 50 per cent (plus National Insurance, of course) for higher earners. Meanwhile, personal allowances will be changed, several times. The slow and faltering moves that have been made towards tax simplification now lie abandoned.

Our relationship with the tax authorities has changed too. Tax inspectors are now incentivized to extract every last penny of revenue from every possible source they can. The tax rules are so complicated that they are often open to different inter-pretations: but the officials' strategy now is to demand the most they can get away with, rather than trying to find some just and reasonable settlement. And the merger between the Inland Revenue and Customs & Excise seems to have brought the heavy-handed approach of Customs – who among other things are expected to stop drug runners – to the scrutiny of personal and small business tax returns. It has all made the relationship between tax officers and the public adversarial, and no longer cooperative.

Stealth taxes

Until recently, the government had stuck to its early promise to keep income tax rates pegged. They wanted to reassure voters in 1997 that they would not soak the wealth creators, nor spend and tax recklessly.

But Gordon Brown was a master at raising tax through stealth. For example, the top rate of tax, at 40 per cent, was originally meant only for the very highest earners. Now over 3 million people pay this high rate – 50 per cent more than in 1997. As their wages have risen with inflation, even teachers and police officers have found themselves creeping into the 40 per cent tax bracket.

Stamp duty, which people pay on the sale of their homes, has also soared because of this stealth effect. Gordon Brown raised the rates of tax paid on the most expensive homes: but as house prices rose in the great boom, more and more people found themselves paying the higher rates – 3 per cent on homes worth over £250,000 and 4 per cent on homes over £500,000. In the five years to April 2007, that neat trick took stamp duty revenues up 140 per cent to reach a record £6.4 billion. As more and more outraged people found themselves paying stamp duty on quite average homes, Brown made a show of re-adjusting the tax bands – but not by enough to compensate for the price inflation that his own boom had generated. Meanwhile, millions of other people found that rising house prices now made their deceased relatives' estates liable to inheritance tax – another tax intended only for the rich.

National Insurance (NI) is another tax which most people don't notice, because it is deducted from their payslip – they don't have to hand over a cheque. The rules for that were changed too, so that poorer taxpayers ended up paying £50 a month in deductions, while all those new top-rate earners faced paying another 1 per cent NI on top of their 40 per cent income tax. A further increase was announced in November 2008 – but it would be paid by employers, in the hope that ordinary voters wouldn't notice.

Meanwhile, pension funds were taxed while public sector pensions expanded. There are new, often hidden, taxes on air travel, petrol, car ownership, insurance, alcohol, gambling and insurance. And alongside these stealth taxes, there have been major rises in charges of various sorts. Fees for university tuition, for example, now bring in about £2 billion. There are more and more charges for council services, and more fines from the growing battery of speed cameras. A standard passport now costs £77.50, and over £100 if you want it within a week.

The effect on productivity

In a positive move, Gordon Brown reduced corporation tax and the capital gains tax paid by people who build up and sell successful businesses. But other countries have cut these taxes more sharply as they square up to the threat of competition from low-cost economies.

That has left Britain's business taxes heavier than many countries. The corporation tax rate of 28 per cent is now higher than the EU average. So it should come as no surprise when companies like the asset management group Henderson simply move their headquarters to Dublin and pocket the difference (about £8.5 million a year in Henderson's case). In fact, not just the high rates of tax, but also its complexity, and the fickleness of Treasury rulings, have led other major companies to go abroad too – or seriously threaten to.

In this context the £30,000 tax on non-doms that came into effect in 2008 was very bad for Britain. Having attracted all these high-flying fund managers, investors and advisers into London, we now hit them with a new tax. For many it is not the scale of the tax that is offputting – many are rich enough to afford £30,000 without too much fuss. It is the arbitrariness of it. They figure that if the Treasury can suddenly impose such a tax on people who generate millions for the British economy, it can probably impose other burdens on them at a whim too. But there are plenty of other places that would like to dent London's supremacy and entice in these wealth-creators. The Gulf states, China, and other countries already aiming to become world financial centres, would love to have them.

It all means that Britain's relative position as a low tax economy, with stable and predictable tax rules, has been eroded. Britain used to be fifth in the league tables of world competitiveness. By 2007 it had fallen to ninth. A year later, in October 2008, it had fallen another three places, and out of the top ten, to twelfth. The World Economic Forum, which compiles the league tables, attributed the fall to Britain's low savings rate, high personal and public borrowing, and large national debt. Indeed it ranked Britain's macroeconomic environment, about which Gordon Brown so likes to boast, as just the 58th most impressive in the world.

Public borrowing
About the only league table that Britain is rising up through is public borrowing. Our public-sector deficit – the shortfall between what the government brings in and what it spends – went from the thirteenth largest in 1997 to the fifth largest ten years later.

The Treasury, of course, always underestimates what it will have to borrow in future years. But the International Monetary Fund and the Organization for Economic Cooperation and Development have been warning about Britain's over-borrowing since 2003.

The Chancellor admits to borrowing around 48% of GDP

this year, which in human terms is around £32,000 per household. That's high by any standards. But there are lots of other obligations on the government's books that he doesn't bother to mention.

For example, there is the £148 billion future cost of all those new schools and hospitals, another £5,619 per household. The 28 billion of guarantees on Network Rail's borrowing, another £1,054 per household. The £73 billion cost of decommissioning nuclear power stations, which adds a further £2,779. And the little matter of the £167 billion, or £6,357 per household which has to be put aside to keep us square with the EU accounting rules.

Then there's all the bank bailouts. Taxpayers have loaned £464 per household to the Northern Rock, and another £217 per household to the Bradford and Bingley. Households have stumped up a further £1,005 to compensate savers who lost money in Iceland. Back in April 2008 the Bank of England pledged another £7,613 per household to shore up the banks, and in October 2008 came a bank recapitalization fund of £1,408 per household, and a credit guarantee scheme of £9,516 per household. There's a £50 billion fund (£1,903 per household) to purchase bank assets, and a £200 billion scheme (£7,613 per household) to mop up toxic debt.

If the Northern Rock, the Bradford & Bingley and the Royal Bank of Scotland really did all go bust and the government didn't get a penny back on them, households would be out to the tune of another £68,000 each. Under the government's own rules, a commercial company would have to show such potential disasters on its books, but of course the government doesn't bother.

It doesn't bother showing its pension obligations, either. State-sector workers have handsome pensions which they will be drawing on well into the future. The cost of all that is calculated at £1,261 billion, or £47,998 per household. Likewise, there are the rather humbler state pensions that the rest of will get – if we're lucky – at a cost of £2,191 billion, or £83,397 per household.

In reality, nobody expects everything to go wrong, or for the government to lose all the money that it has promised to the banks and builders. And it doesn't actually have to stump up our future pensions right away – future taxpayers will have to pay for those. But Gordon Brown has forced pension funds to reveal their future obligations, and claims to be angry that the banks have not confessed the extent of their potential debts. Why doesn't he work by the same rules that he demands of others?

Because the reality is so awful, that's why. If you add up all the liabilities that should be on the government's books but aren't, the total comes to a whopping £277,503 per household. It would take households nearly 19 years of living on bread and water to pay that lot off. But the point isn't affordability: it's honesty. The government claims that its debt is 48.2 per cent of the nation's income (GDP), which is comparable to most developed countries. In fact, its liabilities are nearly ten times that, amounting to 478.6 per cent of GDP. That's what Gordon Brown, under his own rules, should make the Chancellor show in the books – but doesn't.

And as a result of the recession, businesses are closing and the government is collecting nearly 12 per cent less in taxation than it did last year – a fall half as big again as the budget prediction of just 7.5 per cent decline. Hope springs eternal in Chancellors' breasts, it seems. Meanwhile, rising unemployment has seen the benefits bill soar, with benefits expenditure being over 10 per cent higher in mid-2009 than it was in mid-2008. So the government is being driven to borrow even more than ever. Just four months in to the 2009-10 financial year, the government's on-the-books borrowing (and this is just the extra borrowing, not the total) had soared to £49.8 billion, three times the comparable figure of a year before. So it seems likely that in total, the government will have to borrow £200 billion more in 2009-10 than it did in 2008-09. So much for 'Things can only get better'.

The gold fiasco
Not that we have any money in the kitty to pay these debts anyway. And we certainly don't have any gold. On a Friday afternoon in 1999, when MPs were safely back in their constituencies, Gordon Brown announced that he was going to sell half the nation's gold reserves.

That in itself was remarkable, since gold was then at a record low of $290 an ounce (down from $835 in 1980). And it seemed to be news to the Bank of England. Gold dropped another 10 per cent on the announcement.

The reserves were sold at pre-announced auctions, giving dealers the chance to bid down prices in anticipation. So Britain got absurdly low prices for its yellow metal. It was called the Brown Bottom, because by 2007 gold was up again at $670 an ounce. Even the Bank of China made £1 billion out of us. But British taxpayers had lost £2 billion.

Where we are now
In 1997 Gordon Brown promised that he would not build a boom on borrowing, but not only did public debt soar: personal debt soared even more, thanks to those low interest rates, rising house prices, and the prosperity that we all felt — until the inevitable crash in 2008, that is.

After years of rapid growth, the total amount of debt owed by UK households reached a little under £1,600 billion by mid-2008, an average of £59,715 per household — twice as much as people in continental Europe. That means the average household owed more than its annual income – estimated at roughly £51,000 last year. But the picture looks worse when you consider that most of that £51,000 is already spoken for, in terms of taxation, heating and utilities, food, transport, clothing, leaving the average household with a 'disposable' income of just £14,520. Even if they cut out every non-essential, like the odd cinema trip or the occasional pint of beer, it would take the average household more than four years to pay off its debt.

With loans now harder to get, and people cutting back, indebtedness has fallen, though not much, to stand at £1,458 billion (£58,320 per household) by mid-2009. That means average repayment levels of £2,650 a year. Personal indebtedness remains a huge problem, particularly for low-income families. There are almost 300 personal insolvencies a day – 22,087 in the third quarter of 2008, just before the crash, which is a 4.6 per cent rise on the previous year. That figure included 17,341 bankruptcies, and 9.746 cases in which people had made voluntary arrangements to repay their debts, usually to the tax authorities. (Companies are suffering too. In the same quarter, 4001 companies went bust, the fastest rate for eighteen years, up 26 per cent on the previous year. And 1007 companies went into administration, up 51 per cent on the previous year.)

But the picture is even worse when you add on the soaring public debt under Gordon Brown. In March 2008 the Treasury calculated it would need to borrow £42.5 billion in the year 2008-09. Half a year later, that calculation practically doubled to £77.6 billion. The year after that, they expect it to hit £118 billion-or £4,491 per household. And that's just the additional borrowing each year.

Right now, the government figures that its total debt amounts to £729 billion, or £27,748 per household. This, says

Gordon Brown, is rather lower than some other developed countries. But the figure is a fraud, which overlooks a huge number of future costs and obligations that are simply hidden, and never appear in the government's accounts.

Of course, the government hopes the economy will improve, the banks will limp through, and taxpayers will get their money back. We are unlikely to lose everything we have staked on the banks. But we have staked £2,642 billion, and if it all went horribly wrong and we lost every penny, each household in Britain would face an additional bill of £100,551.

No wonder the World Economic Forum thinks that the state of Britain's public finances is shocking – all the government's reassuring talk notwithstanding – and has been issuing warnings, alongside the International Monetary Fund and the Organization for Economic Cooperation and Development, in 2003.

The British economy is going through a mighty economic hangover after a mighty economic boom. But much of that boom, we caused ourselves. We cannot blame our problems on the rest of the world. Meanwhile, Britain's reckless taxing, spending, borrowing, and inflation have left us far less well equipped than many other countries to get through that hangover without suffering too much.

Our economic prospects were another thing that supposedly 'could only get better'. In the event, government profligacy has made them very much worse.

9

LIVING

A walk on the wild side

My journey to work is always a distressing one, because it brings me up against so many things that are wrong with Britain.

As soon as I go into the street I am stuck by the squalor of the place, and the nearer I get to the town centre and the railway station, the more squalid it becomes. Crisp packets blowing down the pavement; plastic bottles on the side of the road; old fridges, tyres and other rubbish just dumped in empty building sites; discarded chewing gum under foot; graffiti on the bridges and other public buildings (though almost never on the private ones).

I don't suppose for one moment that this situation is remotely new. I remember the black-and-white billboards and TV ads from the Keep Britain Tidy campaign in the mid-1950s, which tells me that people must have thought litter a menace even then. If you go to ancient Pompeii, you will also see graffiti, and in the tombs of Orkney's Maeshowe you can see various rude runes carved by vulgar Vikings.

What I do think, though, is that our national and local politicians have actually made these problems worse.

Take a trivial example. Outside the pubs and cafes that I pass on my walk to the railway station, the pavements and the doorways are strewn with cigarette butts. And yes, cigarette

butts have been discarded in the street ever since Sir Walter
Raleigh first brought in tobacco from the Americas. The
difference is that now, of course, we aren't allowed smoke
inside public places – so people are forced onto the street or
outside tables. Since pubs, clubs and restaurants are warned that
providing ashtrays by the door could be seen as encouraging
people to smoke on the premises, they don't dare. The result is
pretty obvious. More cigarette butts in the street.

A system that kills local pride
In addition to national rules like this, the way we run our local
authorities does not encourage pride in the local environment
either. It's not just that councils and those in charge of public
buildings do not obliterate graffiti quickly – which then just
encourages other people to add to it. The problem is that our
councils are largely just agents of the national government,
rather than servants of the local citizens. Three-quarters of
what local authorities spend comes from central government,
and three-quarters of what they do is what central government
tells them to do. They hardly exist to represent real and unique
local interests at all.

The obvious thing would be to shift much more of the
decision-making and the funding down to local authorities. But
of course Westminster politicians and Whitehall civil servants
don't want to give up their control of what happens locally.
And despite expensive government reviews of the system by
Nick Raynesford MP and Sir Michael Lyons, the government
blew its chance to reform local authority finances in ways that
could see more funding raised from local areas, and yet be seen
as fair. Council Tax – a hasty compromise pulled out of the
wreckage of the Poll tax – is definitely not up to the job.
Already people are going to jail rather than pay it.

Since Council Tax began in 1993, it has risen one-and-a-half times as rapidly as average earnings. In a typical year, 2008-9, Council Tax bills in England rose an average of roughly 4 per cent, though some councils put up their bills by nearly 5 per cent. It took the average annual charge on a Band D property – a modest mid-range home – to £1,373. In 2009-10 they rose to £1,414, a 3 per cent rise which council chiefs proudly boasted as the 'lowest in fifteen years'. If only the productive sector of the economy could grow so fast.

Ministers, of course, condemn Council Tax rises and say there is no excuse for them. But they would say that, wouldn't they? The truth is that every day, ministers are loading local councils with more and more responsibilities, but not stumping up the cash to pay for them – just as they do with schools and other public services. It means that councils are overstretched and don't perform well – whereupon, just to convince us all that they are keeping up the pressure on these idle councillors, government ministers come up with all sorts of bureaucratic schemes – 'beacon councils', 'strategic partnerships', a 'neighbourhoods charter', 'community delivery' and the like – which load even more strain onto the Council Tax.

Since everyone knows that it is Westminster and Whitehall who call the shots, and that the councils decide next to nothing, turnout at local elections is pitifully poor. In 2003 it was just 36 per cent in England. It limped up to 41 per cent in 2004, when the European elections were held on the same day. It fared better still in 2005, at 61 per cent when it coincided with the general election. But it seems that if you want more than a third of us to vote for our councillors, you need some other attraction to get us to the polls.

When local becomes authoritarian
The politicians, of course, wring their hands and curse us for not being public spirited enough. And, predictably, they start

devising all sorts of costly schemes and poster campaigns and quangos that they hope will rekindle democracy and enhance the reputation of our councils and town hall officials. But low turnouts have nothing to do with any decline in public spirit: Britain can't really be faulted on that charge. No, low turnouts in local elections are a perfectly rational behaviour as far as the general public are concerned – because they know that whoever they vote for, it is unlikely to make a quantum of difference.

Local authorities, then, aren't really local. Local people don't feel much identity with them, and nor do councils see the local environment as their main problem. Keeping up with all the targets and directives coming out of Whitehall and Westminster is much more urgent. And it shows. Go to many other countries across the Channel and the streets are cleaner, there are flowers and benches and less litter and graffiti – not because French or Germans are genteel and cultured and we are just filthy oiks, but because their systems encourage a much stronger focus on the quality of life in the local area.

Where local authorities do feel compelled to act on the local environment, it is because central government instructs them to, with measures like the Environmental Protection Act 1990. This comes with a 58-page 'Code of Practice on Litter and Refuse' telling councils and other agencies what they are to do. And of course, rather than providing helpful local encouragement for people to do the right thing, it produces instead a rule-bound, heavy-handed persecution of innocent people.

Under the Act is an offence to 'throw down or drop litter'. Local litter wardens have the power to issue spot fines, and failing to pay up can land you with a £2,500 fine. In May 2008, Swinton resident Keith Hirst, 54, spent 18 hours in a police cell after being accused of dropping an apple core – which he denied. So having refused to pay a £50 spot fine, Mr Hirst, who has a heart condition and is a full-time carer for his wife, was surrounded by five police officers, arrested, fingerprinted, DNA-swabbed and banged up. While his family were ringing the hospitals to find out if he'd had an accident, Mr Hirst was being led to court in handcuffs. It was only after much public outrage about the case that the Crown Prosecution Service eventually decided to drop the charges. But not before total bureaucratic cost to taxpayers of this pointless absurdity had reached some £5,000.

Kate Badger, from Wolverhampton, also refused to pay a £60 spot fine for an apple core that she denied discarding. Though you and I might think that apple cores are biodegradable and pretty low on the litter ladder, 'throwing down or dropping' one is in fact a serious charge: the indictment read that she 'knowingly deposited controlled waste, namely an apple core, on land that did not have a waste management licence'. How bureaucratic can you get? Again, charges were dropped – eventually. The judge said he was 'pleased to see that common sense has prevailed'.

Bin Ladens
Perhaps the biggest pieces of unsightly junk on our streets are not the discarded crisp packets and supermarket bags, nor even the apple cores that have been thrown down or dropped, but the ubiquitous wheelie bins and recycling boxes.

I do understand the shortcomings of the traditional black bag – they can burst as they are being loaded, vermin can get into them and scatter the contents, they leak, and so on. But at least you can carry them easily through a small terraced house, which you can't do with a wheelie bin.

This, of course, means it is much easier for people to leave their wheelie bins out on the street all the time. Since they are collected only once a fortnight, they stand there stinking in the summer heat. For passers-by, it is an an unpleasant and unsightly nuisance. So, to correct a problem of their own making, our local authorities have decided to crack down on people who leave their bins out all the time. Now there are regulations that specify exactly when you have to leave your bin out and take it back in, and exactly where you are allowed to leave it – on pain of a £1,000 fine. Council snoopers-known as Bin Ladens by annoyed householders – have been trained to sniff out those of us who break these rules. They have been given protective clothing and empowered to root through our bins for private letters and other documents that prove the address of the perpetrator.

Plymouth man and keen recycler Martin Parnell, 38, found his recycling bin had not been collected because his son had left it three steps up the garden path rather than at the gate. And many other people's bins have been left unemptied – or the householder has been fined – because the lid was slightly open, or because they mistakenly put items into the wrong bin. This is easy to do: the rules are complicated, and they vary between different local-authority areas – so the recycling code in the street where you work may be different from the one in the street where you live.

Mr Parnell's local authority claims that if everyone left their bin three steps up the garden path or put bottles in their paper bins, it would slow down the refuse collection and add to Council Tax bills. It's a fair point. But the question here is who is serving whom? A local authority refuse service is there to serve us, not the other way round. We should not expect it to treat us like criminals.

In my experience, we got a much better service when local refuse collection was contracted out. Private operators, fearful that complaints might lose them their contracts, were much more obliging. But now, many local authorities have taken refuse collection back in-house, and the responsiveness of the service has dropped. One thing that has enabled councils to take back refuse collection under their own control is the so-called Best Value regime, which imposes a detailed service-by-service performance plan on local authorities, backed by independent audit. But it is a vastly complicated and over-technical solution to the simple problem of finding a good-value contractor, and its bureaucratic, box-ticking method doesn't actually deliver best value at all. It measures what the rules force it to measure; and all too often that turns out to be what is best for council staff, not for local service users.

Squeezing the life out of the bus

But, having walked down my litter-strewn, wheelie-bin-cluttered street, here I am at the bus stop. If there were three of us, we'd be cheaper taking a taxi into town, which seems pretty strange economics. Buses have become very expensive. And it is not competition that has done it: quite the opposite. The service is indeed contracted out. But it is contracted out in such a way that the contractor pretty well has a monopoly. And even then my local authority, like many others, is doing its darnedest to bring bus travel back under its own control. The bus company I use has almost no control of its own. The local authority sets down what vehicles it will use and regulates its routes, its timetables and its fares. Just like the old days. No wonder the bus is so expensive.

And in addition, new costs are being loaded on to the bus company all the time. The latest regulation is that drivers now have to have a 'certificate of professional competence' that costs £240 and requires a four-hour theory test. In fact my bus company already demands that its drivers hold the appropriate National Vocational Qualification (NVQ), which covers the same theory, so that's just a useless duplication. But in addition (this regulation emanates from Brussels, after all), the certificate covers not just safety but subjects such as 'customer care', 'transport in the economic context' and the driver's 'role in the company'. Existing drivers will have to undergo periodic training, involving 35 hours attendance, to meet the same criteria.

Once again, Whitehall dream-lists are being written into law, raising the cost for everyone and driving out new competitors, who can't afford the burden of employing all the necessary compliance staff, in particular. While of course I want my bus driver to be safe, this regulation won't improve on what responsible operators do already. What it will do is to load the company with extra costs, which will force the smaller or newer operators out. So competition will be cut back even more, and my fares will rise even higher. Meanwhile, perfectly well qualified part-time drivers will find themselves out of work because their hours don't justify all the cost and training.

Traffic congestion

At last I've made it through the traffic to the railway station. In 1997 John Prescott announced that he would happily resign if he didn't cut the number of car journeys we all made. He didn't, and he didn't. But the promise was crazy then and is still crazy now. The majority of us now own cars, many more of us have access to one, and 85 per cent of all passenger miles are made by car.

In fact 'Two Jags' Prescott came up with a 'ten year plan' to get us all out of our cars and onto public transport. One element of this was a 6 per cent annual rise in fuel duty. But the only effect that had was to bring thousands of protesters, mostly farmers and lorry drivers, out to blockade oil refineries and garages in 2000. In response to all the bad press and public concern, the government quickly froze fuel duties and said it would pass more duties on to foreign lorry drivers, who of course don't have a vote.

The one thing that might curb the peak-hour traffic jams is road congestion pricing. At present, you pay the same to use the road, whether it's a quiet rural lane on a Sunday afternoon or a busy city artery at 8.45am on Monday morning. Some form of peak road pricing would encourage people to car-share, take the bus, or come in before and after the peaks. Downing Street proposed making this a national policy. But it did not first resolve and reassure people about the many questions that the issue raises, like surveillance and privacy, for example. A million-strong online petition promptly scuppered the idea, so no doubt the jams will continue.

Of course, those in power don't need to worry about traffic. Gordon Brown's motorcycle outriders just sweep it away. And when the 'First Lady of Downing Street' got stuck in a traffic jam because of defective traffic lights, her husband was quickly on the phone to the transport minister to tell him to sort it out. If only the rest of us had such powerful friends who were prepared to abuse their office to get us through the jams.

Notwork rail

When the railways were privatized in 1993, the track and stations were put into the hands of a private monopoly, Railtrack. Like all monopolies, its performance was pretty poor, and in 2001 the new Transport Secretary, Stephen Byers, put the company into administration. This was largely an ideological move: Labour politicians never did like the idea of private companies running the railways. It seems clear that this change of policy was planned for weeks, and perhaps months. But true to form once again, there seems to have been no thought given at all to what might replace Railtrack. Eventually Byers came up with Network Rail, a fudge run by an assortment of train companies, quangos, and individuals, which had no clear objectives and whose lines of non-accountability were even more complicated than those of Railtrack.

Network Rail certainly seems to have no control of our money. Byers criticized Railtrack for overspending, but Network Rail has spent billions more. Over the five year period 2009-14, it plans to spend £35 billion of our money. That's more than Railtrack aimed to spend in twice the time (and one of the arguments for ditching Railtrack was that it was costing too much), and does not even count their latest ambitious project for a high-speed London-Manchester-Glasgow train link. A large proportion of the money has gone into minute improvements in rail safety, since, in our litigious culture, Network Rail lives in fear of being sued by survivor groups if there is another accident.

Only about a quarter of Network Rail's spending goes into actually expanding the network, and very little seems to have gone on making my own train less crowded. It is in fact less crowded, because the Department of Transport tells me so. In a stunning move to cut overcrowding, in October 2008 the Department simply re-defined it. Now, a train with 30 passengers standing in a carriage of 100 people is deemed not to be overcrowded; whereas before, 10 passengers standing counted as overcrowding. Problem solved, at the stroke of a pen: things really are getting better – it's official.

Of course, the real problem will be solved only when Network Rail lengthens the station platforms to allow longer trains, and when the planning process allows new lines to be built to relieve the pinch points in the rail network. But we might have to wait a long time for that – probably standing all the way.

Transport policy in Britain has been a sorry saga of plans, consultations, and reversals of policy. It was typified by the appointment of ex-BBC boss Lord Birt as 'Transport Tsar': he had no clear role, and pretty soon resigned, after showering the transport world with the particularly rarefied form of office management jargon that his former colleagues at the BBC had come to know as Birtspeak. Frankly, it's a wonder that any of our trains run on time at all.

Destroying the rural environment
My train journey takes me through long stretches of open fields. It seems a paradox that our farmland, which should be an environmental asset, is now one of the most unappealing and unfriendly parts of the landscape. Over the decades we have done it enormous environmental damage.

Most of this stems from the Common Agricultural Policy, an EU-wide system of agricultural subsidies and support. It is huge – the EU spends about £46 billion a year on this system, around 45 per cent of the whole EU budget.

An additional £5.75 billion or so is spent on other forms of rural aid. And there are other measures too, such as import tariffs and quotas on certain agricultural products from outside the EU, which neatly prevents poor third-world farmers from undercutting our, more expensive, producers.

Around 90 per cent of CAP spending goes as direct payments to farmers. The rest is used to buy food at guaranteed minimum prices, so when prices fall, farmers don't lose too much money. Of course it means that we consumers have to pay more than we should, but that is reckoned to be worth it in order to protect our agriculture.

In fact it protects hereditary landowners and large agribusinesses more than anyone else. Three-quarters of the funds go to just a fifth of EU farmers. Decades of CAP subsidies to encourage farmers to grow more crops have led to a great intensification of agriculture. Big agribusinesses have grown even bigger. In so doing they have changed the rural landscape.

Hedgerows and copses have been torn out, and wildlife habitats lost, because the subsidies make every furrow highly valuable. A fieldscape that had changed little in centuries, a rural environment that was once pleasant and inviting, has been turned into an unwelcoming industrial prairie. And not because of the pressure of progress and of the market, but as the result of the unintended consequences of political programmes designed to help small groups.

Britain's inability to change things

And farmers are indeed a small group. Only 5 per cent of the EU population works on farms – it's much fewer in Britain – and the sector generates just 1.6 per cent of the EU's GDP. Certainly, it is important in a few countries like Poland, where a fifth of the population presently work on the land; but that is likely to shrink as Poland's economy modernizes, develops, and becomes more urban-centred like those of the more established EU members.

Despite their small numbers, our farmers have nevertheless dumped countless lorry-loads of nitrogen fertilizers onto land that would otherwise groan with exhaustion at the effort of all this intensive, subsidized cultivation. Much of this chemical mountain has for years been quietly leaching into our streams, canals, lakes, rivers and reservoirs, where it promotes the growth of weeds, hampers navigation, and makes water purification more difficult and expensive.

It's an environmental disaster. So why don't we just scrap the whole system? To their credit, countries such as Sweden and Britain have suggested just that. But as soon as we seemed to be on the verge of a breakthrough, France – the biggest beneficiary, getting 20 per cent of CAP cash – stitched up a deal with Germany to fix CAP spending without further change until 2012. We were supposed to be 'at the heart of

Europe', but in this case we were well outflanked and left embarrassingly and expensively out in the cold.

Still, even the CAP's proponents feel some embarrassment with the milk and wine lakes and the grain and butter mountains that it produced. So they responded to that problem of their own making with 'set-aside' – which paid farmers not to farm their land. But many enterprising farmers simply set aside land that was marginal anyway. And the number of 'farmers' in Britain rose from 80,000 to 120,000 as all those country home owners discovered they could get subsidies on their daughters' horse paddocks. The Rural Payments Agency, with the best part of 5,000 civil servants to manage all these payments, promptly went into tailspin and subsidies were overpaid, underpaid, or not paid at all for months and even years. In May 2008 the Agency admitted that some 9,000 farmers were still owed a total of £190 million from the year before. Indeed, the record is so bad that the European Commission itself is fining Britain £348 million for the mess-ups.

In the meantime, reforms agreed in 2005 replace the old, crop-specific grow – more subsidies with flat-rate payments based on the cultivated area, provided that environmentally friendly methods are used. In other words, we are subsidizing people to go back to the kind of environmentally friendly agriculture that the subsidies stopped them doing in the first place!

When New Zealand simply scrapped its farm subsidies, agriculture boomed. Can't we learn from that?

Wilting at windmills
But no, the countryside is probably going to get even more like a prairie thanks to the Renewable Transport Fuel Obligation. This obliges suppliers of transport fuels to source 3.5 per cent of it from a renewable source by 2010, rising to 5 percent by

2013. And just to encourage them, there has been a 20p per litre reduction in the duty on biodiesel since 2002 and on bioethanol since 2005. Unfortunately, reaching the 5 per cent target means dedicating 1.2 million hectares – that's a fifth – of Britain's arable land to the production of biofuels. You can be sure that they won't be grown in quaint little smallholdings that encourage birds and butterflies.

And those wind farms – wind factories, really – that I pass by on the train are another environmental disaster. When there were just one or two, they were interesting. But now they blight any number of nice views. The so-called Renewables Obligation adds 8 per cent to every one of our energy bills. The money goes to the big energy companies in order to promote renewable energy – not because they believe in it, but because politicians think it would enhance their green credentials to subsidize it. In 2006-07, that subsidy from every one of Britain's electricity users – rich and poor alike are hit by it – amounted to £217 million. In 2010, the taxpayer subsidy to the renewables industry will reach £1,000 million.

That is an almost 100 per cent subsidy on a wind turbine, which is why subsidy farmers, who have already built 2,033 of them, onshore and off, want to build 3,189 more in 235 sites over the next five years. Indeed, the government says it will fine the power companies if they don't come up to its renewables targets.

We now have more offshore wind turbines than any other country in the world. But far from being 'free energy', wind power is about the most expensive and inefficient way you could find to cut greenhouse gas emissions. It's costing us £50 a megawatt. For up to 30 per cent of the time, turbines are idle because wind speeds are too low to turn the blades, or so high that it would risk damage to them. And since the wind is so unreliable, you have to have conventional power stations to back them up. The 2,327 existing onshore wind turbines, covering hundreds of hectares, deliver slightly less energy than you get from a medium-size conventional power station.

Long term dithering
Politicians have assured us that they are taking 'long term decisions' on energy, but the reality has been dithering and delay. Two energy white papers, in 1998 and 2002, contained few practical answers on how we were going to fill the gap left by falling North Sea production and the retirement of our more ageing nuclear reactors. In 2003 the government decided to close down nearly all of Britain's nuclear generating capacity by 2015. But then Old Labour types like Michael Meacher, who was Environment Secretary at the time, loathe nuclear power. Perhaps they confuse it with nuclear bombs.

But having discovered that Britain is on the end of some very long gas pipelines that start in Russia – which has already interrupted supplies to Ukraine and other countries that it has spats with – in 2008 the policy was completely reversed and now we're to build new nuclear capacity. Commitments to reduce carbon dioxide emissions added to the pressure. The rising price of oil, and the worries about Russia, enabled the government to save face when it did this U-turn. The French nuclear power company EdF was hastily drafted in to do the work: British nuclear expertise is mostly, er, decommissioned.

But all the prevarication means that, even on the government's own most optimistic forecasts, the first of ten new £2 billion nuclear stations won't start producing electricity until about 2018, by which time the lights will already have gone out.

Mean taxes
The politicians have been very pleased to advertise their green

credentials, and we have applauded them for it. But when things have moved from talk to action – which isn't very common in politics – we have been less appreciative. The rise in fuel duties led to those demonstrations in 2000, and the rising price of oil in 2007-08 caused equal alarm. In fact a rising price of oil probably does more to cut carbon emissions than any number of platitudes from Kyoto – because of it, the amount of energy that the US uses to produce each dollar's worth of GDP has fallen 40 per cent in the last thirty years: cars are smaller, lighter, more fuel-efficient, and boilers use less oil. It's just not very popular when it comes as a new tax. A MORI poll in May 2008 revealed that 7 out of 10 voters were not willing to pay higher taxes in order to improve the environment.

I am not surprised. Voters know that many of the government's green taxes seem aimed more at raising revenue than helping the planet. Air passenger duty is a case in point. It taxes air passengers – not old, inefficient, polluting planes. It is a flat charge, so budget airlines like Ryanair, which happens to have an enviably up-to-date and efficient fleet, get clobbered: the tax is often many times the fare they are charging. A rational policy would charge the emissions, not the passengers. And the doubling of the duty in 2007 may well have increased carbon emissions. As longer flights became relatively cheaper, people tended to take more of them. That was not the intended aim. (Of course, the Chancellor resolved this problem to his satisfaction in 2008, by simply raising the tax on long-haul flights.)

In other cases, so-called green taxes have just been another way to soak the rich without breaching the 1997 commitment not to raise income tax rates. One proposal in 2007 suggested raising vehicle duty (which already discriminates against larger cars) to £1,000 for families who drive the largest cars. Our metropolitan-based politicians and civil servants, who mostly have no need to drive, are apparently oblivious to the fact that some larger families in some rural areas actually need larger cars.

But in any case, motorists already pay far more to drive than any plausible cost of the carbon they produce while doing so. If motoring taxes were really green, they would go down. But they're not green taxes: they're mean taxes.

Hitting the buffers
Yes, like everyone, I want a better environment. I just feel that much of it has already been despoiled by the actions of a rotten state. Institutions that do not promote local pride, recycling policies that just get people's backs up, an agricultural policy that has raped (in more ways than one) the landscape, a transport policy with the long-term vision of a newt, even greater short-sightedness on energy – all of these have actually made our problems worse. And now the proposed solutions look equally depressing.

Time for me to get some shut-eye before I arrive in London and have to take the Underground, which of course – thanks to John Prescott and his colleagues – is suffering from the most inept finance and investment plan in the long annals of public procurement. But don't get me started on that.

10

ROTTEN HEALTH

Huge boost in health spending
Health is the largest government department, with a budget of £110 billion for 2009-10. It has also had the biggest financial boost of any department, thanks to the government's 2000 promise to raise National Health Service spending from 6.8 per cent of GDP up to the European average of 9.3 per cent. In fact, it's been raised even beyond that: by 2010, NHS spending will be well above the EU average, and a full 50 per cent higher than many developed countries, from New Zealand to Scandinavia.

Politicians seem to have a touching faith in the power of larger and larger doses of our money to cure their own organizational problems. And the dose in this case was particularly large. Health and personal social care spending has nearly doubled, even taking inflation into account. Spending in England is equivalent to £8,759 for a family of four, and in Scotland it is even higher, over £9,000 for the same family. By 2007, a full third of the rise in Britain's public spending was going into the NHS. Lots of shiny new hospitals and clinics have been built, and by 2006 some 279,454 new staff had been taken on.

For so much more money, you might hope to see a corresponding increase in NHS output. And it is true that waits for cardiac surgery have plummeted from two years to three months, while 'elective' treatments – non-emergency procedures that can be put off for a while, like cataract removals or hip replacements – are down to three months. Nevertheless, 250,000 of us wait for more than 18 months for surgery, according to the official figures – though the real figure is certainly higher, given the notorious amount of cheating that goes on as the hospitals strive to meet their waiting time targets.

Not buying us better health
We're living longer, certainly, and the death rates from the major killers such as cancer, heart disease and strokes have been falling. But neither the present government, nor the extra £300 billion or so that has been pumped into the NHS since 1997, is due any of the credit for that. The figures show a slow, straight-line decrease ever since the 1970s. And much of that is because more of us now recognize the dangers of smoking, and are giving it up.

Meanwhile the chance of surviving these killer diseases is still much worse than in comparable countries. We spend more than any other European nation on cancer treatment, but still have some of the worst cancer survival rates in the European Union. The chance of still being alive five years after you are diagnosed with cancer is 24 per cent better in France and Germany – mainly because cancers are diagnosed and treated earlier in those countries. Of the 200,000 people in Britain who die of cancer and strokes each year, some 30,000 would survive if they lived anywhere else in Northern Europe. We are the fifth richest country in the world, but we are far down the league tables in terms of medically preventable deaths. In addition, our access to life – saving drugs is much worse than in most EU countries. And the health inequalities between different parts of Britain remain shocking.

Even if you do manage to get into a British hospital, your chance of picking up something nasty there is increasing all the time. One in nine hospital patients pick up an infection during their stay. In 2006, the well-known superbug MRSA killed about 500 patients in England and Wales, and was a possible contributory factor in the deaths of another 1,100. The figures fell slightly in 2007, partly due to the massive hospital clean-up campaign that the government was forced into as a result of all the bad media publicity. But deaths from another hospital superbug, Clostridium difficile, have been shooting up. It was recorded as the cause or a contributor in nearly 2,000 deaths in 2003, and more than 8,000 in 2007. Experts believe the true number of deaths from hospital infections has been 30,000 in the last five years alone.

If the superbugs don't get you, NHS doctors and staff just might. In 2008-09 the NHS received 6,080 legal claims for clinical negligence and 3,743 claims for non-clinical negligence, on top of the 76,438 claims that were outstanding. Each year, the NHS pays out hundreds of millions of pounds in damages and costs. The NHS has its own Litigation Authority to deal with this torrent of complaints, and they estimate the total cost of outstanding claims at around £10 billion.

Inhumanity of treatment
And you can't rely on good hospital food to help you fight off the superbugs. Forget all that stuff about superchef Lloyd Grossman being recruited to improve hospital food. That was just spin to buy a few weeks' headlines. A total of 139,127 patients were discharged after being inadequately fed on NHS wards in 2007 – up 84 per cent on the 1997 figure. Most were malnourished when they came in, but the condition of 8,500 people actually worsened while in the care of the NHS.

Around 13 million NHS meals are thrown away each year –

about £35 million worth. Many people are served food which they are too weak to pull towards them, or which they are too frail to cut or chew or swallow.

How, in a civilized country, can this happen? One reason is that the NHS is so badly managed that nurses are rushing about a great deal but achieving less than they might. Another is the 'Project 2000' campaign to make nursing a degree profession. It's part of the politicians' efforts to impress us that they are raising standards in the public services. But in fact it has the opposite effect. Graduates of course command higher salaries (which we taxpayers pay for), but they have less in the way of practical skill and experience. So while the graduate nurses rush about, the wards are full of auxiliaries. There is no joined-up nursing: things are organized around tasks, not patients. So the auxiliaries may not realize that a patient cannot eat because of some medical condition or frailty, and clear away the untouched plate. Despite all the proud miracles that the NHS has achieved, that simple inhumanity should make us weep.

A generation with parents who lived into their eighties and nineties all have their stories. My own mother collapsed and was admitted to one of the nation's top hospitals. They called her Janet – which was her real name, though nobody ever called her that. Hospitals claim that using first names makes patients more relaxed. In fact it is a political act. A lawyer or accountant calls you by your family name, to mark the professionalism of the relationship and your status as a valued client. The NHS use of first names is saying: 'We're all in this mess together, comrade, so don't expect special treatment.'

There was no way of accessing her family doctor's records, so they missed giving her the sleeping aid she was on. The sudden withdrawal sent her temporarily deranged. She wandered off the ward – though nobody seemed to notice – and was found hours later in a distant part of the hospital.

She was soon back to her old sharp self, doing the cryptic crossword in fifteen minutes flat. So the interview with the psychologist went badly. 'Do we know our name?' he asked. 'Well I know mine,' she replied. 'And do we know who the Prime Minister is?' 'Ramsey MacDonald.' I explained to her that this was just process; boxes had to be ticked. She gritted her teeth and answered less sarcastically from then on.

The nurses were unconcerned when they lost her wedding ring. I tried the hospital laundry, but they had a drawer full of uncatalogued jewellery, so it was impossible to know which if any it might be. Then there was the elderly woman in the next bed, crying because she had soiled her bedding; but nobody came. The indignities went on and on.

Most remarkably, there was no joined up case management with the local social services. Everyone knew she must eventually go home, and would need support. But social services resist new people coming on to their budget, so they languish in hospital. Then, without warning, she was sent home, and only then did social services think about what to do.

Many other people have worse stories – like Rose Addis and Mavis Skeet. It was such cases that made Tony Blair realize that words and persuasion were not enough, and to promise a huge increase in NHS funding.

The new money has bought staff, better pay, and new hospitals and equipment. But it has not changed the system's Kafkaesque inhumanity. People approaching the four-hour waiting target for Accident & Emergency (A&E) still find themselves being wheeled into a assessment unit' and dumped there to continue their wait and keep them off the statistics. Others wait outside in ambulances until there is a chance of getting them through A&E in the target time. And when an elderly friend of mine went for a knee x-ray in October 2008, they x-rayed the wrong one – because that's what it said in the notes – and told him he'd have to make another appointment to get the right one done. To them, he wasn't a person. He was a 'knee'.

The medicines apartheid

It is also shocking that cancer patients can't get the life-saving drugs they need. The National Institute for Clinical Excellence (NICE), which approves NHS treatments, spends more (£4.4 million) on communications than it actually does on evaluating new drugs and technologies (£3.3 million). Meanwhile, around £500 million a year is wasted on prescriptions that people don't take, or should not have been given. And hospitals unnecessarily keep patients in overnight, because under 'payment by results' rules they get paid for that, even though it clogs up beds with patients who would be better off at home.

The treatment of Monmouthshire lung cancer sufferer Sue Bentley, 67, was withdrawn when she supplemented it by paying privately for the drug Avastin. This forced her to pay for treatment that was given free to other patients. The NHS is supposed to fight disease: it should have been applauding someone doing her own bit in that battle. But the rule was that you have to be either a wholly private patient or a wholly NHS patient: private 'topping up' would somehow be unfair on NHS patients who could not afford it.

Like so much political decision-making today, this policy was reversed in October 2008 following a court action and a big media fuss. So officially, the public-private apartheid in healthcare is now over, and the NHS will continue to treat patients who try to help matters by spending their own money. But it is a rotten system in which sensible policy comes about only as a way of avoiding bad publicity.

Getting away from it all

Public satisfaction with the NHS is low. Just 7 per cent more people say they are satisfied with it than say they are dissatisfied; and patients who have had a lot of recent dealings with it are the least satisfied of all. People in Switzerland, Sweden, Spain, Norway, the Netherlands, Luxembourg, Germany, France, Finland, Denmark, Belgium, and Austria are all happier with their healthcare systems than we are, according to the 2007 European Health Consumer Index.

Meanwhile, 57,000 operations were cancelled in 2007-08 for non-medical reasons. So it's not surprising that record numbers of people – around 50,000 a year, according to the Department of Health, but over 100,000 according to others – go abroad for our medical treatment. They prefer to pay, not just for their operations but for their travel too, rather than put up with long waits or risk superbug infections in NHS hospitals. People who need heart surgery, hip replacements, cataract removals and other procedures are using the internet to book operations as far away as Malaysia or South Africa.

India is the most common destination: its health system is one of the world's most unfettered, and the country has made a good business in providing surgery for worried and frustrated British patients. The fact that English is widely spoken helps too. But Hungary, Turkey, Germany, Poland, Spain and scores of other countries are also welcoming British 'health tourists' in large numbers.

Of course, 50,000 (or even 100,000) is a small fraction of the 13 million or so who are treated on the NHS every year. But on top of that number we must add all those who have private surgery in Britain. Millions of them have private insurance. Millions more have hospital cash plans that give them money if they are laid up in hospital. And hundreds of thousands each year decide not to wait for treatment in a bug-ridden NHS hospital, but to spend some of their 'rainy day' savings on having their operation in a private hospital near to home.

There may be a lot more of us going abroad for operations after the case of Yvonne Watts, who had her hip operation done in France and sent the £3,900 bill to the NHS because she'd had such a long wait. In a landmark ruling in 2006, the European Court said that the NHS should indeed pay for treatment abroad if patients had to wait too long. The doctors' trade union, the British Medical Association, didn't like that a bit: if everyone went abroad, they complained, British surgical centres might have to close. Well, that's competition – something that the rest of us face every day, and have to respond to by sharpening our prices and raising our quality. But then the NHS is a competition-free zone.

Huge inequalities in treatment

In 2003, with great fanfare, a strategy to reduce health inequalities across Britain was announced. But the billions that have been spent on it have again bought little.

True, life expectancy in the most deprived parts of Britain is rising – up by 2.5 years for men and 1.5 years for women over the last decade. But the gap in life expectancy between women in the most disadvantaged areas and those in average areas was 2 per cent wider in 2004-06 than it was in 1995-97. Life expectancy in London's leafy Hampstead is 11 years longer than in nearby urban St. Pancras. And a boy in the Glasgow suburb of Calton can expect to live on average 28 years less than one born in nearby, affluent Lenzie. That's a remarkable difference: but in fact health inequalities are even wider today than they were before the NHS was founded.

The Health Secretary's dispiritingly predictable response to this news was another initiative, another programme, perhaps another quango: seventy of the poorest areas would now have 'health trainers' to help people improve their health. The announcement may have improved the minister's headlines for a day, but it is unlikely to improve health in Calton or St. Pancras. One reason, among many, is that it is hard to get doctors to go to these places, and they do not get paid more for doing so. But sadly, health policy focuses more on getting headlines onto the front pages than on getting doctors into the back streets.

Where has all the money gone?
With a workforce of over 1,500,000 people, the NHS is, quite simply, too big to manage. This became obvious when its income began to soar under the government's initiative to match European spending levels. Money on such a scale should have wiped out the NHS's financial worries. But in fact the budget deficits recorded by NHS trusts actually rose, from £50 million in 2003-04 to £547 million in 2005-06. A service whose budget had tripled from £30 billion to £90 billion in a decade had somehow got itself into escalating deficits, with one in ten trusts being on the brink of bankruptcy. A truly remarkable feat of bad management.

At that point the Health Secretary Patricia Hewitt, facing enormous media ridicule, told trusts that if they didn't balance their books there would be blood on the carpet. But it all simply showed that pouring taxpayers' cash into an unreformed NHS was like pouring petrol into a rusty engine: it didn't go any faster, it just leaked fuel everywhere. Meanwhile, the possibility of a financial explosion increased – like the explosion in the multi-billion-pound NHS IT budget.

A disproportionate amount of the extra hundreds of billions put into the NHS has gone on administration as managers try to wrestle this leviathan under control. And a disproportionate amount of that rising personnel budget has gone to the higher, most expensive grades. Since 1995, the number of senior managers in the NHS has increased by half. That is against a rise of just 8 per cent in the number of qualified nurses, and a fall in the number of hospital beds. Between 2007 and 2008 alone, the number of managers grew by 9.4 per cent, while nursing staff numbers grew by only 2.1 per cent. Not surprisingly, then, there are now over twice as many managers and support staff as there are nurses, and seven times as many as there are doctors.

And this is the problem. The NHS is driven from the top, through a management bureaucracy. It is not driven by the demands of patients.

Why is it that we have so many people suffering back pain, but not enough physiotherapists and osteopaths to treat them? Because there is no market in healthcare. In other areas of life, when there is demand for something – shoes, bananas, spoons, haircuts, handbags, veterinary services – suppliers step forward to satisfy that demand and take our money for it. We don't expect to queue up to buy a pair of shoes. Our cats and dogs don't have to go on a three-month waiting list to see the vet. So why should we tolerate waiting six months to see a surgeon who then has to turn us away because someone x-rayed the wrong knee?

Then there are the quangos. By 2004, when the Health Secretary at the time, John Reid, promised to cull them, there were 42 different healthcare quangos, employing 22,000 people and with budgets totalling £2.5 billion. They included bodies like the Healthcare Commission, the National Institute for Clinical Excellence, the Human Fertilization and Embryology Authority, the General Social Care Council, and many others. Dr Reid's cull included taking the axe to quangos that his own government had created just a few years before. Forward planning has never been one of state healthcare's greatest strengths.

But it is significant that so many healthcare quangos seem to represent different producers and different parts of the production process. On the other hand, it is hard to think of one with any real power that represents patients.

Staff increases and higher pay

By 2007, the cash boom had bought the NHS 38,500 more doctors and 80,700 more nurses than ten years earlier. But much of the personnel budget went in simply boosting wages. Of the extra funding in the (typical) year 2005-06, for example, 52 per cent went into higher pay, 17 per cent into extra drugs, and only 13 per cent into expanding the services for patients. So of every £100 put in, only £13 got through to front-line service improvements.

Arguably, NHS staff were underpaid back in 1997, and wages needed to be raised. But not to the point of carelessness. In 2004, the same John Reid, under political pressure to bring negotiations with doctors to a swift conclusion, agreed to a new contract that gave general practitioners more money for less effort. They could opt out of evening and weekend work – expensive part-timers now do that – while new bonuses pay pushed the average GP salary to over £100,000.

Another initiative, the Agenda for Change programme, made widespread changes to pay differentials, which proved particularly expensive. A new consultant contract raised that part of the salary bill by an immediate ten per cent. Large increases in the numbers of graduate nurses not only raised salaries there, but required an expansion in support staff too.

Even failure is rewarded. Rose Gibb, the former £150,000-a-year Chief Executive of the Maidstone and Tunbridge Wells NHS Trust – where ninety people died between 2004 and 2006 in an outbreak of Clostridium difficile – sued her ex-employer for £250,000 severance pay after her departure in October 2007.

Lower productivity
While GPs and consultants are earning three or four times the average wage and can now spend more time on the golf course, there is little evidence that the spiralling pay of NHS staff has bought much in the way of greater productivity and improved services.

The very longest hospital waits have been shortened, but the average waiting time for elective surgery has not improved much. It was just 18 days less in 2007 than it was in 2000. By 2008, some 60 per cent of patients were waiting more than four months to see a specialist; and 41 per cent of patients were waiting more than four months for treatment (the comparable US figure is just 10 per cent). Some patients still wait over six months for treatment for relatively serious conditions. And huge numbers of people face very long waits for things like hearing aids (where the wait has risen to 45-48 weeks), and other things that are not covered by the government's waiting time targets.

Not surprisingly, the Office of National Statistics estimates that productivity in the NHS has been falling – though the figure is notoriously hard to measure. But it seems that there has been so much money flooding in to the NHS that there has been no reason for anyone to focus on getting the best value for it. Unfortunately, the cash bonanza is now over. The NHS budget is still rising, and in real terms, but much less rapidly than before. Suddenly, there is an urgent need to make the money go further, but no systems have been put in place to achieve that.

The fact that more and more of the new money has been

spent on the hospital sector might explain some of the fall. Hospitals are expensive to run, the most costly part of the NHS. New hospital medical technology is also expensive. The same money might have bought better value elsewhere.

Meanwhile, the ambitious hospital building programme under the Private Finance Initiative, with 133 new hospitals built since 1997, is proving expensive as NHS trusts start to be hit by the increased costs of repaying the capital – costs that may turn out 15 per cent higher than the old capital charges. And despite all the new billions, the target to replace a third of hospitals by 2022 and upgrade all primary care premises by 2010 always seemed doomed to fail, and the economic downturn makes that failure a racing certainty.

Lack of direction

One reason why so much of our healthcare money is wasted is that the NHS is simply too big and too complicated for single minds to grasp – especially the minds of politicians, who have many other things to distract them, such as keeping ahead in the opinion polls. So there is little understanding, and no vision.

On election eve in 1997, when Tony Blair famously announced that there was just '24 hours to save the NHS', the aim was to cut hospital waiting lists by 100,000. But mere determination didn't seem enough to drive change through the NHS. It was time for a Plan B.

Plan B was published as The NHS Plan in 2000. The new vision was to throw vast amounts of money at the NHS – along with education and other public services – in return for reform of structures and working practices. More nurses and doctors would be recruited, thousands of hospitals would be renovated, and hundreds more built.

It was a hospital-focused plan, so the new money was being directed mainly into the part of the NHS that was already the most expensive. Instead of promoting change, it pumped more cash into the existing structures, which then simply became stronger and more difficult to change. So by the time of the 2003 election, a great deal more money was being spent, but there had been no obvious improvement in delivery – not even with the presence of a new Delivery Unit in Downing Street that was supposed to focus on it. Waiting times had not fallen, nor activity increased. It was obviously time for a Plan C.

The government's effort now shifted onto getting more diversity into healthcare provision, giving new-style NHS 'foundation' trusts more freedom, and hiring private providers to do long-wait NHS procedures like hip replacements and cataract removals. There would be new Independent Sector Treatment Centres (ISTCs) – private clinics taking NHS patients, something not even imagined in the NHS Plan. Patients too would be given more choice. To some it seemed like Tony Blair was painstakingly rebuilding Mrs Thatcher's internal market system after his first Health Secretary, Frank Dobson, had torn it down.

It certainly all looked like policy on the hoof – an attempt to build a new, flexible, local, plural, choice-driven healthcare system alongside the old, centralized, state-run, hospital-focused one. Unfortunately the old, perhaps obsolete, hospital system was already absorbing all the new money and more.

Directionless change
And even within these three broad and incompatible strategies, various other initiatives have come and gone. The architecture of the NHS is being changed by one short-term, media-focused, politically driven programme after another. It is no wonder that those who work in it complain, just as much as the patients. They can hardly work efficiently when the NHS is being torn down and noisily rebuilt around their ears; and then

torn down and noisily rebuilt again.

Meanwhile, scores of health quangos like the National Institute for Clinical Excellence and the Commission for Health Improvement have been created, abolished, merged, reformed or forgotten. Primary health trusts (which were supposed to drive the dynamic provision and procurement of primary healthcare services) were formed, then expanded, then considered under Plan C to be too bureaucratic, then changed and cut back to a third of their numbers. Strategic health authorities, designed to bring large-scale planning into how health authorities worked, were similarly expanded and then cut back by two-thirds. Health Action Zones, which were to improve public health in deprived areas but seem to have had no effect, came and went. Time will tell how the new 'health trainers' succeed in their place.

Resistance to reform

With the extra billions serving to expand and reinforce existing ways of working, rather than forcing reform on them, change has been slow. And it has been resisted.

Where the private sector has been allowed to supply the NHS, it has brought with it enormous innovation – like the million-pound mobile operating theatres that go round the country mopping up waiting lists for things like hernias, varicose veins and vasectomies – allowing NHS patients to be treated faster and closer to home. But it's all a threat to the old order, and many on the Left see it as privatization by stealth.

The development of treatment centres run by the private sector has been resisted for the same reasons. If the diversity agenda and the new flexible ways of working had come before funds had been thrown at the old-style NHS hospital sector, things might have been very different. But now, despite the evident cost and innovation benefits of using private-sector delivery, the programme has been deliberately limited. The original target – made low enough not to put too many Old Labour backs up – was for 15 per cent of NHS procedures to be done by the private sector. And that is where it remains.

NHS trusts too have not been given sufficient freedom to run themselves in new or different ways that are right for the local community. Despite all the bluster that decisions are being devolved from Whitehall to the localities, trusts still spend most of their time pursuing delivery targets set out by Downing Street and working in ways that the Department sets down in minute detail.

Reform is happening here and there, of course. But only gradually, in the hope of not rocking the boat too much: and therefore inadequately. The slow pace of change may reassure the incumbent interests like hospital staff and welfare-state traditionalists, but it slows down any improvement in the delivery of better services to patients: waiting times may fall a little, and quality may be forced up – but all much later than need be, and at much greater cost.

But now, the demand for healthcare is once again rising more quickly than the NHS budgets that supply it. The only thing that can close the gap between demand and supply is innovation, new ways of working, higher productivity, flexibility, and focus.

Grey power

With any luck, the postwar baby-boomer generation won't put up with the healthcare establishment's resistance to reform. As they get older, they will be demanding more health and social care. There are a lot of them, and they are more educated and articulate than any preceding generation. They expect and demand choice. And their health conditions are more chronic than they were when they were young. They might have put up with dirty, ill-managed hospitals and long waits when they just needed an episode of treatment now and again – a hernia operated on, or a knee x-rayed. But now they are living with long-term conditions. Their care needs to be more joined up, and more focused on them as human individuals, not them as a 'hernia' or a 'knee'.

This generation are not going to sit and be told by some health authority which hospital or care home they will die in – they will demand state-of-the-art care that is centred around them as customers, not around the producers. They will demand to be treated in more convenient, high-quality settings, and cared for at home among the people they love. They will want a consistent, integrated package of care-healthcare, social care and social benefits all focused on their particular circumstances, rather than them having to traipse around different parts of the state apparatus to beg for the different things they need.

The producers of all public services, including health and social care, will have to respond to this new kind of demand. Reform will have to accelerate, or politicians and providers will face a spreading rebellion from a lot of angry and articulate electors.

Safer in your own hands

Already, people are taking healthcare more into their own hands. It's not just the rising number that have operations privately at home or abroad. It's prevention too. We're also smoking less, joining more fitness clubs (and sometimes even going to them), cutting back on salt, taking more vitamin supplements. This again is something we drive ourselves, not something led by politicians and the state healthcare system. The NHS budget for health promotion is small, and the number of public health consultants and registrars has actually fallen since 1997.

But the private sector, and not just the traditional healthcare private sector, is coming up with new ideas that will, increasingly, produce greater choice and flexibility without reference to the lumbering, politicized NHS.

In the United States, more than 1,500 retail health clinics are now in operation. Drugstore chains such as CVS, Target, and Walgreens are pioneering them. Wal-Mart – though it took a knock as a result of the financial downturn – plans to open scores more clinics, leasing space in their supermarkets for drop-in clinics run by local healthcare providers. These clinics are run by nurse practitioners, and open seven days and evenings each week – so people can get quick, cheap, convenient diagnosis, and some treatment, at a time that suits them, and without needing expensive insurance.

It cannot be long before the idea spreads here to the UK. The NHS has been building its own drop-in clinics, of course. But it would do better to encourage innovative private-sector initiatives like this, rather than try to reinvent them.

The NHS as agent

The latest change of direction – Plan D – came from the surgeon and minister (now resigned, of course) Lord Darzi. He suggested giving at least some patients their own healthcare budgets so they could buy in the treatment they want, from the sources they prefer, in ways that suit them best.

Undoubtedly it would all be very bureaucratic – the Department of Health set up 97 different work streams to look at the implementation of the proposals. And it would be limited to patients who suffer long-term conditions like diabetes, multiple sclerosis and motor neurone disease – the thinking being that these patients surely know the mix of treatment that works best for them far better than any doctor.

But the move is in the right direction – an NHS that is driven by the wishes of patients rather than the presumptions of providers.

The future of the NHS must be as an agency that ensures we all get a minimum standard of healthcare, and pays for much of it, but which buys in that care from a wide range of nimbler, competitive non-state providers, rather than clumsily trying to deliver all healthcare services itself. Such a change is inevitable. The pity is that it will be slower and more painful because politicians, rather than patients, are currently in charge.

11

ROTTEN EDUCATION

When they entered government, New Labour strategists were adamant that Britain's future living would come from its brains, not its brawn, and that his priorities would be 'education, education and education'.

Twelve years on, we have spent billions on this objective. Education spending rose from £38 billion in 1997-8 to £85.1 billion in 2009-10 – an increase in real terms, after inflation, of 66 per cent, and around 6 per cent of Britain's GDP. It has bought us 40,000 extra teachers and 100,000 new classroom assistants. There has been a profusion of laws and targets, new kinds of schools, recruitment drives, new buildings, taskforces, initiatives, and more.

Yet, after eleven years of compulsory education, under half (47 per cent) of the children leaving state schools in 2008 did so with five good (A*-C) GCSE grades including the vital subjects of English and maths. Just half (50 per cent) got good grades in science, but less than a third (30.6 per cent) got good grades in a foreign language. Around 26,000 kids leave school each year with no qualifications at all, while more than 20,000 leave without having any basic literacy.

Meanwhile we have a school funding system that rewards failure, a bewildering profusion of different kinds of school, teachers swamped by paperwork, schools unable to recruit teachers and heads, over 8,000 kids a year being expelled, 63,000 kids bunking off school each day, another 25,000 or more leaving school each year with no GCSEs at all, more parents going private or hiring in tutors, and school places being allocated by lottery rather than by what is best for the kids. How did education get into such a rotten state?

Opening up the secret garden

Perhaps it was because the state got into education. The postwar education system was a typical nationalized industry, run by supposed experts, gripped by powerful trade unions, and caring little about its customers because most of them had no realistic alternative. But throughout the 1960s and 1970s, parents and academics all suspected there was something wrong. They couldn't find out, because schools doggedly resisted the publication of examination results, saying they were a bad measure of the rounded individuals they aimed to produce.

It took Margaret Thatcher, 36 years on from the creation of the system in 1944, to force schools to publish their results and their curricula. It revealed some appalling results and methods. The secret garden of the curriculum, which educationalists claimed to tend so well, was actually full of weeds.

A second step, in the Education Reform Act 1988, was to allow parents to choose between schools on the basis of the published 'league table' results – or for any other reason they liked. Schools' funding would depend, in part, on how many parents they could attract.

My family was a beneficiary of this choice. One of the many weeds growing in the secret garden was the 'real books' method of teaching reading. The idea was to spare kids the tedious repetition of the John and Jane sort of primers, or having to break down words into syllables in the 'c-a-t = cat' style.

Instead, they would simply pick any book they liked from the bookshelf and – somehow, hopefully – get the feel of the words and the language.

So our son would come home with books of widely varying difficulty. He would learn words from one, then not see them in another for weeks, by which time he had already forgotten them. When we asked teachers why the kids weren't given books that built up gradually in difficulty, we were told that this would give rise to 'school gate comparisons' of performance – which were obviously politically incorrect.

We believed our son needed a more structured approach. So we transferred him to another nearby state primary. Immediately, other parents started asking how to do the same. Their feelings, it turned out, were identical to ours. So we told them. It took only three or four to move before the school had a crisis meeting and completely changed the way it taught reading. Choice is a powerful tool.

The focus on results

In government, New Labour retained the Conservative policies of a set curriculum, regular testing and school inspections. They believed these things gave crucial information to parents and were a vital measure of standards. But to actually raise standards, they thought, would require a firm push from government. Targets would have to be set, and performance monitored.

Within days of the 1997 election they had set up the Standards and Effectiveness Unit (SEU). Education Secretary David Blunkett announced targets for primary-level literacy and numeracy, warning that his 'head would be on the block' if they were not met. Professor Michael Barber, a keen advocate of targets, became a special adviser at the Department for Education and Employment (DfEE) and then went on to become 'Mr Targets' as head of the Prime Minister's Delivery Unit in Downing Street.

But in education, what targets should be set? Professor Barber found he already had a useful set of objective measures – the tests that the Conservatives had introduced at ages 7, 11, and 14, plus the General Certificate of Secondary Education (GCSE) examinations at 16 and A-Levels at 18. For good measure he added another one, the so-called AS-Level at 17.

Tony Blair seemed to think that simply a change in personnel at the top, and a little of his famous persuasiveness, would be enough to improve the public services such as education. But two years later he was telling business leaders 'I bear the scars on my back after two years in government' and complaining of the 'forces of conservatism' that were blocking reform.

Gordon Brown, though, had the far more persuasive weapon of Treasury funding. He instituted 'Public Service Agreements' with the spending departments, tying their budgets to their performance. In the case of education, the target was a 2 per cent annual improvement in the proportion of students getting five A*-C grades at GCSE, or their equivalent (the A* grade had been introduced because so many students got A grades that universities complained they were meaningless).

Getting the rubbish you pay for

Suddenly, we had moved from the 1970s world where results were not even published, to a 1990s world in which they became schools' sole focus.

Indeed, results have become the sole fixation of everyone in education. For the government, hitting its targets is essential for electoral credibility. For local authorities, government funding depends on hitting them; schools too depend on them for funding, and for retaining parents' support. Teachers' careers too depend on how they rank in the results league.

Even the exam bodies have an interest in rising results. They want to maintain standards, but they don't want to lose business to other boards that teachers think might give them more of those vital A*-C grades. A 'watchdog' quango, the Qualifications and Curriculum Authority (or the Qualifications and Curriculum Development Agency, QCDA as we must now learn to call it after one of the inevitable re-naming sprees), is supposed to regulate this; but it too is under pressure from politicians to produce improving results. (Not that it's much good at producing anything: in November 2008 its Chief Executive, Ken Boston, quit ahead of a damning report on that summer's huge mess – up in the teenage SATs tests.)

So the whole upward pressure on results is circular. And these incentives have indeed produced improving grade performance. More and more kids are hitting the five A*-C target. But many people believe that this is just grade inflation.

There is some evidence for this. Teachers can drill and coach kids to pass GCSEs and get results up that way, but they can't drill and coach them for the various international tests that are done from time to time. The Trends in International Mathematics and Science Study (TIMSS) tests children in several countries, including England, every four years. It shows England's primary school maths performance rising. But it shows no improvement at all at secondary school level, despite the fact that schools' GCSE results have been rising rapidly.

The Organization for Economic Co-operation and Development (OECD) runs another testing programme, the Programme for International Student Assessment (PISA). Every three years, it tests 15-year-olds in maths, science and reading. Again, while England's age-14 test scores and GCSE results were soaring, PISA actually showed a slight decline.

You get what you pay for. We pay for a target of five A*-C grades at GCSE, and that is what our education system gives us. But it isn't necessarily giving us better education or real improvements. The international comparisons suggest that it's all an institutional fraud against the public and the kids.

Games teachers play

It's easy for schools to play the targets game and improve their results. The old days when a pupil's results depended on just two or three exam papers are over. Current testing relies much more on coursework. And there are several things that teachers can do on this to get their kids through.

Many schools use 'writing frames' to coax pupils into writing the right things in the right way, with the right language, grammar and formatting. Some teachers set pupils almost identical tasks before the coursework itself so that they know exactly what to do in the real thing. Some get pupils to hand in draft coursework, then hand it back with suggested improvements — several times, if necessary, until it is fit to present. Some teachers also take a lenient attitude to coursework being handed in late. That doesn't encourage punctuality, but it gives the school a 100 per cent completion record. And when it comes to marking, teachers can be a little generous (not too much, though: exam boards will smell a rat if a student gets an A* on coursework and a D on the written examination).

Many teachers go for where they can make the most difference in terms of hitting the A*-C target. However beneficial it might be to stretch a bright student to turn an A into an A*, or to turn another's E into a D, it's pointless in terms of the targets game. Far better to focus on the D student in the hope of getting a C.

Today's smart teachers drill their pupils constantly, not to improve their understanding of the subject in question, but to make sure they regurgitate exactly the right answers for the test without having to think. Textbook writers know this too: they don't waste time trying to engage the interest of pupils with more general information that they won't actually need to pass the tests.

If the worst happens and one of their pupils produces a D, schools still have several options. They can ask for a re-mark in the hope of getting a more lenient examiner and squeezing out a few extra marks. (On-the-ball schools will already have refused to accept examiners who marked them stiffly the year before.) Or, because exams are broken into modules, they can have the pupil re-sit one or two papers, and cram them extensively on that specific part of the subject, so they are not having to take in too much at once.

Profiting from the ratings game

The prize for gaming the examination system went to Kevin Satchwell, the head of Thomas Telford School in Shropshire. He spotted the crucial words 'or equivalent' in the government's five A*-C target. For some odd reason, the QCA (as the QCDA then was) had decided that a pass in one work-related qualification, the General National Vocational Qualification (GNVQ) would be equivalent to four GCSEs. So one of those, plus some 'soft' GCSE, hits the target. A GNVQ may be of little value to many of their students; but by this method, Thomas Telford managed to achieve a perfect 100 per cent A*-C target success in 2000. It went on to make millions by selling an onscreen course that was hugely effective at getting pupils through the Information and Communications Technology (ICT) GNVQ, clicking up four 'equivalent' passes every time.

The fact that Satchwell was knighted for his performance and that other schools were happy to pay £3,000 to get their own pupils through the GNVQ shows just how urgent the official target had become.

In 2007 the government phased out GNVQs, but there are other qualifications that still count. And in response to public concerns about the number of 'soft' subjects being taken, the new target also required A*-C passes in Maths and English. When this new objective came in, schools' overall success rate dropped spectacularly from 59 per cent to just 45.8 per cent.

Spoon-feeding in exams

Schools also game the A-level system. The imposition of AS levels at 17 enables schools to enter students for perhaps four subjects, and then drop the weakest one before they face the A-levels themselves.

And exams are designed to help students pass too. Question-sheets now show how many marks are at stake for answers, method and presentation – which focuses kids on getting the marks rather than showing their understanding. Questions guide the candidate through the steps of an argument, with points for each step, rather than just asking them to prove X=Y and leaving them to work out the steps themselves. And exam boards, anxious to have happy customers, give schools precise instructions on how to get the most out of the marking scheme.

In this system, everyone wins prizes. Until you apply to university. Then you discover that academics are more sceptical about what your results mean. Or until you apply for a job, and discover that your inability to complete work on time, your habitual goofing off, your incapacity to think, and your lack of general knowledge and human communication skills don't get you very far.

How good is it anyway?

Though school examination results have certainly been getting better and better, it's questionable whether this has anything at all to do with the £200 billion or so of extra money that has been spent on education since 1997.

In fact, school examination results improved more rapidly between 1995 and 1999, once the secret garden of the curriculum had been opened up and was starting to benefit from its thorough weeding – despite the fact that no targets were then in place.

Beyond that slight surge, though, exam performance has been on a pretty straight improvement trend since before 1997, making it seem that all the effort spent on 'education, education and education' has made not the slightest difference.

Even the marked improvement in primary-school literacy can be traced back to 1995 with the initiative directed on it by Chris Woodhead, the head of Ofsted at the time.

The directionless drive to be different

Because politicians have found it so hard to reform existing schools, they have invented a wide variety of new ones. Creating diversity in schools was one of Margaret Thatcher's main aims. She knew that education bureaucrats would never drive change; but schools would improve if given the freedom and incentive to do so. So she allowed schools to opt to become Grant-Maintained (GM), leaving local-authority control and being paid on the basis of the number of pupils they could attract.

Another strand of the policy, aimed at improving technical skills, allowed schools to become City Technology Colleges (CTCs). And the plan to use diversity to drive change continued, with all secondary schools being invited to apply for 'specialist' status.

By the time New Labour took office in 1997, there were hundreds of GM schools, 15 CTCs and 245 specialist schools. While Tony Blair was suspicious of this situation – thinking it created a two-tier system – the performance of specialist schools was clearly better, and their execution was stayed. Two years on, frustrated by the 'forces of conservatism' within education as much as those within health, he was championing specialization and diversity as the only way of pushing change through the education bureaucracy.

Naturally, he had to distance the policy from Mrs Thatcher, the Left's main hate-figure. So City Technology Colleges became 'City Academies' and then just 'Academies', and were dressed up as a way of rescuing failing schools from collapse. But Blair knew the intrinsic value of diversity, and by the time he left power, had set a target of 400 Academies.

Specialist school numbers were boosted too. Before 1999, schools wishing to apply for specialist status had to demonstrate their commitment by raising £100,000 in sponsorship from local sources. Now that barrier was halved, and targets for specialist school numbers were raised, eventually to include all secondary schools. Specialist status was broadened to include technology, languages, arts, sports, maths and ICT, science, engineering, business and enterprise, humanities, music, special educational needs, or any combination of these subjects.

Even independent schools were recruited to the cause. On taking office, New Labour closed the assisted places scheme, which paid for kids from poorer families to attend private schools. But within ten years it was back, paying for deserving kids' boarding places, and pushing the independents to expand to meet more of the needs of state pupils. Universities and businesses were encouraged to create yet other sorts of institutions, 'Trust Schools'.

Management: running the diversity empire
All this diversity has certainly made the school system

confusing for parents. But has it actually improved standards? Given the unreliability of examination results, that is hard to answer. But there are grounds to be sceptical.

A 2001 survey by the standards regulator Ofsted judged four-fifths of specialist schools to be highly effective. But specialist status was then still novel, and the schools that sought it – and were able to raise the necessary sponsorship – were probably the more dynamic and well-managed ones. Nevertheless, by 2005 another Ofsted report was claiming that five in six specialist schools were now meeting the programme targets, and did well on measures such as leadership, management, teaching quality and test results.

However, much of the success of specialist schools may be due only to the extra money that is spent on them. Spending on specialist schools more than tripled from £41m in 1998 to over £145m in 2003. They get access to £100,000 for capital projects plus £129 per pupil per year. For a school of 1000 pupils that's a £616,000 boost over four years.

Too much central control

And it does seem to be the extra cash that counts, since their actual specialization is often slight. One study discovered that science schools did not have science teachers who were any better qualified than non-science schools, and often had poorer science results than schools with other specialisms. Central direction from Whitehall is still strong. And they are allowed to select only a minority of their applicants on the basis of academic ability at their specialist subject.

One senior Whitehall mandarin once told me how much he enjoyed running the 'diversity agenda'. He did not see that the point of diversity is that schools ought to be diverse, free to run themselves as they think fit, rather than being run from the centre. But Whitehall continues to specify exactly how schools should operate, with hundreds of different forms and circulars dropping onto heads' doormats each year.

It has become difficult to recruit and retain teachers, and to recruit and retain heads, when they are being subjected to so much form-filling from the centre. Only 4 per cent of teachers say they would consider becoming a head, and half a million children are taught in leaderless schools because they can't recruit new heads.

Despite the fact that spending on teachers rose by 53 per cent between 1997 and 2006, and that over 200 school heads now earn over £100,000, teaching can no longer attract people. Half the students who train to be teachers never actually go into teaching. In the last five years, nearly a third of teachers left the profession, and half are due to retire within the next ten.

Arithmetic: school budgets that don't add up

Britain's school financing system has the effect of rewarding failure. Much of the schools budget stays in Whitehall, to support the education civil service. From there, what's left is paid out to Local Education Authorities (LEAs), who of course take some to maintain their own staff and facilities before passing it to schools.

Secondary schools get about 80 per cent of their funding through this mechanism, which is called the 'Delegated Budget'. The exact amount depends on how big the school is, how may of its pupils have Special Educational Needs, what fixed costs it has, and so on.

But there are three other sources too. Money comes from the Department in the shape of the 'Standards Fund', and more as the 'School Standards Grant'. If the school has sixth-form kids, there is cash from yet another source, the Learning and Skills Council.

Having four different sources of funding is confusing

enough; but it gets much worse. Take the Standards Fund. That might account for 10 per cent or more of a school's budget – a significant amount, and the difference between breaking even or running at a loss. But it's a fickle source of income, which depends on the changing obsessions of ministers.

And ministers have a lot of obsessions. In 2001, there were 107 different project funds within the Standards Fund. Mercifully that was pruned to just 50 in 2003. Today, most schools are seeking money from about 10 or 20 of these funds. Almost £1 billion, for example, has been spent on improving behaviour in schools. Yet it remains dire. Of the 10,000 permanent exclusions each year, almost a third are for persistent disruption, a fifth involve threatening teachers, and another fifth involve violence against other pupils.

Bidding not teaching
Indeed, the funding system almost encourages such failures. For schools, funding is a delicate balancing act. You want to be full so you get the maximum Delegated Budget. But if you can arrange to have large class sizes, a shortage of teachers, lots of students who are failing or who have Special Educational Needs, plenty of exclusions for bad behaviour, and lots of truanting, then you will be better off.

And the system is riddled with bureaucracy. Schools bid for money from Whitehall. They get perhaps 200 pages of bidding forms each year to fill out; and with so much money at stake, having good bidders on your staff is just as important as having good teachers. To get the money, you need to show not how good you are, but how appallingly bad your school is.

Once you have taken the cash you have to report back to Whitehall to say how you have spent it. But Whitehall likes to micro-manage this spending, which means that there are even more complex forms to fill in. One head, for example, tells of receiving £1,700 from one particular Standards Fund programme. That's not a vast amount to a school whose budget is in the millions. But it required him to fill in a 12-page report – back form, detailing exactly how the money was spent, what his objectives were and how far they had been met, and the postcodes and ethnic origins of the pupils who had benefited. He sent the form and the money back.

Often, ministers' priorities are not schools' priorities. The school where I was a governor got a letter from the local authority, explaining a new initiative to improve disabled access in schools, and asking us to bid for some of the money. So we sat around, discussing whether we could take a step out here and put a ramp up there. After about twenty minutes, I ventured to ask how many disabled students we had. The answer was that at that time, we had none.

I pointed out that, with no disabled students, this money would be completely wasted. What we really wanted money for was for improving things like the boys' toilets, which were disgusting. 'Ah,' said our finance officer. 'If we make them disabled toilets, we'd get the money.' And so the bid went in. It's an absolutely crazy way to finance schools.

(In the event, since the council demands £2m of public liability insurance from all its contractors, there were only a handful of builders we could use. They were all busy on other jobs. By the time the work was completed, the disabled access funds had run out and we never got the money anyway.)

Building, but without a plan

But it gets crazier. The grandest spending programme is Gordon Brown's £45 billion plan to refurbish all secondary schools and half of Britain's 24,000 primary schools by 2020.

Half of that money is going on completely new buildings under the Private Finance Initiative (PFI). The waste in this programme is astonishing. Many parents and teachers complain that perfectly good school buildings are being torn down in order to put up new ones in their place.

And the contracts are badly managed. One PFI school in Brighton closed after only three years, forcing the local authority to pay £4.5 million to get out of its PFI contract. Another, in Essex, closed after five years, leaving the local authority with a bill of £370,000 a year for the next twenty years.

In my own case, again, our old school building was 50 years old. It's design life, however, had been just 25 years, so it was crumbling. We had just got and spent a second tranche of £140,000 on new windows, because the old ones made classrooms unusable in wet weather. So we were feeling pretty pleased – until the LEA governor suddenly announced that the government was making millions available to us in order to knock the whole place down and build a new one. Jaws dropped. Some £280,000 of taxpayers' money had been completely wasted, simply because there was no capital planning in the schools finance system at all.

It reminded me of the 1992 TV programme Troubleshooter, in which businessman John Harvey-Jones went to sort out an aircraft factory in Poland, where the old Soviet-era methods were still very much in place. One day everyone had to down tools and clear the place to make room for a large consignment of propellers, which (as usual) simply arrived from the supply factory without any warning. That's exactly how we run our schools.

Mainstream funding mistakes

Even the mainstream part of school funding, the Delegated Budget, is a mess. One of its many problems is that the government pushes extra costs onto schools, without raising the budget to pay for them. Gordon Brown's raising of National Insurance was a case in point: it added to teachers' salary costs. And nearly all the 197,000 teachers who applied for bonuses under David Blunkett's 'payment by results' programme got them: which raised schools' salary costs again. As did his changes to the pay scale so that more teachers got the top salaries.

Nor does the Delegated Budget incentivize schools to improve. It depends on pupil numbers, which you might think would reward the schools that perform well and so attract more parents. But the good schools are already over-subscribed. Indeed, England's grammar schools, which the government would like to turn into comprehensives, are ten times oversubscribed. And local government planning rules make it almost impossible for schools to expand.

The system doesn't even give successful heads any incentive to take over the running of an unsuccessful school nearby. In business, takeovers happen all the time – when good managers believe that they can make money by turning round someone else's failing company. But not in schools. The system would not give a successful head any greater back office support for the extra administrative costs, such as personnel management, logistics, and purchasing. They wouldn't get any reward for success. All they get is the risk of failure. So the talents of good heads are going to waste – but they act quite rationally in sticking to their own patch.

Naturally the bureaucracy has come up with its own second-best solution to the shortcomings that its own systems have created. This is for schools to club together as 'federations' so that good ones can help under-performing ones. In my own governing body, everyone worked hard to keep themselves off the federation board: it was a waste of time. Its only function was to reduce the embarrassing over-demand for the best schools and fill up the under-subscribed ones. We would just offer parents a place in the under-performing school: and since the 'federation' had thereby found a space for them, the better schools could brush their applications aside.

It was like saying you couldn't book a table at the Ritz because the greasy-spoon café down the road had no customers. But that is how the budget incentives work. The state education system desperately tries to prevent parents from applying to good schools, rather than designing incentives that will cause good schools to expand. Brighton even decided to allocate places by lottery, rather than on any needs of the children – which was highly unpopular, and of course leaves bad schools with absolutely no incentive to improve at all.

Must try something else

And that is the rotten state of education today. I lasted only four years as a school governor because I couldn't stand its absurdities. And every teacher of my acquaintance can't wait to take early retirement and take themselves out of all the form-filling, the bossy micro-management of Whitehall and LEA bureaucrats, the constant drilling to pass exams, the bad behaviour they have to try to teach round, the threats of violence and the unwillingness of kids to participate in a system they see no point in. They can't even get disruptive kids expelled, because many local authorities impose financial penalties of up to £10,000 on schools that permanently exclude a pupil. So they put up with it, until they can take the first possible opportunity to retire from teaching and do something else. The staffing gaps they leave are then filled by newly qualified teachers, some from overseas, or even teaching assistants with much lower qualifications.

Inasmuch as rising exam grades mean anything, it is private initiative we have to thank, not the state education system.

Parents have such little faith in the state school system that 11 per cent of them say they buy in some kind of private tuition, though some estimates put the figure at more than twice that. Indeed, tuition has become a boom industry, with various online agencies coordinating it and teachers happily moonlighting to supply it.

And much of the rise in grades is down to the performance of independent schools. It is true that independent schools select brighter children, but even then, their results have been getting better and better, and they far outpace state school performance. In 2008 just 7.6 per cent of pupils in state comprehensives got three A grades at A-level: in independent schools it was 30.3 per cent. Either private-school kids are getting even brainier for some reason, or private schools are doing something right. Or our state schools are doing a lot wrong.

12

WELFARE

Nearly a third of state spending – £193 billion of it in 2009-10 – goes on various kinds of welfare benefits. After a decade of rising economic growth and prosperity – until recently – you might have thought that the need for social benefits was falling. But spending on them actually rose 50 per cent in real terms over the ten years from 1997 – a total of nearly £400 billion of extra benefits spending over the decade.

You might also think that benefits go only to the very poorest. In fact, nearly two-fifths of us (39 per cent) receive one or more of forty state benefits or credits – that's up from under a quarter (24 per cent) in 1997, which seemed pretty high even then.

It's a huge cash roundabout. Millions of us pay taxes into this system, only to get it back again (minus administrative expenses) in benefits. To manage it, the Department of Work and Pensions employs 130,000 benefits staff, while HM Revenue & Customs has another 8,000 working on tax credits alone.

Not only does the system give with one hand and take with the other. It also traps people in poverty by making it not worth them working; it produces the highest rate of single parenthood in Europe; breaks up families by paying two individuals more than one couple; it finds it easier to make disabled people sit at home than find appropriate work for them; and it allows politicians to disguise unemployment as 'sickness' or 'training'.

Disguising unemployment

By 2007 about 21 million people were claiming state benefits, up from 17 million in 1997. That includes some 5.8 million people of working age who are drawing out-of-work benefits. These benefits include Jobseekers Allowance (JSA), paid to adults seeking work; Income Support (IS) for adults who cannot work full-time for various reasons; and Incapacity Benefit (IB) for those who cannot work because of illness or disability. This year, the number of people of working age who live on benefits has risen faster than ever before, to record levels.

Unemployment in Britain is officially around 2.4 million and rising, but more still is disguised by these benefits. For example, many of the 2.6 million people on incapacity benefit are probably capable of some kind of work: indeed, in November 2008 the government announced a new initiative to investigate this. For years the benefit has been abused: doctors have been content to sign people on to incapacity benefits because it is more generous and permanent than unemployment benefits; and politicians have been willing to let them, because it makes the unemployment figures look better. But the IB numbers have become rather ridiculous in a country that is supposed to be getting healthier.

The New Deal

Another tranche of unemployment is disguised under the New Deal. The idea of this is that people should not simply be able to sit at home on benefits, without doing anything to get back into work. Gordon Brown spelt out the options in 1997: get a job, work for a voluntary body, work on the new environmental task force, or be in full-time education or training. There was 'no fifth option' of simply drawing benefits and doing nothing.

In fact the New Deal wasn't so new. John Major had already imposed similar conditions on Jobseeker's Allowance. It was immediately dubbed 'workfare', but it seemed to work: unemployment fell faster during the last years of John Major's government than it did during Tony Blair's.

The New Deal gives skills training, work experience and advice to people who have been unemployed for six months. But it's a bureaucratic monster, much less effective than similar efforts in other countries. In fact there is not one, but six New Deal programmes, though in 2008 the House of Commons Public Accounts Committee calculated that only two of them had produced any savings in the social benefits bill.

In the ten years following its launch in 1998, the New Deal had cost £3,500 million of taxpayers' money and created (the government says) 1,729,000 jobs. That's over £2,000 per job: and many on the scheme would probably have ended up finding a job anyway, so the real cost is even greater. And the unemployment count seems unaffected: it began its rise in 2004, just when the New Deal was supposed to be kicking in and getting everyone off benefits.

But by an amazing sleight of hand, the New Deal allows the government to claim that long-term unemployment has been completely abolished. In fact, it's just called something else. As soon as you threaten to become 'long-term unemployed' – that is after six months out of work – you go onto the New Deal. You move off Jobseekers Allowance and onto a 'training allowance': so you are now in training and no longer part of the benefit count. This takes 40,000 out of the jobless figures. When you have been through the New Deal process and are still out of work, you go back on the dole again, but you're still not 'long-term unemployed' because you start back at the beginning as a 'new' claimant. Ingeniously crooked.

NEETs

Perhaps the most disturbing figure in the statistics is the 1 million young people aged 16-24 who are not in education, employment or training – known as NEETs. That's a sixth of the people in that age group, and twice as many as in Germany or France. The London School of Economics calculated in 2007 that the cost of these young people sitting around at home amounted to £3.65 billion a year – equivalent to a penny off income tax. Average NEETs will cost taxpayers £97,000 during their lifetime, while some will cost more than three times that.

If there is 'no fifth option', how can this happen? Despite all the 'get tough' rhetoric from ministers – including the threat to dock benefits if they refuse a job or a training place – young people signing on to the New Deal spend the first four months talking to a personal adviser about their options. Then they go into training. And if they still don't get a job, they start all over again. For many, it's a permanently revolving door.

In any event, two-fifths of benefit claimants who do find a job are back on state support within six months. It seems the employment 'training' they are given is hardly worthy of the name.

Other efforts to push school leavers into jobs have been equally ineffective. A £100 million reward scheme, which encouraged kids to stay on in education by giving them 'loyalty points' was soon abandoned as a total flop. The much-advertised £500 million Education Maintenance Allowance, which offers £30 a week to young people from low-income families to stay in education, has little impact on Britain's staying-on rate, which remains one of Europe's lowest.

Back to the drawing board

Politicians will never publicly admit their mistakes, but a clear acceptance that the system wasn't working came in late 2008, when the Work and Pensions Secretary James Purnell announced a new welfare package. For people who could not get a job there would be compulsory community work or volunteering. Those dependent on drugs would be forced into rehabilitation. Parents of older children would be obliged to seek work. And there would be tighter checks on those claiming to be incapacitated.

In other words, it was going to do what the New Deal had promised to do back in 1997; had that been properly managed, this further patching-up would hardly be necessary.

But there was a ray of hope embedded in the new proposals. Private-sector firms would be paid up to £50,000 each to get unemployed people into work for at least 18 months. This was a policy stolen from the Conservatives, who in turn stole it from American states such as Wisconsin, where private and charitable organizations help to train and place long-term unemployed people in long-term work – and don't get paid until they succeed. It is a policy that works: private firms can be much more flexible than the state at dealing with people as individuals, and tailoring a package of personalized help around their specific needs.

The right to remain in poverty

The state's problem is that benefits are rights-based. If you qualify on one of a huge number of criteria, you get the money. You are not expected to change your behaviour so as to reduce your reliance on benefits. The money is yours as of right.

As the former Welfare Minister Frank Field has pointed out, this system turns people into benefit cheats. People find that if they can actually worsen their circumstances – or pretend to – they will qualify for additional benefits.

For example, because the government's tax credit system gives particular help to one-parent families, it ends up creating one-parent families. A single mother who works 16 hours a week on the minimum wage and is paid tax credits could achieve an income of £487 a week. But a two-parent family on minimum wages would have to work a hundred hours longer to achieve the same income.

In fact, tens of thousands of families discover that they would be better off by pretending they live apart. In 2007 around £320 million of tax credits, plus another £85 million in Income Support and Jobseekers' Allowance, went to 80,000 couples who fraudulently claimed that they were not living together. The scam accounted for nearly a third of the £1,100 million benefit fraud bill.

And many other couples really do split up, and remain apart, as a result of this brutal economics. And the system actually discourages many more single parents from finding a partner or marrying – even though it could help them out of poverty. The system leaves taxpayers to pick up the bill, not just for the extra benefits but for the child poverty that the system prolongs – some 40 per cent of children in poverty are in lone-parent families – and for the social costs of the troubled children that family break-up often produces.

The tax credits fiasco

Along with the New Deal, Gordon Brown's other flagship welfare measure was the tax credit system. Its motivation was perfectly sound. When you give benefits to people when they don't work, and tax them when they do, many people will be reluctant to leave the security of the benefits system and actually get a job. The idea of tax credits is to create a smooth slope at the margin between welfare and work, so that people find they are always better off in work, and never lose out by getting a better-paid job.

In 1998 Gordon Brown abolished Family Credit, mapped out his own Working Familiess' Tax Credit – and then proceeded to re-jig it several times. In 2000 he replaced it by the Employment Tax Credit for Working Households – soon renamed the Working Families' Tax Credit. And the new Children's Tax Credit became the Integrated Tax Credit, then the Child Credit. At various points, he brought in the Disabled Persons' Tax Credit, a Childcare Tax Credit, an Employment Credit, a Child Tax Credit and a Baby Tax Credit. And at various other points, he abolished the Married Couples' Tax Allowance, the Working Families' Tax Credit, the Children's Tax Credit, the Disabled Persons' Tax Credit, the Baby Tax Credit and the Employment Credit, and brought in a new Working Tax Credit. Got it? Do keep up!

Unfortunately, the system has changed so many times that it is very hard for those who depend on it to keep up with it. More than 700,000 children in poor working households do not receive tax credits, partly because their parents find them unfathomably complicated.

Nevertheless, some 7.5 million families do receive £12 billion worth of Child Credit. It's a ridiculously high number of beneficiaries for something aimed to help the poorest. The reason is that Gordon Brown made the smoothing between benefits and work very shallow indeed. Couples with a combined income of up to £58,000 are eligible. At that level the benefits are small, but it is amazing that the state pays out any money at all to families who earn twice the average wage. It is a sad waste of money that is supposed to fight child poverty. And it makes even well-off people reluctant to criticize a system that they too benefit from.

The IT required to administer all this is a fiasco in its own right. The new tax credits system went live in April 2003, and the IT firms EDS and CapGemini were given £236 million to run it for two years. They got more money for building the software, but the system still paid thousands of families the wrong amounts. In the first two years, some £184 million had been overpaid to claimants – which of course HM Revenue & Customs immediately demanded back, leaving some of the poorest families with bills that they could not possibly pay. Public outrage led to an HMRC retreat, but not before they had spent a further £65 million on repairing the system and cleaning up the mess. HMRC has now admitted that the problems of over-complexity, overpayments and fraud are very much larger, with some £6 billion having been overpaid to families, many of whom are struggling to repay.

The massive expansion of means testing

Though the tax credit system is supposed to make it easier for people to leave benefits and get into work, it still hasn't succeeded. The poorest 10 per cent of the population still see up to 56 per cent of their income going in tax. Even those on the minimum wage face the disincentive of paying tax. And by 2012 an average graduate will face an effective tax burden of 47.2 per cent when student loan repayments and state pension contributions are taken into account.

When other means-tested benefits – Housing Benefit, free school meals, student loans – are added in, the perversity of this system is huge. Of course, we want people to be housed, children to be fed, and young adults to be educated. But means testing on this scale undermines incentives. If you are going to lose 60 per cent or more of any additional earnings because you both pay tax and lose benefits, why bother working? There are more people in this position than before, and for some the effective tax rate can be as high as 90 per cent.

This is one reason why the target of halving child poverty by 2011 won't be met. The 2004-05 target of cutting child poverty by a quarter has already been missed, and things have slipped further behind since then. The best way out of poverty is work, but that just isn't happening.

A 2007 UNICEF report, looking at 40 indicators including poverty, family and community relationships, and health, put Britain bottom of the league table for child well-being across 21 industrialized countries. And the problems are cascading down the generations: one in five children is growing up in homes dependent on means-tested benefits.

The cost of housing policy

Even ministers admit how perverse our means-tested welfare system has become. In 2008, the housing minister Caroline Flint admitted that people were 'working the system' in a 'race to the bottom' to get priority on housing lists over people who hold down jobs. They produce doctors' certificates and other evidence to show that their families are on the brink of collapse. And the worse off they make themselves, the more they succeed. As a result, she noted, some council estates have become a 'parking place' for the unemployed.

Having created this system, the government seems stuck with it, no matter how absurd the results become. Targets to keep down council waiting lists, for example, put a huge strain on local authorities to house people, and lead to bizarre situations where families are farmed out to expensive bed-and-breakfast accommodation rather than being found a permanent home. Private landlords are being paid as much as £1,800 a week to house families in the London borough of Kensington and Chelsea, the country's most expensive and affluent area. In 2008 the newspapers discovered one family, a mother and her children, living in a £1,500,00 four-bedroom mews house which the council was renting at £1,125 a week – £58,500 a year.

In a bizarre contrast, Corporal Marcus Kilpatrick, 31, who served twelve years in the armed forces, including a stint in Afghanistan, was forced to set up home in the back of a Land Rover Discovery. Nearby, in the London borough of Ealing, could be found a family of eight Afghan migrants, housed by the council in a £1.2 million, seven-bedroom property, their annual rent of £170,000 being paid by the taxpayer.

Initiativitis

The government has a long list of initiatives aimed to pull children and families out of poverty, get people back to work, reduce household debt, and promote saving among the poorest.

There was the Universal Bank, by which benefit claimants would have accounts opened for them at post offices. Or the 2002 Child Trust Fund into which the government would put £500 to grow along with the children of poor families. But families are so confused by all these initiatives, that a quarter of them don't actually open an account and claim the cash.

Then there is the Savings Gateway, under which the government says it will match savings made by families on tax credits and other benefits. But pilot projects showed it did nothing to promote new savings. Most families on benefit don't have any spare cash to save.

The Stakeholder Pension has been equally disappointing. It was intended as a simple pension plan, free from the tax complexity of existing private pensions. But all it did was add a new level of complexity to the old system. Stakeholder Pensions are not bought by the poor, but by middle-class families for their children and grandchildren.

The latest cunning plan is Personal Accounts, which go live in 2012 and are supposed to be low-cost workplace-based pension accounts. But actuaries say that the bureaucracy of them will simply cause employers to close existing workplace schemes, many of which are better value. And true to government form, the cost of the scheme is already four times over budget, at £2 billion.

All these ideas emanate from an essentially middle-class Westminster elite who simply do not understand the problems of poorer families. The elite may see saving as a virtue, but most people on benefits have no money to salt away. And about a quarter of the population would be stark staring mad to save for a pension, because the more income they had in retirement, the more they would lose from their means-tested benefits. They are better to spend it all now.

The state pension

Frederic Bastiat described the state as the great fiction by which everyone tries to live at everyone else's expense. And the triumph of this great fiction is the state pension system. When Lloyd George brought it in, the pension was a form of emergency insurance against the rather unlikely risk of anyone reaching the age of 65, by which time they would probably be incapable of earning a living.

But now we all live to 100 or beyond. Or quite a few of us do. There are 11,580,000 folk over the pension age of 60 for women and 65 for men – just under a fifth (19 per cent) of the population. The fastest-growing age group is the over-80s, who number 2,700,000 – around 5 per cent of the population. The number of over-80s is expected to double to 4,900,000 within 25 years, and could be 7,000,000 by mid-century.

That would be fine if the state pension was on a sound financial footing. If the government invested our National

Insurance contributions, then there might be some future cash around when we retire. But in fact the system is a gigantic chain letter. The money that workers put in today is not invested to pay their future pensions. It is paid straight out again to today's pensioners. When you pay your contributions today, your only hope of getting a pension in the future is that the next generation will agree to join the chain letter and pay in tomorrow.

The state pension system shows how the get-now-pay-later principle on which government buy votes has been around for over a century. Lloyd George himself promised contributors that they would get out more than they put in – 'sixpence for fourpence' – an early example of government spin. For a time there really did seem to be an ambition to build up a proper investment fund; but as the payouts spiralled upwards, every pound of contributions went straight out again.

So far, the chain letter has worked. But in 2008, for the first time, the number of pensioners exceeded the number of children under 16. So quite who is going to be around to pay the pensions of the baby-boom generation is a worrying question.

Today the Department of Work and Pensions has to find £47 billion a year (and rising) to pay state pensioners. If the actuaries are right in predicting how long we're all going to live, that means that future governments will have to find about £1,200 billion to pay the pensions of everyone who is currently retired. That is the huge scale of the liability that a hundred years of chain-letter pensions has saddled us with.

Things would be even worse if the pension was higher, as it is in most of Europe. In Britain, the state pension is equivalent to just 17 per cent of average earnings, against an EU figure of 57 per cent of average earnings. Our retirement age is also one of Europe's highest. But that just means they have an even bigger funding gap for future generations to worry about.

In fact Britain's state pension is so low that, on its own, it leaves recipients below the poverty line. The government therefore created a means-tested benefit, the Pension Credit, to top up the incomes of the poorest pensioners. There are now 2.7 million pensioner households, some 3.3 million individuals, being paid an average £52 in Pension Credit. Many more are due it, but don't claim – about 1.8 million pensioners, who would get up to £1,500 a year each. If you saw the application forms, you would know why.

It is this means-tested benefit that makes saving irrational for around a quarter of the population. If you save throughout your lifetime, it does you absolutely no good at all, because you simply lose this means-tested benefit when you retire. Instead of encouraging thrift and self-reliance, the Pension Credit encourages profligacy and state dependency. It really is a rotten system.

Private pensions
Britain used to have an exceptionally successful system of private occupational pensions, based around the workplace, which helped millions of people escape poverty in retirement. Employers would pay part of each worker's salary into the company pension scheme. The funds would be managed by independent trustees, and would pay a pension when the employee retired – usually two-thirds of the worker's final salary. It was a very easy and popular way for workers to save: nearly everyone who had the opportunity to join a company pension scheme did so. By 1997, British had more money invested in these private pension schemes than the rest of Europe combined.

That is now all gone. The 97,900 work-based pension schemes that existed in 1997 have now shrunk to just 53,801 –

and falling. Of those, 18,990 no longer accept new members, 4,354 are frozen, and 1,779 are being wound up. Less than a third of the 1997 figure are still active and open to new employee members. By the end of 2007 there were about a million less active members of occupational pension schemes than there were just three years earlier. Less than half of those who work in the private sector are now paying into a pension. At the current rate of decline, there will be no contributors at all by 2020. The demise of this once-thriving savings sector is one reason why more and more people now face hard times when they retire.

The sole person responsible for this is Gordon Brown. It goes back to that announcement, of the ending of dividend credits on advance corporation tax, which Brown slipped into his first Budget speech in 1997.

Of course, most people hadn't the faintest idea what dividend credits on advance corporation tax were, so losing them didn't seem much of a big deal. And it was a week or two before pension experts finally got the media to cotton on. It was in fact a very big deal for the occupational pension funds, and the millions of workers who paid into them. Until then, pension funds had not paid tax on the dividends that were generated by their investments. Pension investments grew free of tax. Now they would start paying tax as they went along, which would mean that there would be a lot less in the pot when workers actually retired.

It was a typical Brown stealth tax – one that few people understood, and which fewer would even notice until they came to retire many years later. And it was big money – over £5 billion taken out of the pension funds in the first year alone, and more each year since then. Over the last dozen years, it amounts to a total of around £175 billion that has been taken out of the pockets of pension savers and put into the

Treasury's. That is equivalent to a tax of £16,600 on every private pension saver.

Treasury officials knew that this stealth tax would have a severe effect on the pension funds, and on the stock market too. Pension funds were large investors in British industry, but they had less money to do that after Brown's raid. Of course, Gordon Brown denied that he was ever given any such advice from his officials. But that proved to be a lie. In 2007, thanks to the Freedom of Information Act, Treasury correspondence was revealed, indicating precisely that.

By around 2001, when New Labour's public spending splurge was underway and the public finances were deteriorating, Brown was completely dependent on the billions that the new tax was bringing in. But he still wasn't finished. New rules were announced, supposedly to improve the financial solidity of pension funds and to make sure that they reported their liabilities in full. Known as FRS 17, they were not debated in Parliament, but simply announced in a Treasury circular. They loaded the trustees of company pension schemes with a huge amount of extra regulation and cost, including new solvency and disclosure rules. Solvency and disclosure rules, in fact, that the government's own pension schemes for public employees would never have any hope of passing.

The new rules accelerated the number of pension schemes that the tax changes were forcing into closure or collapse. Companies could not afford to maintain their pension funds; some went bankrupt, taking workers' pension promises with them. Some 125,000 people were left without any pensions savings at all.

A Financial Assistance Scheme was set up, and by mid 2007 it had paid out £4.6 million to the 1,200 people who were in this predicament and who had actually retired – though in typical fashion, the scheme cost more than that to run, £5.2

million. It is a sorry tale of political greed, deception and incompetence.

Public sector pensions

While the number of people with company pensions has plummeted, the number of people in public sector pension schemes is actually rising. There has been a rise of about a million in the number of civil servants that this government employs, and about ninety per cent of them have defined – benefit pension schemes – usually, again, providing a pension of two-thirds of their final salary – run by the government. Unlike the majority of private pensions, most of these pension benefits are indexed against inflation, which roughly doubles the cost of providing them.

Police, judges, Whitehall mandarins, BBC staff, teachers, firefighters – there are now about 5.2 million public employees who are members of some 313 separate schemes. The cost to taxpayers was £45 billion in 2008. (This is billions more than Brown estimated in his Budget three years earlier, which shows a degree of carelessness with our money.)

Indeed, private-sector workers now pay more to fund public pensions than they save into their own. And when it comes to retirement, the average private sector worker now retires with a pension pot – if they have one at all – worth £25,100, enough to fund a pension of about £1,700 a year. By contrast, the average public sector worker retires with ten times that – a pension of £17,091 a year.

The cost of public sector pensions pushes up the cost of public sector services. One reason why council tax is rising so fast, for example, is the cost of paying pensions to retired council officials. A large part of the taxes we pay for policing goes to pay the pensions of the 140,000 retired officers rather than the 165,000 serving ones. Some of Britain's biggest police forces – Lancashire, Leicestershire, the City of London, and Northern Ireland – actually pay out more in pensions than they do in salaries.

Civil servants pay just 3.5 per cent of their salaries into the civil service pension scheme, but the government pays a whopping 22 per cent on top. Thanks to all this taxpayers' largesse, a top civil servant, say the Permanent Secretary of the Department of Work and Pensions – the person in charge of paying married couples their pension of £198.45 a week – who has a salary of £158,929 (plus perks, of course) could expect to retire with an inflation-proof pension of £105,000 a year, for life, which is over ten times as much.

Nice work, if you can get it. Though of course in the private sector, you can't. Another of Gordon Brown's stealth taxes was to cap private sector pension funds at £1.5 million (rising to £1.8 million in 2010). Save more than that, and you pay punitive rates of tax. But with interest rates at their current levels, a pension pot of £1.5 million would buy you a pension about a quarter as generous as that enjoyed by a Permanent Secretary, and it wouldn't be indexed against inflation, either.

This is why the total liabilities of public sector pensions are something over £1,000 billion – the exact figure depends on how long our bureaucrats go on living. To his credit, the Pensions Secretary Alan Johnson attempted to reduce the size of this black hole by making public servants work until they were 68. But he was met with outrage and strike threats, and so quickly shelved the idea.

Another big cost in public sector pensions is their generous sickness provisions. About 20 per cent of private sector workers retire early on health grounds. In the public sector, nearly 70 per cent of firefighters do, along with 50 per cent of police officers and 25 per cent of doctors and teachers. But the whole thing is a scam on the public. Many public servants who

retire on full pension at age 50 get full-time work elsewhere –
or are even hired back as 'consultants' to do the same job.
Police officers facing investigation over their actions take early
retirement so that they are no longer open to questioning.
Virtually every teacher I know takes advantage of the
profession's generous sickness pensions to retire early – not
because the job has made them sick, but because the kids do.

If only our politicians would take the hint and all retire early
too.

13

SOCIETY

Our social benefits system does everything wrong. The politicians throw money at the very things we want less of, and seem to be surprised when they get more of them. Then they conclude that the answer must be to throw even more money at the problem. But it is the very fact that they are throwing so much money around that is the problem. The more we tax work and reward idleness, the more idleness we are likely to get.

It's not that people on welfare benefits are bad, feckless, or even workshy. Far from it. It's just that the brutal economics of our social benefits system does not help anyone to help themselves. The system traps people in unemployment and poverty, discourages prudence and saving, and treats people as cases rather than as human individuals.

This is why society is no more equal or mobile than in 1997, according to the most recent figures. Given the vast amounts spent on social infrastructure, tax credits, urban regeneration programmes, back-to-work schemes, parenting classes, and much else, that's a shameful result. The fact is that more people are in the very deepest poverty than there were in 1997, that millions of people of working age are claiming out-of-work benefits, and that the amount that taxpayers have to stump up to pay those working-age benefits has risen by a quarter.

Our social apartheid
Worse, our welfare state has created a social apartheid. National and local government housing policies have concentrated our poorer, workless, single-parent or problem families into grim urban estates and dismal, neglected inner-city areas.

It's a world that most of Britain never sees. The majority of people live in middle-class, sociable, stable families; they live in homes and communities they care for alongside neighbours who are much like them; and like their neighbours, they teach their children the habits of self-improvement, diligence, honesty, respect, thrift, moderation, and self-reliance. They know the names of places like White Hawk, Gorbals, North Peckham, Easterhouse, Toxteth, Moss Side, St. Pauls, or Handsworth only from the news reports of crime, or occasional rioting.

Our urban estates, in particular, have been turned into concentration camps of despair. Life there is completely different from what most middle-class families know. There you will more commonly find lone parents and single workless men, all living on benefits; problem families whose members cannot hold down a job; gangs and drug abuse; and decaying and untended buildings that depress the soul. The children who grow up there never learn the habits or advantages of work because they rarely meet friends or neighbours or even family members who have a job. A higher proportion of British children live in workless households than anywhere in Europe. Many of them will not know what it is like to have the role model of a loving, resident father.

It's not because their parents are lazy or unwilling to get work and stick together. It's because our social benefits system encourages them to do the exact opposite. Many people on benefits will be scarcely better off by getting a job, and by the time travel and other expenses are paid, some will be worse off. And fathers find they can make themselves better off by absenting themselves and leaving the welfare system to pay for the upkeep of their children and former partners. But the strain this puts on single mothers simply adds to the problems of debt and alcohol or drug abuse that are all too common in poor neighbourhoods.

Instead of teaching children self-esteem and self-help, our urban ghettos are passing dysfunction through the generations. Rootless families turn out children who cannot cope with social situations. They form street gangs rather than constructive social relationships. Their badge of honour is crime, bullying, violence – and what comes across to many people as sheer bloody rudeness. These symptoms of the disease are what middle-class Britain sees. But the cause of the infection is that sixty years of our rotten welfare state has created, not hope, opportunity and aspiration, but a forlorn, unsocialized underclass.

Family breakdown

The most malign effect of our welfare system is that it breaks up families. Tax credits are assessed on the income of both parents, which has the result that roughly three-quarters of the poorest households would be better off splitting up. And when money is tight, that is exactly what happens. The UK has the highest divorce rate in the Western world; though of course the rate of split-ups among unmarried partners is much greater still. One in twelve marriages will break up before the first child is five years old; half of cohabiting relationships will do so.

And the problem of family breakdown is much bigger than just the £20 billion or so that we spend on benefits to support children and lone parents. The real problem is the effect on the children themselves. Children who have suffered family breakdown, for example, are 75 per cent more likely to suffer educational failure. They are more likely to have mental problems and drift into crime, or alcohol and drug abuse – all of which puts a heavy burden on both them and on the rest of society.

The welfare benefit support that stems from having dependent children has become more significant for lone parent families over recent decades. It now provides just under a third of the disposable income of lone parent families – compared to just a tenth of the disposable income of an average couple with children. So – as fathers who split from their partners know and take advantage of – it is perfectly possible for lone mothers with children to survive.

It's possible, but not easy. Household debt has become a huge problem in Britain. It is not just those middle-class households who have run up rather a lot on their credit cards. There are around four million people with serious debt problems, and many of those are in the poorest households, single parents or families on social benefits, who struggle to manage their budgets. Personal debt in Britain is the highest in the world, and it is higher now than ever before.

The effect on children

The family dysfunction that our welfare system promotes manifests itself in other ways too. Serial partnerships, which the system encourages, produce confused family relationships that cause real identity problems for children. My local school used to send out admissions forms that had simply two spaces for the names of the parents. Now the same form has five spaces for the names and addresses of any adult who might conceivably have some interest in the child as a result of the natural parents drifting in and out of different relationships.

And the form advises applicants to use an extra sheet of paper if there are more than five. It may be a wise child who knows its own father, but many children today must struggle to understand their family structure at all.

It is not surprising that such rootless relationships add to the problem of domestic violence – almost one million children are thought to live in such circumstances – and the abuse of alcohol and drugs. It seems that we have succeeded in brutalizing a generation. As parents fight, or feed their addiction, children become neglected or abused, families split, and the children get taken into care. Indeed the numbers in care have risen by a fifth over the last decade, to 60,000, though the numbers of 'children in need' who receive local-authority support of some form are five times higher still.

But being in care is not the same as being in a loving natural family. The statistics make depressing reading. Children in care are four times more likely to have mental health issues. Children who have been in care are more likely to abuse drugs, more likely to abuse alcohol, and more likely to have problems at school. Girls who leave care are four times more likely to fall pregnant within the first year. People who have been in care account for a third of Britain's homeless, a third of children in custody, and a quarter of the adult prison population.

And even the financial cost is alarming. With millions of people out of work and on benefits, millions of lone parents, millions of people in debt, perhaps a million of those in really deep poverty, possibly eight million people with serious drug or alcohol problems, the cost to the taxpayer is not far short of £100 billion.

Drug and alcohol addiction
Despite the best anti-drug efforts of the government of Columbia and the United Nations in Afghanistan, the price of

cocaine and heroin is falling. So too is the price of alcohol – at least in supermarkets, though not in our over-regulated pubs. But this is only one reason why the problems of drug and alcohol addiction are spreading, and not the main one: alcohol is far cheaper in France, and cannabis can be bought legally and cheaply in the Netherlands, but they have a mere fraction of the addiction problems that we have.

There are an estimated 280,000 problem drug users in Britain, mostly users of heroin or crack cocaine. Drug abuse accounts for around 2,500 deaths a year. Around a quarter or a third of a million children (nobody knows for sure) are living with parents who abuse drugs, and many more live with parents who have problems with alcohol. These things may themselves be the results of family breakdown; but they exacerbate it too. And children who, as a result, are taken into care are much more likely to abuse drugs and alcohol. Nearly three-quarters (73 per cent) admit to smoking cannabis, a third (34 per cent) of those daily; a tenth (10 per cent) say they have used heroin or crack cocaine within the last month; and nearly one in six (15 per cent) say they have used ecstasy in the last month.

Britain's standard treatment for heroin addiction – to prescribe the substitute methadone – isn't working. We give addicts 1.8 million doses of it, at a cost in 2006 of £22 million. But it is also a nasty drug, arguably more addictive than heroin. Many heroin addicts avoid it as being even worse than what they are on. It doesn't help people to beat their problem. Addicts can be on it for years – 97 per cent are still being prescribed it five years on – when what most addicts say is that they really want to get off drugs altogether.

Addicts who are treated in residential rehabilitation centres are far more likely to kick the habit. Almost 30 per cent are drug-free three years later. The Netherlands, where the choice for addicts is either jail or rehabilitation, has a third of the problem we have. Zurich has seen an 82 per cent fall in addiction in a decade by giving addicts injectable heroin in designated clinics. The drug has now become medicalized and has lost its old glamour. Addiction is now regarded as a health problem, not a badge of honour.

Prescribing methadone, which costs around £6,000 a year, looks much cheaper than the £15,000 cost of prescribing heroin. But addicts will be on it for longer, and heroin users do not readily volunteer to step forward for treatment when that is the main option on offer. Therefore the cycle of addiction, debt, social breakdown, domestic violence, and crime simply widens further. A typical addict has to steal property worth £45,000 or more to feed the habit for a year. So the social cost of this short-sighted and inhumane form of treatment is high.

Inadequate support for children

Meanwhile, those we rely on to support the distressed children that our rotten system has created are themselves under-valued and under-supported. Only a third (34 per cent) of foster carers say that they are satisfied with the quality and nature of the assistance that they receive from local authorities.

Nearly three-fifths (59 per cent) of people who had been in care as children say they felt that their social workers didn't really care about them, and almost as many (58 per cent) believed that their social workers were poorly equipped or trained for the job they had to do.

For sheer bureaucratic incompetence it is hard to beat the dismal case of Victoria Climbié, an eight-year-old girl from the Ivory Coast, who was abused and in 2000 finally murdered by her guardians in North London. Although the local police, hospitals, and Haringey social services departments noted the signs of abuse, the information was never properly coordinated, and the case was never properly investigated.

The case was so shocking that a £4 million public inquiry was set up to review how Haringey council and other public bodies could have missed the warning signs that led up to Victoria's death. The inquiry heard a depressing catalogue of mistakes and bad practice. The social services staff hid difficult cases from the social services inspectorate; many families who needed their help were turned away; money had been diverted from social services into higher-profile, vote-winning programmes such as education; and Metropolitan Police resources were diverted from child protection to the high-profile murder of Stephen Lawrence.

The inquiry found that there was no joined-up information between welfare and health services; social services departments were under-staffed and badly managed; restructurings had paralyzed Haringey's child protection functions; staff were poorly trained and were overworked. It was a catalogue of systematic failure and incompetence.

The government responded to the inquiry with several initiatives, including the Every Child Matters programme, the Children Act 2004, the ContactPoint project, the creation of a Children's Commissioner, and the new database holding information on all children in England and Wales.

The former deputy leader of Haringey council, Ian Willmore, was sceptical about what good any of this might do. The script for such inquiries, he said, is 'almost traditional': ministers demand action, everyone agrees that lessons have been learned, but essential changes'.

They certainly did not change to any effect in Haringey social services, which were back in the news in November 2008 following the death of the 17-month-old boy 'Baby P' from multiple injuries inflicted in his home, including eight broken ribs and a broken back. Yet this boy had been well known to social workers. He had been on the child protection register for seven months and was seen about twice a week by health or social workers. His natural father went off and, unknown to the authorities, his mother was now living with another man, who (along with another male friend) violently abused the boy. A judge said social workers were too trusting in taking the mother's assurances that the toddler was just clumsy and kept stumbling into things.

Even after a £4 million inquiry and a dozen new laws or initiatives since 1997, some 29,000 children are on the national register of children at risk, and still one child dies at the hands of a parent or guardian each week – 450 since the Victoria Climbié case. Children from dysfunctional families like these are 33 times more likely to suffer violent abuse. Nothing has changed. Nor is it even likely to, until we change the system that creates the dysfunctionality in the first place.

Educational failure

The one time when the middle classes do get to see the existence of the human dustbins that the state welfare system has created is when their contents spill out onto the streets. Socially, their leafy suburbs are a million miles from the problem estates, but as they go about their business they cannot escape seeing the gangs of youths, crime, drunkenness, drug abuse, and rudeness.

They see it in the disruptive pupils who stop their own children from learning and make teachers' lives a misery (that's why teachers all retire at the first possible opportunity). At one time, disruptive children were removed, in an attempt to educate them separately where, again, the middle classes didn't see them. Now a politically correct idea of social inclusion puts them in the same classes as other children. The theory was that the example of being surrounded by other children who were willing and keen to learn might socialize and reform them. In fact, the experience is that it takes only one disruptive child to break up a lesson and prevent the whole class from learning anything at all. School finance officers love it, because these children all come with generous Special Educational Needs funding. But teachers hate it and are frustrated by it, as are parents.

Should we press on with the policy, in the hope that classroom inclusion might indeed turn around the lives of such children? Should we, as David Cameron famously didn't say, hug a hoodie?

The reality is that by the time some disturbed children get to school, it is already too late. Family breakdown, rootless relationships, neglect, domestic violence, debt and addiction all too often produce kids that are not properly socialized in their critical early years and from then on are unsocial and impossible to socialize. It has even got to the stage where more than 1,500 children under five are now suspended from school each year for disruptive behaviour, including physical assaults on teachers and fellow pupils.

When I was a state secondary school governor, the collective agreement of my colleagues, based on long experience, was that when pupils' behaviour was so bad that the school had to exclude them, we might as well have told the Home Office to reserve them a jail place in ten years time. It was a shocking indictment of the system.

That is the measure of our failure. Children in care are the lowest achievers of any social group, and despite more than £1,000 million being spent on them in the last decade, less than one-eighth are able to obtain five or more GCSEs at grade C or above, compared to nearly two-thirds of pupils overall. Of pupils whose family income is low enough to entitle them to free school meals, just under one-fifth (19.5 per cent) get five good GCSEs. And schools with high proportions of children on free school meals are nearly three times more likely to be scored as under-performing by the schools inspector, Ofsted.

Lack of skills and worklessness

It all means that a third of adults in Britain today have left school with no meaningful school leaving qualifications at all – double the proportion of, say, Germany. Without useful qualifications, it is hard for school leavers to find work. Teenage unemployment is up by a third over the 1997 figure: there are 230,000 16-18s not in education, employment, or training, and three-quarters of a million more in their early 20s. Too many school leavers find themselves unqualified, unable to get a job, and then trapped in poverty from which the New Deal and other state programmes cannot save them. They become yet more chronic victims of our state welfare system.

For one thing, they find that employers don't regard them as worth the minimum wage that they are forced to pay. Over half of firms in the Confederation of British Industry (53 per cent) say they cannot find people with adequate skills. Only 28 per cent of British workers are qualified up to apprentice, skilled craft or technical level, compared to over half (51 per cent) in France and two-thirds (65 per cent) in Germany.

Naturally, the politicians' predictable answer is to set up a quango to tackle the problem. Mrs Thatcher's Employment Secretary, Lord Young, did just that by setting up the Manpower Services Commission in the 1980s. It was huge and costly, and it was billed as a welfare-to-work programme. But its real function was simply to give young people some of the skills that the state school system should have taught them in the first place – but didn't. Gordon Brown's equivalent was the Learning and Skills Council, set up in 2001. Among other things, it funds Further Education colleges: but despite the skills shortage, the numbers of people enrolling in those has actually fallen by quarter of a million since 1997, to 745,000 – largely because they aim at a narrow range of target qualifications which demand long courses, which is not what people without skills actually want or need.

Then we were going to have 'Modern Apprenticeships'. The 2003 Budget promised 320,000 such places by 2006. But in reality only two-thirds of that number were created. Now the government says it wants to have 400,000 new apprentice places by 2020, which looks like yet more spin without substance. There is also 'Train to Gain' – subsidies to employers for training staff over the age of 26. It was rolled out in 2006, with a budget rising to over £1,000 million in 2010. But much of the programme is just about ticking boxes – confirming on a questionnaire the skills that people already have. It takes an average 33 hours of training to be awarded a Train to Gain qualification, but the majority of contact time is spent on assessment – box ticking-rather than training. And around 90 per cent of the money is thought to subsidize training that employers would have undertaken anyway, even without the state subsidy.

Crime and the fear of crime

People in the UK fear crime more than most other countries – much more so than in the United States, for example. Knife crime is spreading and illegal handguns are rife. But crime is highest where people are poorest: the twenty poorest local authorities suffer three times the crime of the twenty richest. And again, it is the children and young adults who have suffered family breakdown who are most likely to be involved in crime. Just six children in a thousand are in care, but those who have been in care account for around half of the twelve thousand under-21s who come into contact with the criminal justice system. It's just like the schools: by the time children appear before the justice system, it is already too late to help them.

Many of these young people will go on to be repeat offenders. Just 4 per cent of young offenders account for 70 per cent of the spending by the Youth Justice Board. Many of them will be sent to Young Offenders Institutions, whose appalling record on rehabilitation, education and welfare does nothing to improve matters. Within a year, 92 per cent of them will offend again.

And public budget considerations get in the way of humane policy. It's cheaper for local authorities if children in care who offend are actually put in jail. And that is exactly why so many young people end up that way. We lock up more children than any country in Western Europe. It all helps to explain why the youth justice budget, at £495 million, is up by 20 per cent over 1979, and why the cost of criminal justice and policing have all soared too.

We are spiralling round the drain of dysfunction. Our welfare system traps people in poverty; it encourages families to break up; kids go into care; they are inadequately supported; they fail at school; they cannot get a job, even if they wanted one; the New Deal and other government initiatives do not help; they fall back on benefits; and they enter into casual relationships that produce yet more children whose prospects are little different.

Gang culture

About the only place where young people in this position can enjoy any status or respect is in the hard street culture of gangs.

In 2008, more than fifteen teenagers died violently in gang violence in London alone. And even the general public get caught up in such violence. In 2003, Marcia Shakespeare, 17, and Charlene Ellis, 18, were caught in the crossfire when a gun battle broke out between two Birmingham gangs. Two other 18-year-old girls were injured.

The death of 31-year-old lawyer Tom ap Rhys Price near his home in Kensal Green, London, brought this home to the general public even more starkly, since he was also an innocent member of the public, but was deliberately murdered. In January 2006, on his way home from work, he was chased and stabbed in the back by two youths, aged 17 and 19. It was reported as robbery, though only his mobile phone and his Oyster card (used to travel on London's buses and Underground network) were stolen. But these items were not very valuable financially. They were much more valuable as trophies – something that could be shown around as a statement of the assailants' hardness.

(In another incident, a cousin of one of the murderers was jailed for life for the point-blank shooting of a 27-year-old man who 'showed disrespect' to members of Mus Luv Crew, his Harlesden gang.)

Tom ap Rhys Price's murder caused particular shock to middle-class Britain for two reasons. First was the thought that it could happen to anyone. This was an ordinary person, going home from work, after all, and murdered just yards from his front door.

Second was that they could not understand how his killers could show not the slightest remorse for what they had done. But on the streets, emotions such as remorse, sympathy or consideration get you killed. Kids who have never been socialized fall into gangs with others who have none of the normal social skills either. Empathy unnerves them; remorse does not come naturally at all. Their bond comes, not from getting close, but on the contrary from being prepared to back off, leave alone, show 'respect' and so confirm each other's status.

Lack of respect?

That kind of bond doesn't depend on the social grooming, the iterative and coherent conversation, the little courtesies that help bond the society of the middle-class majority. And perhaps some of this seemingly uncouth way of acting has spilt over into the general public, especially among teenagers – who may be perfectly law-abiding but are naturally rather unsure of their status and anxious to protect it.

According to surveys by the genteel Polite Society, nearly 90 per cent of people in Britain think we are generally ruder than we were a decade ago. More than half believe that bad manners are the biggest problem in the country today and blame parents for not stamping it out. Three-quarters (73 per cent) think that manners should be taught in school. A 2008 survey for Bernardo's found that 54 per cent of us think children now behave like animals, and 40 per cent think that adults need protection from them.

One of society's most persistent myths is that our children are more rude, feckless, violent, and unsocial than we ever were. It goes back at least to Aristotle, and was just as wrong then. In Richard II, which I was forced to read at school – luckily, the experience didn't quite put me off Shakespeare – Henry Bolingbroke asks the whereabouts of his 'unthrifty son', and suggests trawling the taverns that the youth and his 'dissolute crew' of 'loose companions' frequent. Yet this same 'wanton' and 'effeminate' boy grew up to be Henry V and defeated the French at Agincourt. I remember being pretty insufferable to my parents too, but I like to think I still turned out all right.

Two things have changed, though. First, prior to the creation of the welfare state, we did not actually encourage family breakdown and personal irresponsibility by means of a dysfunctional benefits system. Indeed, we did the opposite. Marriage was applauded – for most women there was no other feasible way to raise a family – and divorce was thought deeply shocking. Certainly, that was a highly restrictive social ethic that trapped many adults in unhappy relationships; but at least it gave their kids the chance to grow up in something resembling a stable family home, with parents who loved them even if they didn't love one another. It meant that we weren't actually spreading a plague of disturbed, disaffected, unsocialized kids whose only solace and status is found in street gangs, casual violence, and a shared contempt for the weakness of the socialized majority.

Second, we find these things more threatening than we did. Officials tell us not to intervene when we see things that are wrong, because it could be unsafe. To some extent they have a point: in September 2008 the senior banker Frank McGarahan was kicked to death when he went to the aid of a homeless man who was being picked on by a gang of youths in Norwich. But much of it stems from officialdom's desire to prove to us that they are indispensible. So they leave in our minds the suggestion that getting involved in even the most minor incident – rebuking a teenager for dropping litter or insulting someone, for example, is dangerous and best left to the experts.

Fearing fear itself
This tough talk on crime – and even on anti-social behaviour – has the opposite effect of that intended. It just convinces us not to be good citizens because it makes us fear for our lives. It's meant to reassure us that our political leaders are doing something, but in fact it just makes us even more worried about the seriousness of the problem. The politicians have succeeded in increasing the fear of crime even beyond its shocking reality.

Like all kids of their generation, my son and his pals used to go round in hoodies. I asked him whether old ladies crossed the road when they saw them coming. Not just old ladies, he replied; grown men would step out of their path too. None of these boys would hurt a fly, of course. Each of them were studious kids who are now all enjoying life in some of Britain's better universities. They were just following the fashion. But people feared them, because the politicians' rhetoric of toughness has not reassured us that crime is being dealt with. It has just scared us into imagining that crime is everywhere, and that anyone in a hoodie must be a thug and that two people in hoodies constitute a gang of thugs.

Well, they might be, just as any middle-aged man might be a paedophile, something else we have been made disproportionately worried about. But the chances are against. In the 1990s, my elderly mother, who was almost blind, always used to say that if you wanted help crossing the road, the most obliging people were the skinheads.

Characteristically, the politicians have been attacking the symptoms of the problem, not its cause. In doing that, they make it worse. But until we replace our rotten, means-tested, rights-driven welfare system, we will never stop the steady growth of social dysfunction.

14

VALUES

In the cult 1960s television series The Prisoner, Patrick McGoohan plays an agent in some secret government organization, who has a row with his bosses and wakes up next morning in a kind of fantasy village. It's a place where everyone is known by number (his is Number 6), not names. Nobody knows or imagines anything outside The Village – as the place is called. The maps don't even show anything beyond it.

It's always a beautiful day in The Village. Everything there is benign, and faultless harmony prevails. Spontaneous parades and events take place all the time, and everyone seems keen to participate in them. But Number 6 just doesn't fit in. He does not see why he should follow the strange rules and rituals of the others. He sees no merit in the strange things they think important. One of them chastises him: 'You have no values.' He responds tersely: 'Different values.'

The analogy with Britain today is chilling. Everyone is expected to fit in, to conform, and to rejoice in their conformity. Those who do not conform are thought immoral, and are scorned or vilified. But who is more bizarre? Those who follow the mainstream conventions imposed on us by the myopic political correctness of officialdom and the state? Or those who regard that as shallow and dysfunctional, and prefer to trust values based on experience and common sense? As

Britain's values become subverted by the trite, dysfunctional, and bizarre values of the Westminster Village, I begin to feel for Number 6.

Formalizing Britain's informal networks

A sea change has come over British society. Values do of course change as circumstances change; and it is entirely right that they should evolve in this way. But the values that society has painstakingly evolved over years of experience are now being replaced by the values of the political clique. They seem to believe that their own narrow wisdom is better than that of millions of individuals whose ideas and values and conventions are tested every day. They are replacing values that, from experience, we know work with values that simply make their authors look good.

A society that could deal spontaneously with anything that life threw at it is being fast replaced by one that always has to look up to the state to know what to do and how to act. This in turn makes it incapable of correcting the dysfunctional mess that this very system causes.

Take, for example, the institutions of social care. Britain is full of people who would like to help children and others in difficult circumstances – by working with them, caring for them, even adopting them. Indeed, politicians praise this voluntary sector: they recognize it as something genuine, unlike their own efforts to connect with the real public.

But when people do try to help others, they find obstacles put in their path. They have to sign up for the state's entire rulebook of health and safety regulations and Criminal Records Bureau checks for anyone who comes within sight of a child under sixteen. The politicians want to capture the voluntary sector's more flexible, more personal, more targeted, more efficient way of caring for others. But by the time the voluntary sector has signed up to all the state's rules – ticked all the state's boxes, passed the state police checks, had all the state's inspections, and followed all the state's equal opportunities guidelines on age, sex, ethnicity, and sexual orientation – it becomes no different from the state bureaucracy itself.

Instead, we have simply nationalized voluntary social care. We have formalized networks that only work if they are informal and based on natural human feeling, rather than on a list of rights and procedures. We have eaten the soul out of the voluntary sector by making it merely an agent of the state and a servant of the official values of the political clique.

Today, more and more kids sign up for voluntary work in their gap years. But they don't do it principally because they simply want to benefit society and have time to spare for it. They do it because they know it will look good on their personal statement when they apply to university. We have created a gap year volunteering industry, not a thriving and useful voluntary sector driven by the natural public spirit of young people.

Companies too tick their corporate responsibility boxes, and produce their annual corporate social responsibility reports, as the regulations require. They do what officialdom demands they do, not what their owners, managers, customers, suppliers or workers believe is actually right. This too has become its own self-sustaining industry. It attracts staff who are focused on complying with the regulation, not staff who bring entrepreneurial flair and innovation to the task of running a business both profitably and responsibly.

Imposing bureaucratic values

This top-down imposition of values from on high leaves us with a set of rules that are applied to everyone, bureaucratically and inflexibly. It smothers the evolutionary process that works through, and indeed promotes, a diversity of different approaches that, between them, can solve our problem.

An example of the inflexible bureaucratic mind was the rule that Catholic adoption agencies should be forced to consider homosexual couples as adoptive parents, even though most Catholics believe that homosexuality is a sin. So more kids languish without loving families because of an ideological point of political correctness, a rule from which there are to be no exceptions. Why instead can we not just accept that different people, and different religions, have different views on these things, and work with that diversity, rather than trying to outlaw it?

What makes this politically correct intolerance all the more remarkable is that councils go to great lengths to place adopted children with people of the same ethnicity. This again can cause lengthy delays while suitable parents are found. It seems Catholics are supposed to be blind to sexual orientation, while councils themselves are not blind to colour. Councils maintain that a sense of ethnicity is important to a child; Catholics maintain that having parents of the opposite sex is too. Who's to say one is right and one is wrong?

But the political intolerance goes further than this. Many middle-class white couples, in particular, feel that they miss out on adoption because of it. Certainly, many such couples do manage to adopt – over 3,700 in 2007. But many others say that local authorities reject them for being 'too posh'. One couple some years ago discovered that social workers objected to them as potential adoptive parents because they had 'too many books' in the house. After delays and frustration, many such couples end up adopting from abroad.

Others think they are rejected for being 'too white'. But then Barak Obama, the President of the United States, had a black Kenyan father and was brought up by his white mother and grandparents; and he did pretty well.

. The latest political correctness sees councils rejecting adoptive parents if they are smokers. It's true that smoking does not benefit the physical health of a young child. But languishing in an institution, or being shunted from one foster home to another, does even more harm to a child's mental health. Like many of my generation, I was raised by parents who smoked heavily; but I'm glad that I had the benefit of their loving, stable home. No doubt council officials will soon be snooping through people's dustbins to see whether they drink more than 21 units of wine a week or take the Daily Mail. But people are just different. The political clique should get over it: the kids do.

Misunderstanding discrimination

America is a melting pot. People are rightly proud of their ethnic roots, but don't consider them an obstacle to integration. They sink their differences into a greater ideal that everyone shares. In Britain, the state imposes on us the rules of values of multiculturalism – that people of all cultures have a perfect right to live and work alongside each other. That is of course correct: and, left to themselves, most different cultures can work out the compromises by which they can coexist.

The problem comes when, in typical bureaucratic fashion, it moves from being a desirable value to being an inflexible rule. Attempting to treat all ages, sexes and races equally as if their differences were of no importance or interest, the state has made itself ageist, sexist and racist. Public bodies spend vast bureaucratic time and effort on checking the age, sex, and ethnicity of those they employ. And of the people who use their services. And of the suppliers who take their money to provide them with goods or services, or sign any kind of contract with them. Everyone that they deal with gets sucked into their vortex of discrimination.

The fact is that people do indeed discriminate, and in most circumstances this is perfectly natural and harmless. Young men, by and large, pick out young women as their life partners. Black, white, and Asian men tend to prefer black, white and Asian women. But the bureaucratic state applies the same rules in all situations, as if there was harm and malice in everything. If the state were in charge of the dating process we'd all have to fill out a checklist proving that we had tried both sexes and all ages and races, and sign a declaration that our final choice was not based on any of these things.

But this is exactly what we are being required to do more and more. None of us want to see people passed over for jobs solely because of their ethnicity. We would all prefer it if employers were colour-blind, and took people on merit. But the bureaucratic solution is precisely to insist that people are passed over on the basis of their ethnicity – or other characteristics – precisely to benefit those who are seen as the minority. Very few men want to become midwives, and few women in childbirth want a male midwife: should we really force the issue and have quotas to get the numbers of male midwives up to fifty percent?

Again, the bureaucratic mind infects the rest of society too. People are given jobs, not solely on the basis of their ability, but on the basis of their age, or their sex, or their race. Employers have to do that, so that they can prove how even-handed they are and not get caught by the discrimination rules. In other words, to stay within the anti-discrimination rules, they have to discriminate.

And of course, anyone who is a supplier to the public sector, or a customer of it, or who is regulated or subsidized by it, now finds themselves having to tick the same boxes. And since, in industrial tribunals, the burden of proof is shifted on to employers to show that they have not in fact been guilty of discrimination – another huge erosion of three hundred years of legal protections – it is no surprise that they tick furiously.

This positive discrimination causes a huge amount of resentment – and not just from better-qualified people who are passed over so some equality box can be ticked. It also irritates many people who are themselves in the privileged minority, who would really prefer to prove themselves in an equal and open contest, not one that is skewed in their favour. They would like their colleagues and the public they deal with to know that they were there on merit, and not just because they happened to fill some ethnic quota.

Positive discrimination is still discrimination. In the recent past, it may have had a temporary benefit in terms of forcing a change of entrenched attitudes in a world that was changing fast. But as a long-term way of running your country it has nothing to commend it, and can only help to deepen tensions.

Distortion of institutions

Yet this is precisely what is happening in some of the most important parts of the state. Take, for example, the magistrates system. It's impossible to find magistrates who exactly represent the local community in their attitudes to keeping the peace. So traditionally the selection of magistrates has reflected a broad party balance, which in turn probably reflects local attitudes to crime and punishment. But of course the magistrates tended to be white, middle-aged and middle class. So now there is an active effort to get a new balance, based on age, sex, and race. This, however, doesn't reflect local attitudes to crime in the slightest: people of the same age, or sex, or race are not homogeneous groups who are equally tough or equally tender – or who necessarily share any political or social attitudes at all. All it does is impose an official value system on the selection of magistrates, one which does not help get to grips with local crime in the slightest.

Take another example. The politicians have at last recognized that much of the unsocial behaviour of wayward children is down to bad parenting. So what is their solution? Not to reform the social benefits system that makes bad parents out of otherwise good people: the only opportunity to do that was lost when Frank Field was fired as welfare minster in 1998. No, it is 'parenting classes', organized by the state.

It's amazing that anyone should believe a sort of classroom course on parenting could have the slightest effect on our problems. It certainly did not help in the case of Baby P. But it is fully in line with the middle-class, metropolitan view of family life that is shared by Westminster's politicians and civil servants. And who exactly will be running these courses? It will be civil servants, and a particular kind of civil servant at that – civil servants who are completely comfortable in promulgating all the attitudes and values that are deemed politically acceptable. Once again, support that should be delivered spontaneously by concerned friends and neighbours has been hijacked by ideological professionals.

When good practice becomes inflexible law

There is a pattern to all these nanny-state interventions. In all areas of life, there are good standards that people strive for, even if they are not always met. These are made into a formal code of practice, which people are urged to achieve. They then become items on an official checklist, where your failure to tick all the boxes puts you at risk of some penalty. This in turn becomes the law, and you are fined or imprisoned for any deviation from it at all. Before long we'll all be facing spot fines for not changing our kids' underwear every day.

You can see it unfolding before your very eyes. Under a draft code stemming from the Animal Welfare Act 2006, pet owners are advised not to give dogs chocolate, raisins or grapes, or to allow them to beg at the table, or to get fat; while cats should be kept out of washing machines and given somewhere to scratch. We are told that this is just 'guidance' and that breaching the code will not be a crime. But doing so could prove to be the deciding factor in whether you are found guilty in court of pet welfare offences.

It's clear where this is going. My grandfather was a gamekeeper and dog trainer; I've always lived around dogs and I hate to see them being treated cruelly. But a dog is only a dog. I'd really prefer that friends, neighbours and newspapers give people advice on how to treat their pets, rather than have a law which can imprison you for six months or fine you £20,000 on the 'deciding factor' that you fed your pooch a square of Fruit & Nut. It's the usual story: if you give state officials the powers, they will use them. They might say that they're going to use surveillance only in the worst terrorist cases, but then they're using CCTV to check whether you left your bin open four inches or put the wrong things in your recycling box.

The shame is that through the animal welfare legislation, the government had the chance to prevent real animal cruelty. But they blew it on this nonsense. They could have had our trust and cooperation in the fight against crime and terrorism too, but they've blown that by the heavy-handed way in which they use their powers against us.

The loss of decency

If Britain stands for any single virtue, it must be tolerance. But this is corroded by the imposition on us of rules and values from above. We want to live in a world where people get along without causing upset or insult to each other. But people are different, and often, conflicts do arise. Traditionally, we have dealt with such conflicts through tolerance and mutual respect. We may not agree with what each of us say, but we respect the other's point of view, we compromise, and we work out ways of dealing with and cooperating with each other. And that is what makes a diverse society able to function.

To some extent conflict is the inevitable result of diversity: and diversity is one of the most important drivers of social change and development. It's an unfortunate symptom of something that is both great and positive. But conflict doesn't sit easily in the middle-class mind of politicians and officials. They seek to outlaw it entirely. And in so doing, of course, they repress the diversity that makes human life work – and makes it so enjoyable, stimulating, and productive.

So primary schools have cancelled their traditional nativity plays in case non-Christians take umbrage. Office parties are a rarity, since employers fear they may be taken as religious discrimination, and worry that they will be held responsible for any sexual or other harassment that might occur (and that tipsy staff who have accidents on the way home will sue them). Councils rename the Christmas holidays 'Winterval' and advise councillors not to eat snacks in front of Muslim colleagues during the fast of Ramadan.

I can see the point of rules to protect people's safety. But laws to protect against their hurt feelings? People have to recognize their differences and work out such conflicts between themselves. It is no place for the state to intervene with its clumsy rules. If rules and regulations tell us exactly how to behave with others, we will never learn, responsibly, how to get along together. When we find ourselves in circumstances that the rules don't cover, we will not know what to do. This is a way of heightening, not reducing, tensions.

Less than glittering

The way that these top-down rules and values come about shows just how political, rather than practical, they are. If politicians really cared much about crime, for example, they would throw resources at rehabilitation, to try to reform the few persistent offenders who are responsible for much of it. But no: their indignation and their rules are all designed to show how active and how tough they are at tackling some supposed social menace.

When Gary Glitter – former glam rocker and convicted paedophile – was released from a Vietnamese jail and deported, the reaction of the then Home Secretary Jacqui Smith was comically predictable. She announced a package of 'tough' new measures on sex offenders. They would face more stringent police monitoring. Restrictions on their travelling abroad would be extended. They might even have their passports confiscated.

It seems that when even the humblest sparrow falls, the government feels compelled to announce some new initiative about the problem, and so convince us all that they're on top of it.

And what does it matter if they haven't bothered to think it out beforehand? The UK's restrictions on sex offenders are already some of the world's 'toughest'. Why do they need re-visiting again? Did the Home Secretary get it all wrong the last time? And since only 1 per cent of offenders go on to commit another serious sex crime, aren't the current measures pretty effective? If it's 'evidence-based policy' you're after, that's pretty good evidence.

Harassing innocent people

Ministers compete to demonstrate their outrage against human sex trafficking. But the rules they put in place on it are just used to harass innocent people. The last set of laws did nothing to find any traffickers, but they caused a lot of aggravation to prostitutes, who are easy victims for police in pursuit of targets.

In high-profile raids, like the one on a Birmingham sauna in 2005, the police proudly proclaimed to have 'saved' innocent girls from traffickers. Some were indeed here illegally, but none had been forced, as very few are: prostitutes just prefer to work away from home and where the money's better.

So in November 2008 Ms Smith (she of the 'porn on expenses' scandal) announced that the law would get even tougher in the hope of finding someone to prosecute. It's going to be men who use prostitutes 'controlled' by another person. Bizarrely, the announcement came within a week of the Metropolitan Police closing down their human trafficking unit, so the cops must think there are better things to do. No doubt the new law will again hit the easy targets – clients of girls in clean, safe saunas where the girls are actually protected by a manager.

So a perfectly voluntary trade will be forced deeper underground, which is where its bad effects are more likely to occur. Not that the politicians mind: they regard prostitution as like boozing and smoking – something they disapprove of, and which other people should therefore be stopped from doing. That's despite the fact that they throw large numbers of asylum seekers into prostitution by forbidding them to get a job and telling them they are not entitled to benefits. What kind of a system of values is this?

Perversion of human rights
It was not surprising that in 1948, after the horrors of the Second World War, European nations adopted a Convention on Human Rights. It was an affirmation of basic rights – such as not being rounded up and killed because you happen to be

Jewish. Such liberties were already well established in Britain, most of them for hundreds of years, thanks to Magna Carta, civil war, common law and the parliamentary tradition. But in an effort to show what good Europeans we were, the Blair government decided to sign up to this new version with the Human Rights Act 1998.

Ten years later, the cost of this legislation is reckoned to be £100 million a year, and over a thousand human rights lawyers live off the back of the Act and the Legal Aid money that is given to fight cases under it. But too many of the 4000 cases that have come up under the legislation are a perversion of what most of us would recognize as human rights.

For example, in February 2000, a plane was hijacked in Afghanistan and flown to Stansted Airport. The nine hijackers and their relatives were simply fleeing the Taliban and wanted asylum in Britain, so they were soon taken off the plane and arrested. But Britain has always been tough on resisting hijacks, and you might think the standard policy would be to put them on the next plane back to Kabul. But the courts gave them indefinite leave to stay, in case they came to harm from the Taliban back in Afghanistan. That was even though British troops were supposed to be in charge of the place.

In May 2008 Abu Qatada, a Muslim cleric, was released on bail from Belmarsh prison, where he had been held as a threat to national security. The courts ruled that he could face execution if deported back to his home country, Jordan. He sounds exactly the sort of character who should be sent home, but the Human Rights Act stopped it.

But it's not just the risk of execution that lets unsavoury characters stay in Britain under the human rights legislation. In November 2008, the courts ruled that a man whose dangerous driving had killed a student here could not be sent back to Pakistan because it would part him from his family life in

Britain – despite the fact that he was here illegally. In August 2007 Learco Chindamo, who murdered teacher Philip Lawrence outside his school in Maida Vale, London, was also given the right to remain in Britain when his jail time was up, because his ties were mostly in Britain rather than his native Italy. Mr Lawrence's widow was naturally upset. And a St. Kitts drug dealer was allowed to stay here because his homeland does not have a good healthcare system.

Then there was the case of Anthony Rice, who raped and murdered Naomi Bryant in Winchester in 2005. He had been serving a life sentence for another rape, but was freed on licence by the Parole Board, which seemed more concerned about Rice's human rights than the safety of the female population of Winchester. Haven't the general public got human rights too?

Taxpayers shelled out £750,000 in compensation to 197 drug addicts in Lancashire jails when they were denied the heroin substitute methadone and put through 'cold turkey' detoxification treatment. That, said the prisoners, was 'inhuman or degrading treatment' that breached their human rights. Facing large legal costs, the government decided to pay up before the case got to court. But it was only one of a number of human rights claims by prisoners, which cost taxpayers millions of pounds each year. Such is the absurdity that politicians get us into, when they start turning their vague values into blanket legislation.

The origins of respect and tolerance

These are not isolated cases. To many people, it seems that common sense has been supplanted by a system of rules and laws that simply undermine what most people would regard as justice, or even self-preservation. And indeed, it has.

Britain's legal tradition was for centuries rooted in common law, where people resolve their conflicts in court and judges decide what is just. The actual rulings are by no means simple – often coming down to what seems 'reasonable' – but then most conflicts themselves are by no means simple, and all kinds of special circumstances make each case slightly different from the next. Decisions are based on hundreds of actual cases over hundreds of years.

What this system gradually built up was a very elaborate but very effective system of justice, by which people came to understand what was reasonable and acceptable. They had a feeling for what was thought just, even though they could not necessarily explain or write down what the precise rules actually were. It was like the rules of grammar, which we use all the time without even having to think about them. Most of us can tell right from wrong, fairness from unfairness, politeness from rudeness, courtesy from giving offence. It has given Britain its characteristic identity: not warm beer or the flag as prime ministers seem to think, but a mutual respect and tolerance, within the limits of what is reasonable.

The dangers of bureaucratic law

Things are quite different, though, when values and the law do not evolve out of the slow distillation of justice from case upon case over a period of centuries. Right is what the law says it is, not what people feel it to be. People can act like utter swine, but as long as they can tick all the boxes, the law is on their side.

And who decides what the law should be and what boxes are to be ticked? Not judges and juries of ordinary people who have to live under that law, and have had a say in shaping it; but politicians and appointed officials who can insulate themselves from the real world, and often act as if they are above the law.

This system of fiat law is inept and heavy-handed precisely because it has not come about through any lengthy and painful process of testing and debate. It matters not whether it's reasonable to arrest someone for shouting at a government minister or reciting the names of fallen soldiers at the Cenotaph: rules are rules, and you're nicked.

At least, you might be nicked, or you might not. Because the second way in which this fiat justice system has undermined real justice is that it is the police and officials who decide which rules should be enforced and which not. That leads to some bizarre outcomes, many based on their own convenience, prejudices, or even arrest targets, rather than justice.

At a 2006 demonstration outside the Danish embassy following the publication of cartoons of The Prophet in a Danish magazine, the police did not intervene – despite the demonstrators calling for the slaughter of non-believers. They did, however, threaten to arrest an onlooker who tried to take a picture of one demonstrator who was dressed as a suicide bomber. Obviously, ill-tempered demonstrations need to be handled cautiously; but threatening people with death is plainly beyond the pale, while taking pictures of demonstrations isn't.

Most people know the difference between threatening behaviour and free speech. There's a big difference between calling someone names and putting them in fear of their lives. But leaving it to the police to decide which laws should and should not be enforced simply perverts the idea of justice that our common-law system has built up over a number of centuries.

In February 2008, Christian evangelists Arthur Cunningham and Joseph Abraham were threatened with arrest by a Muslim Community Support Officer for handing out bible texts in Muslim areas of Birmingham. True, this action might indeed provoke some Muslims. But our society works – and only works – on the basis of the long evolution of mutual respect and tolerance within the limits of reason. I guess that most

Christians wouldn't much care to see Jesus being insulted in cartoons, or to be handed Islamic texts as they came out of church either. Yet they would at least tolerate the right of other people to do it.

But by leaving officials to decide what our rules and values are, and how they are enforced, things like free speech and the values of mutual respect and tolerance have been suppressed. To them, the value of mutual respect becomes the rule that we should not be allowed to give offence to others under any circumstances. But it is solely because we do irritate and offend each other that we gradually learn to live together with tolerance. If our force is equal, then we have to get along, like the cowboys in the saloon who are each carrying a Colt 45. But if the Sheriff and all the deputies stand behind the big, noisy loudmouth because it's easier and safer to be on his side, that's hardly equal. In that sort of world, intolerance comes to dominate, and a lack of respect prevails.

And worse, the majority of us come to respect the law and its agents even less than they do the loudmouths.

15

STOPPING THE ROT

Nobody is safe from the executive

In November 2008, police sensationally arrested an opposition frontbench MP, Damian Green, for receiving documents leaked from the Home Office – documents which posed no risk to the nation, but merely demonstrated how our security was being compromised by the government's incompetence. Astonishingly, the Speaker and Serjeant At Arms allowed a squad of police to search Green's House of Commons office, where they seized computers, phones, files, and correspondence with colleagues and constituents.

In one swift move, centuries of Parliamentary privilege, established to protect opposition MPs from government harassment, were swept away. But if leaking documents that might embarrass the government can get MPs arrested, Gordon Brown would have been in jail for most of the Thatcher and Major administrations: and his own colleagues have no hesitation in leaking public information for their own gain.

With the principle of Parliamentary privilege breached, no MP who criticizes the government can feel safe. Nobody who blows the whistle on ministers' inept and improper use of state power can feel safe. None of us can feel safe that our private correspondence with our representatives will now remain confidential. Our broken democracy is looking more and more autocratic – like Robert Mugabe's police beating up opposition leaders, or Charles I trying to arrest troublesome MPs. That last move precipitated the Civil War – that's how important these things are.

Curbing executive power
One reason why we are in such a rotten state is that much of the power that was once wielded by monarchs such as Charles I is now in the hands of the Prime Minister. Or at least, it is in the hands of the Prime Minister and scores of party workers who are installed in Downing Street at public expense.

Through the power of the Prime Minister, this highly political machine controls all the great levers of state. The Prime Minister deploys the armed forces, authorizes the use of nuclear weapons, takes Britain to war, and signs foreign treaties. The Prime Minister also effectively appoints bishops, ambassadors, senior judges, and quango members, and decides who will get peerages and other honours. (Formally, these names are put forward by independent panels and the Queen makes the final appointments; but everyone knows where the real power is.)

The Prime Minister also has huge political power, appointing the Cabinet, ministers, government whips and other payroll jobs, and controlling the various grace and favour homes that go to ministerial colleagues. Being the leader of the largest party in Westminster, a Prime Minister also has a strong influence in Parliament and dominates the ruling party's policy decisions.

Plainly, too much state power lies in the unrestrained political machine that is Downing Street. Inevitably, power corrupts those who wield it, and state power comes to serve private interests.

Curbing Downing Street's power would require either a constitution, or a great deal of self-restraint from an incoming Prime Minister. Constitutional solutions bring their own problems – like the proposed EU Constitution, they tend to sprawl. They start as a simple set of management rules and grow into a vast catalogue of favours for special interest groups. And few Prime Ministers actually want to give up their power, especially when they have been in office a few years.

But a few simple changes would help re-establish the divide between what is party and what is state. Party appointees in Downing Street should not have power over civil servants: only elected representatives should have that. The appointment of judges, diplomats, bishops, and quango members should be a job for Parliament, probably in open hearings, not for the Prime Minister behind the closed doors of Downing Street. And it should be Parliament that decides whether Britain goes to war, and approves foreign treaties.

Strengthening Parliament

To balance the power that has grown up in Downing Street, we need a stronger – and less corrupt – Parliament. MPs will only ever stand up to executive power when their own careers, salaries and pensions don't depend on its patronage. So that is the place to start. MPs should be paid equally, whether they are ministers or not. Many of them would still aspire to become ministers, but their fortunes would not hinge on it. They would then be more willing to stand up to the executive, and vote as they thought best for their constituents, rather than as the government whips demanded. They would be more independent as ministers too, willing to resign or face the sack for their principles.

Term limits for MPs might also increase their independence, since they would know that politics could not be a long-term career for them. Some people worry that Parliament might lose experienced people if MPs' time there was limited. But in fact it might gain some. Today, Parliament is full of political careerists who have no experience of the real world outside Westminster. If becoming an MP was not a lifetime career, it would attract more people who already had some outside career but thought they had something positive to contribute to public life.

The House of Lords needs to be strengthened too. It cannot continue as a quango appointed by the Prime Minister: that's undemocratic, and adds further to Downing Street's power and patronage. It needs to be elected, but not on the same basis as the House of Commons; we need to find a system that elects those with real merit and experience, not just political ambition. Perhaps it should be based on regions, counties, or cities, rather than existing constituencies. A limited term might help preserve members' independence there, too.

We should pay MPs properly and cut back on their expenses. Since MPs decide their own pay, you might expect that they would give themselves generous wages. But in fact they were so terrified of looking bad in the press that they limited their headline pay and voted themselves generous expenses instead – with shocking results. It would be far less corrupt to pay MPs a fixed multiple of the average wage and cut out all of the expenses they use to buy themselves second homes and employ their families.

Strengthening local authorities

Britain's local authorities are the feeblest in the developed world, raising only a quarter of their spending locally. So they too are in thrall to ministers. We need local authorities that raise all their own money (apart from any block grants made to particularly needy areas on the basis of equity) and make all their own spending decisions.

The present Council Tax is not up to this job. People are already willing to go to jail because they think it so unjust. The best solution is probably to replace VAT with a local sales tax, like that in the United States, though this would require some tough talking in Brussels, where the VAT rules are decided. A local income tax is less good – taxes on work are never good – but it might still be fairer than Council Tax.

Whatever happens, we should be paying less in central taxes and more in local taxes. And more decisions should be made locally too. All the ring-fencing and auditing and other financial rules like best-practice tendering should be torn up, and local authorities should be judged at the ballot box by their electors.

People worry that local councillors are not up to the job. But the reason why local councils are so mediocre today is that they have little power to decide anything. People of calibre regard local government as a waste of time and do not stand for election. But if councils were both raising and spending all their own money, their debates would be of great local importance and local democracy would be livelier.

Elected local mayors would help strengthen local democracy too, providing people with a single person that they could blame when things went wrong, or re-elect when things went right. And mayors, having popular support, would again provide a local counterweight against the autocratic power of central government.

Putting police back under public control
Much more power should be devolved from national government to these newly strengthened local authorities. English counties should have much the same powers as the devolved Scottish Parliament, over health, education, agriculture, and justice.

Police powers should certainly be devolved. When the Adam Smith Institute polled police forces to find out what their priorities were, they listed things like recruiting more officers from minority groups, counselling victims of crime, and issuing more speeding tickets. What the public wanted was for them to catch local villains. But the central, bureaucratic targets have crowded out local priorities. And catching violent thugs is much harder than issuing speeding tickets.

Local police must be made properly accountable to local people. They should come under the control of local Sheriffs, elected by counties or cities. The Sheriffs should set local policing priorities and manage forces' budgets. They should set down the local sentencing guidelines and take over the management of prosecutions from the Crown Prosecution Service.

Reasserting our legal rights

The Human Rights Act was a costly mistake that hinders Britain's ability to deal with extremism. It should be scrapped. Some have suggested replacing it with a Bill of Rights, but like constitutions, such things can turn into a real mess. Already a joint Lords-Commons committee on human rights has suggested a Bill of Rights that includes rights to housing, education, healthcare, a healthy environment, and a good standard of living. And it proposes special protection for the elderly, children, and people with learning difficulties.

But a Bill of Rights should not be about trying to dream up all sorts of new things that government might do to help special interest groups. Governments are quite good at doing that on their own. Instead, a Bill of Rights should focus on making sure that our rulers treat us fairly and equally without discrimination, protect us from the threat of violence, don't bully and harass us, and don't interfere arbitrarily in our lives.

A Bill of Rights should protect us from those in power by giving us the right to due process of law, to be presumed innocent, to remain silent, to be tried by a jury, and to expect confidentiality from the police and other officials. It should give us the right not to be arrested without cause or for trivial offences – particularly not under some grossly disproportionate measure such as anti-terrorism laws – and not to be held for weeks without charge or trial. It should guarantee that we won't be carted off to some other country, on the basis of no evidence at all, to spend a year in some reeking cell while local prosecutors think about whether they've actually got the right person – EU treaties notwithstanding.

And a Bill of Rights should ensure that the enforcement of regulations takes account of local circumstances. So when Norwich licensing authorities tell hairdressers – as they did in November 2008 – that they face six months in prison and a £20,000 fine for giving their customers a glass of mulled wine at Christmas, it's not the salon owners who find themselves in jail.

Stopping heavy-handed regulation

Our state is rotten not just because central government authorities have too much unrestrained power. It is rotten because there is too much law too. Nobody can possibly keep up with the torrent of law and regulation that comes out of Westminster – or from Brussels, through Westminster.

Postwar Germany boomed after the 'bonfire of controls' lit by Ludwig Erhard in 1948. Britain too needs a bonfire of controls, and not just the insignificant ones. We need to look at the three sources of regulation – the EU (which produces red tape mountains as proficiently as it does butter mountains); Westminster and Whitehall (where much 'gold plating' of EU regulation comes from); and the regulators themselves (who always seem to find new things to regulate, and so justify their existence). We then need to look, for each, at how we can scrap their old or over-burdensome regulations; streamline and rationalize the remainder; make sure that new regulatory proposals are cost-effective; and ensure that regulations are sensibly, rather than rigidly, enforced.

The Netherlands has an ingenious system to deal with regulation. Departments are given regulatory budgets: the cost of regulations is totted up, and before a new one can be introduced, an old one has to be dispensed with, so that new regulations do not add to the total burden. And another idea that should be standard in regulation is the sunset principle – that a regulation is given a set life of maybe five years, and expires unless Parliament votes to save it.

On enforcement, the public would have much more respect for health and safety, licensing, and other regulations if there were not so many petty officials trying to enforce them in silly ways. We should rely more on insurance – which looks at both risks and costs, and so prompts businesses and others to manage their risks far more cost-effectively than any civil servant can achieve through blanket regulation. And if, instead of those countrywide regulations, councils had more power to make and enforce regulations locally, they would probably be made and enforced more sensitively than they are now; and we would all be able to enjoy a glass of mulled wine at the hairdresser or a slice of home-made birthday cake when we visit granny's care home.

Getting Britain working again

Just as more regulation cannot save us from every risk, greater borrowing is not going to get us out of the rotten state that our economy is in. The first priority must be sound money – because without a stable value of money, people cannot make any calculations about the future, so cannot plan and invest at all. That means giving the Bank of England a much more sensible inflation target, which includes the cost of housing – and a much tougher one.

Banking supervision should also go back to the Bank, which had a much better feel for what was happening in the financial markets than do current regulators. But the banks should build their own regulatory structure rather than wait for heavy-handed politicians to do it for them.

Public expenditure has to be reined in too. Inevitably, it is paid for out of taxation – or out of borrowing, which has to be repaid through taxation in future years. But high taxation depresses an economy. So too does the situation where people can be better off drawing benefits than getting into work. Despite an enormously complicated tax credit system, millions of people today conclude that work just isn't worth it. The speediest remedy for that is not to fiddle around with tax and benefit rates, but to take the poor out of tax entirely by raising the tax-free personal allowance to match the minimum wage, about £12,000 a year.

And taxes need to be much less complicated. Instead of having four different rates of income tax, as we are promised, we should have just one at, say, 20 per cent. The upper rates bring in little revenue – people simply hire accountants, or stop working, or emigrate, or send their money abroad, to avoid them. We would be better off making Britain a haven for wealth creators, and letting them keep some of the fruits of that wealth creation, instead of scaring them overseas with high and arbitrary taxes.

Taxes are unpopular, so it's asking a lot for any future politician to bring stealth taxes out into the open. But it has to be done. National insurance, for example, is hidden because employers pay most of it. It was originally designed as an insurance premium for health and pensions; but real insurance premiums don't rise along with your income, as national insurance does. In reality, it has become just another tax on wages – and a complicated one because its rules don't match the income tax rules. It would be better simply to add it on to income tax, and require employers to pass on in wages the amount they save on the contributions. Then people would know what they are really paying.

Tax Freedom Day is a simple measure to show the total burden of taxation on the public. Chancellors should be obliged to publish the impact of their tax changes in such simple terms, so that the impact of stealth taxes is brought into the open. Hidden taxes, like VAT and fuel or alcohol duties, should be declared openly as part of the price of what we buy – as in America, where sales tax is specifically added to the cost of goods. Then people would know what they are really paying in tax, and could decide whether they thought they were getting good value for it.

Just as taxes should be simplified, so should benefits be simplified too. Employers don't ask your household outgoings or how many children you have before they hire you: they pay you the going rate. Similarly, we need more standard welfare benefits, rather than a confusing array of different rules to deal with every small detail of each person's different lifestyle. This would aid simplicity and transparency. Charities could help if this caused hardship in particular cases. But the change would make benefit rates much plainer, making it easier to construct a system that ensures people are always better off in work.

Schools

Our education system is a failure, largely because we pay schools to fail. School funding should come from a single, predictable source, dependent almost wholly on the age and number of the children. The only adjustments should be for issues like rural schools with small pupil numbers, or urban schools where many pupils do not have English as their first language. There may be temporary funds to help overcome failure, but not long-term funds that promote it.

School funding should encourage schools to succeed, become popular, and grow. It needs to incentivize the heads of good schools to expand, and maybe take over other local schools that are not currently performing so well. That means giving schools the funds and letting them decide how best to spend them, rather than trying to dictate everything from the centre. And alongside the funds for current costs, there needs to be proper capital budgeting so that schools can plan the replacement of old buildings and equipment in a rational way.

The politicians' idea of accountability is that schools should report to central bureaucrats and be driven by central targets. It's about time that state schools became accountable to parents and driven by parents' ambitions for their kids instead. To achieve that, we could simply give parents the cost of a state education, and let them shop around between schools – state and private – to find the sort of education that they think is most appropriate for their own children. Or what amounts to the same thing, we could adopt the systems that are revolutionizing the school system in Sweden and Denmark. There, parents can send their children to any school they choose, and an amount of money reflecting the cost of their education goes with them to the chosen school. So the schools that provide the kind of education that parents want get more money and can expand, while the schools that don't have to mend their ways and improve – or face closure.

In Sweden, parents are not allowed to pay anything on top of what the state sends to their chosen school. Even so, thousands of new schools have started up, many of them established by groups of parents and teachers who were dissatisfied by their local municipal school. Others have been started by private companies, including chains of schools which are able to use their size in order to keep down costs – and which give parents a branded education product that they know they can trust.

In Britain, private schools could be encouraged to participate, expanding their places and taking the state's money to educate state pupils. This would get the system working quickly. But we could grow new schools too, if they were not thwarted by rigid planning rules, and were free from the detailed regulations and targets that Whitehall currently imposes. Denmark (where top-ups are allowed, incidentally, though they are usually modest) insists that schools teach Danish, English and Science, but otherwise, schools largely decide their own curriculum.

Health

Healthcare suffers from the same dysfunctional central planning as education. Again, there is little choice, and the NHS is a competition-free zone, run from the top by supposed experts, and unresponsive to the wishes of its users. The solution again is to put the financial power into the hands of patients – though this is more difficult than in education, where the costs of educating each child are fairly standard: in healthcare, some patients may have very expensive medical conditions, while others may never see a doctor in their lives.

Health is surely a sector where there is room for personal savings, insurance, and the state. Plainly, the state has to pay for long-term medication such as dialysis, which are hard to insure because of the uncertain costs. Most other procedures, from hip replacements to heart surgery, can be covered by private insurance. People could be obliged to take out private insurance rather than paying for the NHS through taxes – though the state would have to pay the premiums of those who could not afford the cost.

The great bulk of routine medical expenses, however, can probably be paid for out of savings. An attractive option here is medical savings accounts, an idea that originated in Singapore and is now sweeping into other countries, including America, where the over-regulated insurance sector has proved expensive. The idea is that people are obliged to save part of their income into a savings account that they can use for medical expenses. They could spend the money in the public or private sectors, on whatever kind of treatment they thought best. Some part of their contribution could also fund insurance for the larger items. And if they reached retirement with unused money in their medical savings account, they could use it to fund a larger pension, and so retain the benefit of their spare savings.

While this system is being built, NHS funding needs to be put into the hands of patients. Instead of funds being dished out from Whitehall to NHS providers, they should be managed by family doctors, who should buy services – again from the public or the private sector – on behalf of their patients.

Ultimately, the actual provision of healthcare services should migrate from the state to the non-state sector, where competition will bid down prices and bid up quality. The NHS will no longer run hospitals and clinics, but will be there to make sure that everyone has access to healthcare, providing funds where needed. So patients would have their pick of treatments and providers, knowing that they would not be refused medical care simply because they could not afford it.

Making welfare work
Welfare is another function that should be taken out of national

bureaucracy and placed under local control. America did this under President Clinton in 1996, shifting welfare responsibility from the federal government to the states. The results have been positive. Florida and Wisconsin, the two states that devolved responsibility for welfare even further, to county and local welfare boards, have made the most progress in getting people off welfare and into work.

Local authorities should determine the entitlement levels that they felt were appropriate in their area. So in areas with low average wages, benefits would not be so high as to be a disincentive; while in wealthier areas they would not be too low to live on. And local authorities would probably have a better grasp on the local employment market than central government, so programmes to get people back to work would be likely to be more successful.

One technique that has helped some American states more than halve the number of families on welfare is that they have largely contracted out the process of helping people off benefits and into work. Private agencies, including charities and church groups, have proved far more understanding of what people need in order to get themselves back into the labour market, and far more flexible in providing it. They can put in place the exact package of counselling and support that a family needs, rather than being able to provide only the specific training or other programmes that the state specifies.

These agencies are paid specifically to get people back to work. Most of their payment comes only when someone on welfare does actually get a job, and has held it down for three months – and so is likely to stay in work. That all amounts to a big saving for taxpayers, a big boost to the economy, and a rise in self-esteem for the people who are helped.

Restoring the pension promise

It's absurd to have a state pension that millions of people rely on but which is below the poverty line. The top-up pension credit, being means-tested, makes it pointless for many people to save, because they would just lose this benefit when they retire. A quick solution would be to ring-fence personal pension savings so that people get the full value of everything they save.

A better long-term solution is to raise the state pension to a non-poverty level. Something near 40 per cent of the average wage would compare with much of Europe. That would be very expensive, because there are millions of pensioners. But it would be affordable if the pension age were raised to 68, and indexed to general longevity. The pensions secretary Alan Johnson bravely suggested a retirement age of 68 for all new civil servants, but quickly withdrew it when threatened with widespread strikes. But people in the private sector are more realistic. They know that state pensions have become unaffordable, and that we are all living longer, so a later retirement age makes sense.

It is difficult to know how to revitalize the private pension sector, since the Treasury now relies so heavily on the stealth tax that Gordon Brown imposed on them. Ideally the tax credit would be restored. And the pension regulations should be scaled back to something more affordable. More simple tax treatment – for example, simply matching people's contributions from taxes, rather than the present system of rebates based on your age, occupation and tax rate – might help to create a system that people understood and were glad to participate in. Saving your money into a pension should be no more difficult than blowing it on the National Lottery.

Power back to the people

The themes behind all these proposals are to take power from the top and devolve it to local decision-making, and indeed back to the people wherever that is feasible. What's rotten in Britain is certainly not its people. They are as proud, inventive, outgoing, fair-minded, tolerant, and enterprising as they have ever been. What's rotten is a system of government that has concentrated power at the centre so comprehensively that these virtues can no longer flourish.

It probably all came about with the best of intentions. In order to serve the will of the people, you need to have the power to deliver what they want. In a country built on conventions rather than constitutions, on give and take rather than explicit rules, this power has been very easy for those at the centre to accumulate. They have thought it perfectly proper to push aside any convention that gets in the way of delivering the people's will – Parliament, the civil service, the monarchy, the courts, the fair handling of public information, the existing laws, the legal rights that can sometimes let guilty people go free.

In so doing, they may have served for a while the populist demands of the public, or at least the tabloid media. But they have also weakened or discarded any legal restraints upon their own actions. They have begun to believe that they, as elected representatives, are the sole judges of what the public wants, and are mandated to achieve it, without anything standing in their way.

And now we discover that it is their will that prevails, not ours, for there is nothing left to restrain them. There is no part of our lives that they are not prepared to pass an opinion on, and – since they have the levers of control at their hands – to pass legislation on to stop us living as we please. We cannot give our customers a glass of mulled wine, cuddle a crying child, enjoy a violinist at our restaurant table, organize children's outings, smoke in a private club, feed the dog grapes, or sing a song at the pub piano without their permission – if at all – even though these activities do no harm to anyone else at all and are part of the fabric of social life. And if we get on the wrong side of any of the tens of thousands of rules they impose on us, we can find ourselves arrested for the most minor transgression, held without charge, and punished by official fiat without any court or jury being involved.

It's a rotten state we're in. We need action to restrain our leaders. We need to assert the rule of law and the principles of justice – rules that may well stop governments acting as we would like them to in the heat of the moment, but which in the long term dispassionately safeguard our lives and our liberties. We need to take power from the centre and disperse it to the localities where we live, and where possible, back to ourselves, the people.

ADDITIONAL READING

The rotten state we're in

Larry Elliott and Dan Atkinson, *Fantasy Island: Waking Up To The Incredible Economic, Political, And Social Illusions Of the Blair Legacy*, Constable, 2007.

Christopher Foster, *British Government In Crisis: Or The Third English Revolution*, Hart Publishing, 2005.

Andrew Haldenby, Peter Hoskin, Helen Rainbow and Henry de Zoete, *Key Policy Lessons Of The 'Blair Years' For Future Governments*, Reform, 2007.

Anthony Selden (ed.), *Blair's Britain 1997-2007*, Cambridge University Press, 2007.

Geoffrey Wheatcroft, *Yo, Blair!*, Politico's Publishing, 2007.

The sleazy state

Martin Bell, *The Truth That Sticks: New Labour's Breach Of Trust*, Icon Books, 2007.

Iain Dale and Guido Fawkes (eds), *The Big Red Book Of New Labour Sleaze*, Harriman House, 2007.

Nicholas Jones, *Trading Information: Leaks, Lies And Tip-Offs*, Politico's Publishing, 2006.

Peter Oborne, *The Triumph Of The Political Class*, Simon & Schuster, 2007.

Peter Oborne, *The Rise Of Political Lying*, Free Press, 2005.

ADDITIONAL READING

A state of injustice

Chris Atkins, Sarah Bee and Fiona Button, *Taking Liberties Since 1997*, Revolver Books, 2007.

Melanie Phillips, *Londonistan: How Britain Created A Terror State Within*, Gibson Square, 2006.

Madsen Pirie, *Freedom 101*, Adam Smith Institute, 2008.

Dominic Raab, *The Assault On Liberty: What Went Wrong With Rights*, Fourth Estate, 2009.

The nanny surveillance

Ross Clark, *How To Label A Goat: The Silly Rules And Regulations That Are Strangling Britain*, Harriman House, 2006.

Ross Clark, *The Road To Southend Pier: One Man's Struggle Against The Surveillance Society*, Harriman House, 2007.

John and Sarah Midgley, *The Politically Incorrect Scrapbook*, John and Sarah Midgley, 2007.

Christopher Booker and Richard North, *Scared To Death: From BSE To Global Warming: Why Scares Are Costing Us The Earth*, Continuum, 2007.

Stanley Feldman and Vincent Marks: *Panic Nation: Exposing The Myths We're Told About Food And Health*, John Blake Publishing, 2006.

The state of public services

Inspector Gadget, *Perverting The Course Of Justice*, Monday Books, 2008.

Matthew Elliott and Lee Rotherham, *The Bumper Book Of Government Waste 2008: Brown's Squandered Billions*, Harriman House, 2007.

Adrian Butler, Gabriel Stein and Nicholas Boys Smith, *Funding Failure: How Schools Pay For Success*, Politeia, 2003.

Warwick Mansell, *Education By Numbers: The Tyranny Of Testing*, Politico's Publishing, 2007.

ADDITIONAL READING

The state of the economy

Alex Brummer, *The Crunch: The Scandal of Northern Rock and the Escalating Credit Crisis*, Random House Business Books, 2008.

David Craig, *Squandered: How Gordon Brown Is Wasting Over One Trillion Pounds Of Our Money*, Constable, 2008.

Nigel Lawson, *An Appeal To Reason: A Cool Look At Global Warming*, Duckworth, 2008.

Will Hutton, *The State We're In*, Jonathan Cape, 1995.

A better state

Douglas Carswell and Dan Hannan, *The Plan: Twelve Months To Renew Britain*, Douglas Carswell, 2008.

Daniel Hannan and Douglas Carswell, *The Localist Papers*, Centre For Policy Studies, 2006.